5/21 2X 0/23/19 c 2018

Perfect Days in...

ST PETERSBURG

MARCO POLO

D0326797

Contents

★ TOP 10 4

That St Petersburg Feeling 6

For chapters: See inside front cover

TOP 10

Not to be missed!
Our TOP 10 hits – from the absolute No. 1 to No. 10 –
help you plan your tour of the most important sights.

⭐1 HERMITAGE ➤ 54
The Hermitage, one of the world's greatest art museums, is housed in the splendid Winter Palace.

⭐2 PETERHOF PALACE ➤ 156
'Russia's Versailles' is a synthesis of the arts: a magnificent Baroque palace and gardens with numerous fountains and cascades located right on the seashore (➤ fig. left).

⭐3 NEVSKY PROSPEKT ➤ 130
This grand boulevard, the city's permanently vibrant main artery with a rich mixture of culture and commerce with churches in between, is flanked by historical façades the whole length.

⭐4 STRELKA ➤ 80
Elegant architecture meets the mass of water carried by the Neva and divides it into two. The tip of Vasilyevsky Island epitomises the resplendent St Petersburg of old in all its glory.

⭐5 CATHERINE PALACE ➤ 162
The stunningly beautiful Catherine Palace in Tsarskoye Selo has much more to offer than just the famous Amber Room.

⭐6 BRONZE HORSEMAN ➤ 104
Dynamic monumental statue of Russia's moderniser – and a famous landmark in St Petersburg – the Bronze Horseman depicts Peter the Great, riding his horse as it rears up at the edge of a ravine.

⭐7 ST ISAAC'S CATHEDRAL ➤ 106
The colonnade around the dome of this grand cathedral provides the best panoramic views of the city.

⭐8 MARIINSKY THEATRE ➤ 111
The most spectacular venue for opera and classical ballet. The world-famous Mariinsky Theatre under the direction of Valery Gergiev now comprises three stages all on Theatre Square.

⭐9 PETER AND PAUL FORTRESS ➤ 82
Peter and Paul Fortress, founded in 1703, is 'Peter's *Burg'* (castle). As the city's stronghold it houses the tombs of the tsarist family, has the highest church tower – and a lovely sandy beach too!

⭐10 CHURCH OF THE SPILLED BLOOD ➤ 61
Also known as the Church of the Resurrection of Christ, its brightly coloured onion towers and stunning mosaics is both eccentric and magical – while at the same time commemorating a brutally assassinated tsar.

THAT
ST PETERSBURG

Experience what makes this city what it is and soak in its unique atmosphere – just as the people of St Petersburg do.

THE WHITE NIGHTS PARTY FEELING

When the sky no longer gets really dark at night, things take on a magical feel on the Neva: when the bridges are open cargo ships glide past the historic façades bathed in the pastel colours of twilight. And when nature turns night into day the locals do the same – it's party time especially around Palace Bridge!

SEE AND BE SEEN

Fancy an evening with friends over a cappuccino, craft beer or a cocktail? It wasn't even so long ago that it was difficult to think of just where to go. But now 'Piter's' young and dynamic café, clubbing and pubbing scene has created its own hotspots on **Ulitsa Rubinshteyna** (➤ 150), in **Small Gostiny Dvor** (➤ 150) and on **Konyushennaya Square** (➤ 74). The culture centre **Golitsyn Loft** is very much up and coming (➤ 32).

THE OPERA HOUSE – NO PHANTOMS HERE

St Petersburg is not called Russia's cultural capital for nothing. Opera and classical ballet are of intrinsic importance – nurtured predominantly by the **Mariinsky Theatre**

Night-time spectacle: The opening of the bridges over the Neva

FEELING

(►111) with its three stages, a symphony orchestra and an ensemble of world renown. And those who visit it are not elitist but simply culturally interested.

WATER, WATER EVERYWHERE

St Petersburg's city centre is dominated by expanses of water: the Neva forms a fresh-air oasis and open-air stage set against the backdrop of elegant bridges, groups of buildings and palaces – and is referred to by the people of St Petersburg as the *Aquatorium*. Let your eyes roam over the wide Russian horizon right in the middle of a major European city – from the **Strelka** (►80), the beach below **Peter and Paul Fortress** (►82) or **Trinity Bridge**.

That St Petersburg Feeling

ISLAND HOPPING

St Petersburg has a number of islands to explore. **Yelagin Island** (➤ 187) has a landscaped park, a rollerskating rink and rowing boats for hire; across the water is **Krestovsky Island** with its amusement park **Divo Ostrov** (➤ 187), brand-new sports arenas (including the futuristic Krestovsky football stadium (also known as the Zenit or Peter Arena) with a capacity for 68,000 spectators and a retractable roof (one of the venues of the World Cup in 2018) – and lots of space for cycling. Afterwards you can relax in **Karl & Friedrich** beer garden (➤ 98).

SOVIET MEMENTOS & RELICS OF THE BOURGEOISIE

Where do St Petersburg's gastro designers come across all their old bits and bobs? The answer can be found not far from Udelnaya metro station. There is only one flea market in the whole city and, as a consequence, it's huge and a place of pilgrimage for all retro fans (to the right of the station over the railway crossing, then keep right. Sat, Sun approx. 9am–3pm).

NORTHERN RIVIERA

St Petersburg actually lies on the Baltic – but you can neither see nor smell the sea. The locals remember this at the latest when the heat of summer gets too much in the city and they head for the sand and beach bars on a 15km (9.5mi) stretch of shoreline between **Solnechnoye** and **Selenogorsk** (40–55 mins. on the *elektrichka* from Finland Station or by bus 211 from Chyornaya Rechka metro station). By the way, even in the height of summer, it never gets full on weekdays. And, while here, you can visit Penaty, the villa and estate where the painter Ilya Repin (1844–1930) once lived (Repino, Primorskoe Shosse 411, Wed–Sun 10:30am–6pm, entrance fee: ₽300).

THE 'NEVSKY PERSPECTIVE'

Expansive vistas can be enjoyed right in the city centre without ever becoming boring. The wide Nevsky Prospekt (➤ 130) runs dead-straight for three kilometres (1.9mi) and, behind the representative façades, you can shop (and party) 'til you drop. The people of St Petersburg feel drawn to the Nevsky – so simply drift along with the masses.

A sunny day out on the Northern Riviera

The Magazine

ONE MAN, ONE IDEA, ONE CITY

Even if St Petersburg is not actually named after him but after his namesake, Saint Peter, the city owes its existence to the most dynamic ruler Russia ever knew: Peter the Great who, however, decided to build his 'paradise' in one of the most unfavourable spots imaginable.

It was 1703. Russia and Sweden were at war, as so often before. Sweden, the major power in the Baltic, had ruled over the Gulf of Finland for a century now – and this included the mouth of the Neva.

Its flat, swampy delta is the gateway to Russia's inland waterways with their many branches. Since time immemorial it had been part of a trade route to the Orient. Russia's young, cosmopolitan tsar, always eager for knowledge, had set himself an ambitious target. He wanted to create a port on the Baltic Sea to bolster the fortunes of his realm – a 'window to Europe' as the national poet Pushkin later put it. And this port was to be the base of a fleet and Russia was to become a naval power.

Russia's Opening

The young tsar had picked up the maritime bug in the outlying areas of Moscow where many foreigners lived and taught himself to sail on a small boat he managed to ferret out locally. In 1697 a group of Russians – the 'Great Delegation' – set off for central Europe to recruit specialists and gain greater technical skills. The tsar travelled with them, incognito, as 'Artilleryman Pjotr Mikhailov' and completed a course of training as a shipbuilder in a shipyard in Holland.

After the Russians had succeeded in driving the Swedes out of Shlisselburg Fortress (▶ 181) at the head of the Neva on Lake

The founder and his city in 1728

The magnificent Winter Palace on the Neva

Ladoga one year earlier, the Swedish fortress Nyenschantz, situated where the small River Okhta enters the Neva, capitulated on 1 May 1703 too.

The Russians celebrated their victory three days long. Then two Swedish sailing ships came up the river, each with 18 cannons. The Russians, however, who only had rowing boats, managed to board them after a series of manoeuvres and tricks.

The Founding of the City

Even if Peter did win his first naval battle this way, he knew only too well that the mouth of the Neva had to be protected. He decided to build a fortress (►82) as quickly as possible on tiny Zayachy Island – also called Hare Island – in the main navigation channel on the river. Building started on 27 May 1703 and one month later, on 29 June, a little church surrounded by ramparts was consecrated and dedicated to Peter and Paul. Documentary evidence shows that it was this fortified structure that was the first given the name 'Saint Petersburg'.

In time the church's name was used for the whole fortress and this, in turn, gave its name to the settlement that grew up outside its walls. From an urban planning point of view the site could hardly have been more unsuitable. The Neva delta consisted of 100 mosquito-infested islands that

---

RENAMED THREE TIMES

In 1914, after the outbreak of World War I, it was thought that St Petersburg sounded too German – and so the city's name was changed to Petrograd. The next name-change came in 1924: after the death of the revolutionary leader, Lenin, Petrograd became Leningrad. In 1991 55% of the city's residents voted in a referendum for a return to the original name.

were submerged whenever there was a strong west wind. The ground was a swamp, the climate damp and cold. Stone had to be brought from a long way away as did the workers as, up until that time, only a few fishing villages had ever existed there. The things to be found in abundance were water, wind and space.

Brutal Modernisation

Peter used his dictatorial powers to push his project through despite severe opposition. Serfs were forced to work, had to live in primitive dugouts and straw huts and perished by the thousand. Noble families were obliged to build townhouses in this remote wasteland. A huge shipyard, the Admiralty (➤ 118), was made from nothing. And instead of roads the tsar had canals dug – after all, the Russians were to be made fit for life as a seafaring nation.

The down-to-earth populace thought all this was the work of the devil. Petersburg was built on human bones, so it was said. For Peter, however, it was 'paradise' where his ideas for an effectively administered, technically and culturally developed city could be turned into reality without having to face the conceit of *boyar* aristocrats in Moscow. Critics and adversaries had to face the full force of the tyrannical reformer's wrath. In 1712, when St Petersburg comprised but a handful of stone houses, Peter pronounced the huge building site to be his capital. To this aim his personal architect Domenico Trezzini drew up a general plan in 1715. The visionary on the throne, who died in 1725, was to be proven right. Some 100 years later his dream city already had a larger population than Moscow – and, for two hundred years, it was here that Russia's wealth was reflected in its magnificent buildings and art treasures. Even if St Petersburg has not been the capital since 1918 it owes its very existence and attractiveness to one tsar's vision. It is not for nothing that the whole of the historical city centre is a UNESCO World Heritage Site.

THE TSARS
A 'Who's Who'

You meet them – or rather their names and testimonies to their reigns – all over St Petersburg wherever you go. To put everything in its historical perspective it is useful to know who's who in the imperial family.

By the way: the title 'tsar' for rulers of Russia during the Petersburg Era was only used colloquially. In 1721 Peter the Great actually raised his own position and that of his successors to emperor – Emperor of All Russia

Name, year of birth	Ruled from – until	Buildings/monuments with a personal connection	Miscellaneous
Peter I, the Great (1672)	1682–25	• Peter and Paul Fortress • Cabin of Peter the Great • Summer Garden • Cabinet of curiosities • St Alexander Nevsky Monastery • Peterhof Palace • Bronze Horseman	Founded St Petersburg in 1703 and made it into the capital city in 1712. Passionate artilleryman, handworker and ship-builder. Opened Russia up to Europe and funda-mentally reformed the country.
Catherine I (1684)	1725–27	• Catherine Palace • Menshikov Palace	Born Marta Skavronsky. The Livonian maidservant became Peter I's mistress and, in 1712, his wife. After Peter's death Prince Menshikov was de facto the regent.
Peter II (1715)	1727–30		Grandson of Peter I; moved the capital back to Moscow in 1728 where he died of smallpox aged just 14.
Anna (1693)	1730–40	• Spire of Peter and Paul Cathedral and the Admiralty • Samson Fountain Peterhof Palace	Niece of Peter I. Left government business in the hands of various advisors and moved the court back to St Petersburg in 1732.
Ivan VI (1740)	1740–41	• Shlisselburg Fortress	Toppled from the throne as a baby. Was imprisoned until murdered in 1764.

The Magazine

Name, year of birth	Ruled from – until	Buildings/monuments with a personal connection	Miscellaneous
Elizabeth (1709)	1741–62	• Winter Palace • Grand Palace at Peterhof • Catherine Palace • Smolny Convent • Academy of Arts	Daughter of Peter I and Catherine I. Last member of the original Romanov dynasty on the throne. Initiator of many representative buildings.
Peter III (1728)	1762	• Grand Menshikov Palace and Peterstadt Fortress in Oranienbaum	Born Karl Peter Ulrich von Schleswig-Holstein-Gottorf, grandson of Peter I and Catherine I. Was deposed and murdered after just 6 months on the throne.
Catherine II, the Great (1729)	1762–96	• Chinese Palace • Agate Rooms and Cameron Gallery • Small and Old Hermitage • Marble Palace • Memorial on Nevsky Pr.	Born Sophie Auguste Friederike von Anhalt-Zerbst, wife of Peter III. Founder of the Hermitage. As an intellectual reformer she ruled in the spirit of enlightened Absolutism.
Paul I (1754)	1796–1801	• Pavlovsk Palace • St Michael's Castle	Son of Peter III and Catherine II. Murdered by conspirators.
Alexander I (1777)	1801–25	• Kazan Cathedral • St Isaac's Cathedral • Old Stock Exchange, Strelka • Alexander Column	Son of Paul I. Played a significant role in the victory over Napoleon in 1814.
Nicholas I (1796)	1825–55	• New Hermitage • Winter Palace (interior) • Cottage • Equestrian statue on St Isaac's Square	Son of Paul I. Suppression of Decembrist Revolt after ascending the throne. Built Russia's first railway line.
Alexander II (1818)	1855–81	• Mariinsky Theatre • Farmers' Palace • Church of the Resurrection of Christ	Son of Nicholas I. Abolished serfdom in Russia. Killed in bomb attack.
Alexander III (1845)	1881–94	• Equestrian monument in front of the Marble Palace	Son of Alexander II. During his reign Russia waged no wars.
Nicholas II (1868)	1894–1917	• Russian Museum • Alexander Palace • Fyodor Church • Villa Kschessinskaya • Vitebsky Station	Son of Alexander III. Abdicated as the last sovereign of Russia in February 1917. Murdered with his family by the Bolsheviks in 1918.

THE ★ SIEGE OF LENINGRAD

For one-and-a-half years during World War II the city remained under siege by the Wehrmacht – the unified armed forces of Nazi Germany. Hitler did not want to take the city but to starve it out. One million people died. This traumatic period in Russia's history is in-extricably linked to the name Leningrad.

The museum exhibit is as plain as it is moving – a small, worn wooden breadboard – on which someone engraved: 'Winter 1941. Hunger. We used to slice bread on this board.' During the Siege of Leningrad bread was more valuable than gold, even if sawdust and cellulose made up to half of every loaf. For the first five weeks at the beginning of the 'Winter of

Starvation' in 1941/42 the daily ration was just 250g (8.8oz) for workers and 125g (4.4oz) for children and everyone else. This was not enough to be able to survive and there were hardly any other foodstuffs available. Supply routes had been cut off and warehouses full of provisions had been destroyed during air raids by the Germans in the first few days of the siege in September 1941. The wooden breadboard can be seen in a deeply moving exhibition in the underground Room of Remembrance in the 'Monument to the Heroic Defenders of Leningrad', erected forty years

ago on the southern outskirts of the city. The enemy moved in so close to the city that still had a population of three million at that time, that Red Army soldiers could travel by tram to the front which was roughly where Pulkovo Airport is today.

The 'Winter of Starvation'

The first winter during the blockade was extremely cold, even by Russian standards, and there was no electricity, no coal and drinking water was scarce. The authorities strove to distribute what food rations there were and to ensure that laws were upheld, as well as overseeing the organisation of troops of volunteers who looked for people buried in the rubble, put out fires and took the sick and injured to hospital. In this way the outbreak of epidemics was largely contained. Nevertheless thousands of people starved to death every day – in bed, while collecting water or walking to work. "The people were so weak from hunger that they could not put up a fight; they died as if they were just falling asleep. And other people around them, more dead than alive, did not pay them the least bit of attention," the writer Elena Skrjabina recorded in her memoirs.

In the course of spring 1942 the situation slowly improved. More and more provisions arrived by lorry along a corridor that was permanently under fire – and, little by little, 1.3 million residents, including most of the children, were evacuated. The 40 kilometre (25mi)-long supply route led eastwards out of the city and crossed the ice on Lake Ladoga. In the summer ships were used. Later it was even possible for an oil pipeline and electricity cables to be laid

across the lake. Eleven months after the outset of the blockade Dmitri Shostakovich's 'Leningrad Symphony' was performed in the city's concert hall.

Breakthrough and Liberation

The actual blockade lasted seventeen months before troops managed to regain control of a strip of land near Shlisselburg on the shore of Lake Ladoga and a provisional railway track to the city was laid. But it was to be almost one more year until the last German troops and their guns moved back from the city boundary. A fireworks celebration on the Neva marked the end of the siege on 27 January 1944.

In the centre of St Petersburg there is virtually nothing to remind people today of this terrible period. An inscription on the wall at Nevsky Prospekt number 14 has been preserved. It reads: 'Citizens! During artillery fire this side of the street is the more dangerous one'. Scars in the granite walls of St Isaac's Cathedral and Anichkov Bridge caused by shelling have been left on purpose. The most impressive monument for the genocide committed against this city with a population of millions is, however, Piskaryovskoye Memorial Cemetery. 70,000 soldiers and 420,000 civilians were buried here in mass graves during the years of the blockade.

The Siege of Leningrad **painted by J.A. Korneev, 1951**

MUSEUMS AND SITES TO COMMEMORATE THE BLOCKADE

Piskaryovskoye Memorial Cemetery: Pr. Nepokoryonnikh 72; tel: 812-297-5716; www.pmemorial.ru; daily 9am–6pm, in summer until 9pm, metro: Pl. Muzhestva and then by bus 80, 123, 138, entrance free

Monument to the Heroic Defenders of Leningrad (Room of Remembrance): Pl. Pobedy; tel: 812-371-2951; www.spbmuseum.ru, Thu–Mon 10am–6pm, Tue 10am–5pm, metro: Moskovskaya, entrance fee: ₽150

Museum of the Defence and Siege of Leningrad: Solyanoy per. 9; tel: 812-275-7547; www.blokadamus.ru, Thu–Mon 10am–6pm, Wed 12:30pm–8:30pm (except last Thu in month), bus 46, 49 (Letniy sad), entrance fee: ₽250

Blockade exhibition in the Villa Rumyantsev: Angliyskaya nab. 44; tel: 812-571-7544; www.spbmuseum.ru, Thu–Tue 11am–6pm, bus 3, 22, 27; trolley bus 5, 22 (pl. Truda), entrance fee: ₽200

Underground
PALACES

No underground railway network in the
world is as deep as that in St Petersburg
between 50 and 100m (165–330ft)
below ground level. And architecturally
speaking the metro is a world of its own.

THE MOST BEAUTIFUL METRO STATIONS ON LINE 1

Ploshchad Vosstaniya: The most 'ideological' of the stations. Its walls are
decorated with motifs from the October Revolution together with any number
of hammers and sickles, red stars and oak leaves.

Pushkinskaya: As elegant as a hotel foyer. Standard lamps light up the
plasterwork ceilings and the granite ornamentation on the floor. And Pushkin
sits musing in front of a painted park landscape.

Baltiyskaya: Lots of grey marble and a colourful mosaic at the end of the
hall celebrating the year 1917 with sailors, soldiers and workers before the
storming of the Winter Palace.

Narvskaya: Reliefs paying homage to the workers of twelve different pro-
fessions including textile workers, artists, horse breeders and, of course,
metro construction workers.

Avtovo: The metro trains pass under chandeliers in this station that was
once the terminus. Covering the columns in glass tiles with reliefs which
are polished like mirrors proved more difficult than originally thought. As a
result, only 16 of the 46 columns have this cladding.

By the way: You are allowed to take photographs in the metro but without
using a flash or a tripod!

The 'Triumphal Arch' at the entrance and...

In most cases a journey on the metro in St Petersburg starts with a two-to-three minute ride on one of the seemingly endless escalators. Only seven of the sixty-seven stations in the city are above ground or just below ground level. To be able to build an underground system at all in the soft alluvial soil in the Neva delta meant that the Soviet engineers had to dig very deep indeed.

Writing about the metro in Moscow which opened in 1935, the philosopher Boris Groys describes it as "a u-topia based on a u-topos". At Stalin's behest the new form of transport for the masses was to exude a magnificence that had only previously be seen in the palaces of the aristocracy and in churches.

...a wall relief at Narvskaya Station

UNUSUAL STATIONS

Tekhnologichesky Institut 1 and 2 (1955/1961): Lines leading into and out of the city share a central platform in this station which, for many passengers, makes changing trains much faster.

Sportivnaya (1997): This station is on two levels as is was built to connect up with a circle line that has existed on paper now for sixty years. Since 2015, a 300m (985ft)-long pedestrian tunnel with moving walkways has provided an alternative access route to Vasilyevsky Island.

Admiralteyskaya (2011): The deepest station within the St Petersburg Metro network is 86m (282ft) below ground level. The main escalator goes down to a depth of 69m (226ft) and is 125m (410ft) long – a world record!

The stations were to be like cathedrals for the working people and the daily commute to work like High Mass celebrating Communism's golden future. The same is true for the St Petersburg Metro.

Stalin Grandeur on Line 1

Within this context it is fitting that the inner city terminus of the first Leningrad Line was given an entrance pavilion in the form of a round Classicist temple, for which a church on the site had to be demolished. Construction started at the beginning of 1941 but work on this huge project was interrupted by the war. The first line ran ten kilometres (6.2mi) from Moskovsky station in a southwestern direction as far as Avtovo, passing through eight magnificently designed stations; the red Line 1 is now three times as long. It was opened in November 1955, eighteen months after Stalin's death, at the same time as a decree was passed by the Central Committee of the Communist Party of the Soviet Union (CPSU) 'to forgo any unnecessary excesses in planning and building'. This forbade the customary bombastic architectural style of the Stalin era and ordered the plain Socialist style to be adopted from then on. The oldest part of the Leningrad Metro, however, was left as it was as a final monument to Stalinist Classicism ('gingerbread' style). It has remained an architectural site of interest to this day – an ideal place to explore on a rainy day!

Pushkinskaya (top) and Admiralteyskaya　　**Avtovo Station in all its magnificence**

THE
RESURRECTION
OF
THE
CURCH

The influence of the Russian Orthodox Church has grown quite considerably in the post-Soviet era and it is now staking its claim to several church buildings in St Petersburg that are being used as museums at present.

There is always a lot of coming and going in a Russian Orthodox church the whole day long. Some church-goers quickly light a candle in front of an icon which they then kiss before reciting a short prayer; others follow the chants of the priests during services, deep in thought and frequently crossing themselves. Everything takes place standing – there are no pews: everyday religious life in a country that, during the Soviet era, was officially an atheist state. In keeping with Marx's theory that religion was the 'opium of the people', Russians were weaned off their belief as soon as possible after the revolution – later, in the 1930s, with Stalinist brutality. The majority of clergymen were sent to prison camps or were executed straight away. Almost all ecclesiastic buildings, regardless of religion, were closed. Many

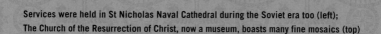

Services were held in St Nicholas Naval Cathedral during the Soviet era too (left);
The Church of the Resurrection of Christ, now a museum, boasts many fine mosaics (top)

were destroyed or put to other uses as warehouses, sports halls or for cultural purposes. The best fate for a desecrated church was for it to be turned into a museum as, for example, with Kazan Cathedral (► 131), in which a 'museum of religious history and atheism' was opened. It was not until World War II that the church was allowed to re-establish some form of organisation, tentatively at first, as a means to further the 'morally patriotic consolidation of the people'. It continued to lead a backwater existence until the end of the Soviet Union.

The Church and the Kremlin
Since then religion – and primarily the Russian Orthodox Church as Russia's traditional religion – has experienced a remarkable renaissance. According to the constitution of the Russian Federation it is a multi-religious state with a strict division between the church and the state. The church, therefore, has to finance itself from donations and through its own business activities. However, since the beginning of the Putin era at the latest, the Kremlin and the Patriarchate have been advocating common values, views and traditions in perfect harmony. At Christmas and Easter the President and Prime Minister can be seen attending a church service broadcast live on television. In practice the Orthodox

The Magazine

church has taken on the role of the state church once again, as it did in the days of the tsar.

In St Petersburg there are now some 200 orthodox church communities. Some have been given back their old churches and have renovated them, as in the case of Feodorovsky Cathedral (▶ 143), for example, which had been used for decades as a dairy. Many churches have been built in new

residential areas where four-fifths of the total population of the city now live. Nevertheless it is still difficult to ascertain how devout Russians really are today. Nobody has to register as a member of a church. Even opinion polls vary – between 40 and 75 percent of the population are supposed to be Russian Orthodox. The number of regular churchgoers (including members of other religions who attend their respective institutions) is, however, around ten percent. Depending on the opinion poll, between five and twenty-five percent consider themselves atheist.

Restitution

The church is conscious of its growing influence in society and, in the meantime, has made demands for the return of prominent houses of prayer, as permitted by a law passed in 2010. As a result Smolny Cathedral (▶ 144) that had been used as a concert hall up until 2015 was restituted to the church that same year. The municipal govern-

The festive atmosphere in a church service

ment has promised the Head of the Church, Patriarch Kyrill, that St Isaac's Cathedral (▶ 106) will be returned in 2017 – something that had been refused point blank two years previously. Not only the museum management that has been responsible for the restoration and maintenance of this major tourist attraction for decades has protested against this decision, but many local residents as well. There have been demonstrations and petitions. Peter and Paul Cathedral (▶ 83) with the tsarist tombs that is used as a museum will also probably become a bone of contention. It is here that Russia's worldly monarchs are buried. The last emperor Nicholas II who was murdered together with his family by the Bolsheviks has since been canonised as a martyr. His mortal remains are now both a relic and an exhibit.

For members of the Russian Orthodox church the interior of a church is an image and foretaste of Paradise (here: Kazan Cathedral)

VODKA + CAVIAR

There are two things to eat and drink that one immediately associates with Russia – one is for the masses and one for the more elite – despite the fact that these two culinary classics, vodka and caviar, complement each other perfectly.

Whether it was actually the Poles or the Russians who invented 'little water' (as *vodka* means in both languages) is something the two nations still debate today! The first documentary evidence of this beverage was in 1431 in Russia and its popularity soon spread. By the middle of the 15th century the production of this cereal grain-based spirit in Russia had become a state monopoly. For centuries, the national beverage has not only warmed the stomachs and relaxed the minds of the ordinary people but also ensured the state coffers are well filled. This has not changed to this day. The minimum price, prescribed by law, for a half-litre bottle is at the moment around 190 roubles, of which 118 roubles are tax and duties. Up to 62 percent tax is, therefore, payable on genuine Russian vodka which always has exactly 40 percent alcohol by volume.

The Mendeleev Myth

This ideal strength – a mystically romanticised equivalent to the German beer purity law – was laid down in 1866. The famous chemist Dmitri Mendeleev is alleged to have determined that alcohol of precisely this strength can best be ingested by the human body – or at least this is what Russian vodka fans say. This is, however, merely a legend! Although Mendeleev did publish his dissertation 'A discourse on the combination

INSIDER INFO

- Background information on the drink's history and tasting sessions are available at the **Vodka Museum** (Konnogvardeyskiy Bulvar 4; tel: 812-943-1431; www.vodkamuseum.su; daily noon–7pm; bus: trolley bus 5, 22 as far as Pochtamtskaya Per., metro: Admiralteyskaya; entrance fee: ₽170).
- To help protect the species and also to ensure that you are neither palmed off with produce of dubious origin or quality nor unwittingly supporting the fish mafia, only buy black caviar in serious shops and restaurants – such as at **Caviar**, the caviar boutique in **Gostiny Dvor** (➤ 148) or the food hall at **Eliseyev** (➤ 148).
- Caviar is perfectly served as it should be in the **Caviar Bar** at the **Grand Hotel Europe** (➤ 42) and in the restaurant **Tsar** (Sadovaya Ul. 12; tel: 812-640-1616; www.ginza.ru; daily noon–midnight; metro: Gostiny Dvor).

of alcohol and water' in 1864, he kept purely to chemical and technical questions. The 40 percent rule was thought up by government officials as this made it much easier to work out how much excise had to be paid. The very popular *polugar* before it had an awkward 38.5 percent.

In Russia vodka is always made of water and a rye distillate. Two to three percent may be made up of other types of grain such as barley, oats or buckwheat (but never potatoes, as is often claimed). Producers may add aromatic ingredients such as herbs, honey or birch bark sap to give their products an individual flavour.

Drinking Rules

And how is 'little water' to be drunk in true *po-russkiy* fashion? The most important rule is that you never drink vodka alone but always with others – and then only after a toast to someone or something. And, whatever you do, don't throw your glasses at a wall! That only happens in the song 'Moscow' produced by the pop group Genghis Khan. Vodka is never

Luxury by the spoonful...

INSPIRED TOASTS

In Russia never ever say 'Na Zdorovie' or 'Nostrovia' when proposing a toast! First of all it's not even Russian but a vodka myth, possibly corrupted from Polish or Czech. And secondly, there is no real Russian equivalent to 'Cheers!' Instead you're expected to think up your own inspired toast.

sipped but drunk in large gulps and never without eating *zakuska*, little nibbles of various sorts. Vodka is best drunk with something sour such as pickled gherkins and it is neither an aperitif nor a digestif – it is drunk with a meal. Liquid intake levels can be balanced out by drinking juice or *mors*, a fruit drink prepared from berries. And, by the way, vodka should be put in a fridge before serving but never in the freezer.

Caviar as *Zakuska*

Taste-wise, vodka and caviar complement each other perfectly but by today's prices for sturgeons' roe that seems a little decadent. The older generation can, however, remember how black caviar was used in the 1970s as a household remedy to pep up sick children – and for that reason lots of Russians can't stand the taste to this day!

The Russians' 'little water'

Back then the USSR produced 2,500 tons a year; in 2015 production was regulated by law to just 43 tons. It comes exclusively from recently established aquaculture farms as the stocks of native types of sturgeon are severely threatened by extinction due to negative environmental factors, overfishing and poaching. For this reason there has been a total fishing ban in Russia for years. Today, a 100 gram tin (3.5oz) costs around 5,000 roubles (about £65) or more in a high-street shop. In exclusive restaurants that have fish roe on their menus, one can expect to pay about 2,000 roubles for a 10 gram spoonful. For the roe of large species of sturgeon (*kaluga* from eastern Siberia and *beluga* from southern Russia) double or even three times that price may be paid – if it is available at all. Caviar is usually served on ice and is eaten with black bread and little pancakes.

Vodka and *zakuska* at the bar in the Grand Hotel Europe

Dachas

For many Russians it is not their flat in the city or their workplace that forms the pivotal centre of their lives but their dacha. The little houses and their gardens are a kind of occupational therapy – they are a holiday destination, supply base and hobby room all in one.

There are an estimated 500,000 dachas in the area around St Petersburg. According to surveys, half of all Russians who live in towns have such a little private oasis in the country. A dacha can be a skew-whiff, wooden hut, battered by the elements, without running water, on a crowded allotment where every working person was given a 600m² (6,500ft²) plot to grow their own vegetables during the Soviet era. Or it can be an old farmhouse in a village. It may even be a genuine, architect-designed villa behind high walls with a separate guest suite and pool.

Luxury versions of the dacha also exist

Strawberries from the garden of one's own dacha taste the best...

There is a saying: 'There's a farmer in every Russian'. This is proven by all the dachas. Four out of five *dachniks* use their dacha to grow fruit and vegetables for their own use. It was for this reason that the Soviet government established dacha colonies, some of which have thousands of allotments. In times of difficulty, such as at the end of the 1980s, the private plots prevented the country from going hungry. The dacha is also a base for a life outdoors – from here you can go fishing in the ponds or pick mushrooms and berries in the woods and marshland in the area.

Even if the yield of home-grown vegetables and fruit from one's own trees might not cover the costs and all the effort, gardening triggers all sorts of positive emotions, creative freedom and material for a chat over the garden fence. City-dwellers also still their need for individuality in the environment they live in, as there are only limited possibilities for this in the heavily populated housing estates they come from. Every week they saw, hammer and paint until the house, the pergola, the *banya* (Russian sauna) and garden fence are all just as they want them to be.

INSIDER INFO

A trip on the *elektrichka* line, departing from Finland Station and heading towards Priozersk, can be recommended to get an impression of typical dacha life. After 45 mins., near **Kavgolovo**, a lake popular for swimming is reached. The train then carries on over a dam. 1½ hours later you arrive at **Orechovo**, from where superb forest hikes through hilly countryside can be enjoyed. From the next station, simply known as '67km', signs point to **Norway Park Orech**, a very well laid out forest climbing ropeway with routes of varying difficulties.

SPACE FOR CREATIVE DREAMS

In St Petersburg everything always seems just that little bit bigger – the streets, the houses, even restaurants and shops. But those restaurateurs and other creative innovators setting up new businesses, enterprising young have to start small here too. The best way to begin exploring is to visit one of the vibrant creative centres which buzz with energy night and day. Such communal start-ups in St Petersburg are taking over courtyards and even a veritable city palace.

Creative coffee' from a food truck

Barely opened, **Golitsyn Loft** quickly advanced to become *the* hotspot in the St Petersburg scene in summer 2016 – and not just for one particular scene. The nostalgically-minded were more than enthusiastic, as this meant that one of the city's palaces on the Fontanka (the left branch of the Neva), right opposite St Michael's Castle (▶ 69), was accessible once again – even if it had subsided and was derelict. It still had a wealth of ornamental plasterwork, parquet floors, high ceilings and an historical aura. Regular guests at the house of the Counts of Golitsyn even included Pushkin. A new venue has evolved for gastrofans with numerous and bars (such as Fresco ▶ 72).

Relaxing at the 'beach bar' Dyuny

Performance in the art centre at Pushkinskaya 10

inner courtyard provides enough space for mobile food vans too. Fashion junkies can rummage through boutiques stocking unconventional designer labels and those who like listening to good music in a bar in the evening or dancing in small clubs will find what they are looking for here. The operators of at least 70 different shops, projects, pubs, studios, snack and shisha bars have been able to rent a few square metres here cheaply for their business start-ups. Sometimes that means a mini café in a niche in the stairwell, a 'pod' hotel or a tattoo studio squeezed into the corner of a former chapel.

Anti-cafés

The two largest and most magnificent rooms in the main building with any amount of period furniture and a wonderful balcony have been taken over by **Ziferburg** (daily 11am–midnight). It belongs to the (now international) **Ziferblat** chain of anti-cafés (other branches: Nevsky Pr. 81, www. ziferblat.net) – and was once just a small start-up. In 2010 the young artist Ivan Mitin from Moscow had the whacky idea of setting up a café where you don't pay for what you eat and drink but for the time you spend there: 3 roubles a minute (after 2 hours just 2 roubles, after 4 hours you can stay on free of charge). For that you can have breakfast, coffee, tea and use the Internet free of charge. If you like you can bring your own food or buy it somewhere else in the complex. Laptop users love it as a place to work with others for a little while; others use it as a living room for a few cosy hours alone or with friends. Sometimes there are concerts and talks in the evening.

Inside the restaurant Selyonaya komnata in the Etashi cultural centre

Considerably smaller creative oases run by the same organisers are **Fligel**, with unconventional bars and cafés as well as interesting fashion and accessory outlets, and **Tretiy Klaster**, where the inner courtyard full of plants exudes something of la dolce vita in summer with its wine bar, beer temple and street food kiosk. Façades painted in psychedelic colours can be found here and there.

Unwinding on the roof terraces at the Loft Project Etashi

Ligovsky Prospekt

Lots of space for dozens of micro-shops, be they for fashion, jewellery or food, but also for larger exhibitions and events can be found in the **Loft Project Etashi**. The whole of this old bread factory has been taken over and now includes an open-air stage on the flat roof with a wonderful view, especially at sunset. A popular meeting place there is the restaurant **Selyonaya komnata** with its strong organic leanings and large roof terrace. A 'container street' is gradually becoming established in the courtyard. Some 30 redundant freight containers that have been partially glazed and cleverly extended now provide a home for start-ups: record shops, hairdressers, steak houses, dressmakers and tailors, shops, cafés…

400m (1,300ft) further on is Ligovsky Prospekt 50. An inconspicuous entrance leads to a complex of old, two-storey warehouses which have developed into an insider address for night-life lovers without even ever having had a master plan. Some of the hippest bars and clubs in the city lie hidden between dance studios, car workshops, wholesalers and a Serbian snack-bar in this latently crumbling environment. It makes little sense naming names as 'in' venues come and go quickly. However, at the far end, St Petersburg's only sandpit serving alcoholic drinks has become a firm fixture over the past few years: the totally informal 'beach bar' **Dyuny** (daily noon–3am, Sat, Sun. until 6am) is located in a little building right next to the tracks at Moscow Station. During the day children play around in the sand in front of the building; in the evening DJs work the turntables and guests have fun either inside or outside, depending on the weather. Noise in this area is not an issue.

CREATIVE CENTRES

Tretiy Klaster: 8 Sovietskaya Ul. 4;
http://luna-info.ru/spaces; metro: Pl. Vosstaniya
Fligel: Ul. Vosstaniya 24 (2nd courtyard);
http://luna-info.ru/spaces; metro: Chernyshevskaya
Golitsyn Loft: nab. reki Fontanki 20;
http://luna-info.ru/spaces; metro: Gostiny Dvor
Loft Project Etashi: Ligovsky Pr. 74;
www.loftprojectetagi.ru; metro: Ligovsky Pr.
Ligovsky Courtyards: Ligovsky Pr. 50; metro: Ligovsky Pr.
Artmusa: 13 line 70; www.artmuza.spb.ru;
metro: Vasileostrovskaya (esp. galleries and artists' studios)
Pushkinskaya 10 (the classic among the artist communes, ▶ 140):
Ligovsky Pr. 53; metro: Pl. Vosstaniya

Coffee break on the balcony of the anti-café Ziferblat

Finding Your Feet

First Two Hours

Almost all visitors to St Petersburg arrive by plane. The overland route by coach or train is long and tiring and there are very few possibilities by ship.

Arriving by Plane

■ St Petersburg's airport **Pulkovo** (www.pulkovoairport.ru) is right on the edge of the city and has an architecturally attractive terminal building that serves its purpose well. Security and passport checks as well as luggage retrieval can all be dealt with very quickly. However, the airport has no railway connection; an express tram link to the metro station Kupchino is still only at the planning stage.

Insider Tip ■ There are ATMs and a bank in the **arrivals hall**. If you intend travelling on from here by bus then you'll have to exchange money here at the latest. Several car-hire companies and a branch of the city's tourist information office have desks here too.

Travelling on by Taxi

Insider Tip Shake off any 'private taxi drivers' who may be lurking around, even if they do have official-looking badges on their lapels! Taxi Pulkovo operates desks at baggage reclaim, in the arrivals hall and outside the terminal building where you can book a taxi to your destination, without any hassle, run by one of the companies accredited by the airport and pay for it straight away (also by credit card). Prices are based on zones and are very moderate: ₽1,000 roubles for a 20km (12.5mi) journey into the city centre; ₽1,400 to districts in the north; baggage is included. More luxurious limousines cost 25 percent more. You will be given a receipt with the number of a taxi on it which you take with you to the taxi stand.

Travelling on by Bus or on the Metro

Bus stops for lines 39 and 39e (express non-stop bus) and the *marshrutka* K-39 minibus taxi line are located opposite the terminal. Buses (₽40, journey time 20–35 mins.) run every 10–12 minutes during the day; the *marshrutka* (₽40, journey time 15–20 mins.) every 5–10 minutes. Large pieces of luggage cost an extra ₽40 in buses; in the *marshrutka* there is no room for anything that you can't hold on your lap. All lines terminate at **Moskovskaya metro station** on the Blue Line 2 that goes straight to the centre (station: Nevsky Prospekt). Any onward journey by metro costs ₽45 (one token, Russian: *zheton*). Large pieces of luggage cost another *zheton* and you may use the pram entrance next to the turnstile. To find the right bus stop when **returning to the airport**, leave the station in the direction of the train, go through the pedestrian tunnel to the far end and take the stairs to the left.

Arriving by Ship

■ The St Peter Line ferries (www.stpeterline.com) come in to the old **Sea Station** (*morskoy Vokzal*, Ploshchad Morskoy Slavy 1). To reach the centre (6km/3.7mi) use the shuttle service run by the ferry operator or, alternatively, take trolley bus no. 10 or 11 (₽30).

■ Most cruise liners dock at the new **Morskoy Fasad passenger terminal** (Mitchmanskaya Ul.). It is also on Vasilyevsky Island but much further away, on a recently constructed site. Bus 158 will take you to Primorskaya metro station. Smaller liners can dock at moorings on the banks of the Neva nearer the city centre. From the pier on Angliyskaya Embankment it is only 1km (0.6mi) to St Isaac's Cathedral; from Lieutenant Schmidt Embankment about 2.5km (1.5mi).

Arriving by Train

■ Trains from Latvia, White Russia and the Ukraine terminate at **Vitebsky Station** (➤ 116). The metro station Pushkinskaya (Line 1) is right next to the station.

■ Coming by train from Finland you arrive at the Vyborg side of **Finland Station**. The entrance to the metro station Pl. Lenina (Line 1) is in the station building but only accessible from the street.

Arriving by Bus

International long-distance coaches from the Baltic States generally head for the Baltic railway Station, used just by suburban trains, with its connection to the metro station Baltiyskaya (Line 1). Then carry on to the **Central Bus Station** (nab. Obvodnogo Canal 36) – it is however a 500m (1,600ft) foot march to the metro station Obvodny Canal (Line 5).

Tourist Information

The municipal tourist information department has several information desks and kiosks. The central office is in Gostiny Dvor (➤ 148; Sadovaya Ul. 14); another branch is in the old Guard House on Hay Square (➤ 190; Sennaya pl. 37, both: Mon–Sat 10am–7pm). Info kiosks and desks can be found outside St Isaac's Cathedral (➤ 106), the Hermitage (➤ 54), Moscow Station and Peter and Paul Fortress (➤ 82), as well as at Pulkovo Airport (all: daily 10am–7pm) and at Smolny Cathedral (➤ 144; Mon–Fri 8:30am–4pm).

Getting Around

Compared to the centres of most European cities the distances in St Petersburg are huge. To rest your feet and save time you should make use of the public transport system after exploring things at first on foot to gain your bearings. Fares are very reasonable compared to those in the West, as are taxis. Cycling is still something rather exotic but is becoming more popular from year to year.

Metro

The metro or underground network is quite extensive and gets top marks for cleanliness and the frequency of trains. The sixty-seven stations at present are laid out along just five lines. While residents in some new housing districts have been waiting for decades for the once promised metro link, the city centre is well served. This is where all stations for changing lines are located.

■ The **fare system** is simple: For the price of one token (*zheton*) that you can buy in the entrance area in every metro station and which you insert in the turnstile, you can travel on the metro as long and as far as you like. A *zheton* costs P45 and there are vending machines and manned windows in every station. Despite the enormous variety of cards available for multiple journeys on the metro system, none of these are particularly attractive for visitors staying just a few days in the city.

■ The **metro operates** from around 6am with trains running every 1½–5 mins. The last trains of the day depart from the ends of each line just after

Finding Your Feet

midnight. At 3 mins. past midnight you can no longer change from one
line to another. On a few important public holidays/festivals the metro
runs until 5am. In addition, a shuttle service operates every 20 mins.
between the stations Admiralteyskaya and Sportivnaya during the
summer months (when the bridges have been opened; fig. ➤ 6/7) and
from 1am–3am on Sat and Sun mornings and on public holidays.

■ **Orientation:** 2 million passengers use the metro every day so it is often
very crowded – just move with the masses! As the long escalators (time
needed: 2–3 mins.) run faster than normal you might need to pluck up
a bit of courage when jumping on and off. Please note: stand on the right
and walk on the left. All signs are now in English too; the different colours
used for the various lines also helps you keep your bearings.

Buses and Trams

■ Above ground the **fare system** is equally simple. On every vehicle there
are conductors who sell and check tickets (₽40). Tickets cover any
distance but are not valid in another bus or tram if you change en route.

Insider
Tip

■ The **timetables** at *avtobus*, trolleybus and tramway stops are very spartan
and merely indicate the route and how often they run. Many lines run
parallel along the Nevsky Prospekt so you never have to wait long. Small
city maps with public transport routes and lines (incl. the *marshrutki*)
can be bought in bookshops and may help you through the labyrinth of
possibilities.

■ **Night buses** marked with an 'M' operate every 30 mins. and follow the
route of the metro lines. In summer, when the bridges over the Neva
have been raised, they can obviously only travel so far before turning
round again.

■ **Marshrutki** are privately run minibuses marked with a 'K' number. They
operate along fixed routes but have no timetables. They can be stopped
at any appropriate place other than official stops by raising your hand or,
during a journey, by telling the driver in advance where you want to get
out. The fare (₽34–₽40, on suburban lines up to ₽80) is paid when you
get on or immediately afterwards (your fare will be passed from row to
row in front of you and you and your change comes back the same way). A lot
of *marshrutka*-drivers are often quite aggressive – speed saves time and
time is money.

■ Tickets for the *elektrichka*, the indestructible but often noisy suburban
trains, can be bought at the ticket offices at stations and – only if it is
not manned – from the conductor.

Taxis

■ **Fares** are extremely reasonable thanks to a huge increase in competition
and a well thought-through online service – unless, of course, you get
in a taxi at one of the strategically favourable spots (Opera House, night
club, up-market hotel) which has been waiting for ages for a clueless
passenger!).

■ The cheapest and yet fastest to arrive and the most reliable companies
are **Wesyot** and **Rutaxi** (www.spb.rutaxi.ru; tel: 812-318-0318). A 5km
(3mi) journey costs just ₽240; online reservations are 25 percent cheaper.
Yandex.taxi (www.taxi.yandex.ru) is slightly more expensive as are the
companies **Taxovichkof** (http://taxovichkof.com; tel: 812-333-0002).
These companies also have (English) apps for calling a taxi that minimis-
es the language barrier. You will be told the fare due when calling and
no bartering is allowed.

Cycling

Although there are hardly any cycle paths St Petersburg is attractive for cyclists. There are no hills and cycling can be fun along the river banks, in parks and down side roads. The municipal online bike-hire system **Velogorod** (www.spb.velogorod.org) operates from some 100 automatic 'stations'. The blue city bikes, however, are only cheap if you rent them for short periods. The yellow **Cafebike** rental bikes (www.cafebike.org) can be found outside many pubs and hostels where you will be given a key. The rate is ₽2 a minute or a maximum ₽500 a day. Bikes better suited to longer tours are available from this price upwards from bike-hire companies such as:

■ **Skatprokat:** Gontsharnaya Ul. 7; tel: 812-717-6838; www.skatprokat.ru
■ **Rentbike:** Ul. Marata 25a; tel: 812-981-0155; www.rentbike.org
■ **Velorodeo:** Petergof, Ul. Sverinskaya 6; tel: 812-974-7431; www.velo rodeo.ru

Sightseeing Tours

■ **The best way to see the city** in summer is from the top of a **Citytour** (www.citytourspb.ru) open-top, double-decker bus. Buses depart for the circular tour lasting just under 2 hours every 30–60 mins. A commentary is given via headphones in a choice of 11 languages. You can hop-off at any of the 14 stops and hop-on one of the next buses to pass. The official starting and finishing point is Ostrovsky Square in the middle of Nevsky Prospekt but you can begin at any stop you like. Tickets are valid for one day (₽700) or two (₽900) and can be bought on the bus or at theatre ticket desks. A combined ticket for a bus and boat trip is available too. This also operates on a hop-on, hop-off principle (₽1,200 or ₽1,500). Easy to confuse: **City Sightseeing** (www.city-sightseeing/led) also has a fleet of red double-deckers but is more expensive (₽1,000 valid for 2 days) and the buses only run on the south bank of the Neva.

■ **Canal and Neva trips:** Excursion boats operate from the end of April until early October wherever streams of tourists end up on the water's edge and there are suitable moorings, such as at the canal bridges on Nevsky Prospekt, along the banks of the Neva and at Peter and Paul Fortress. Round trips last 1–1½ hrs. (₽600–₽700); boat trips in English run several times a day from **Anichkov Bridge** (➤ 133; www.anglotourismo.com, nab. reki Fontanki 27, ₽1,000).

■ **Sightseeing flights:** 10-min. sightseeing flights on a 20-seater Mi-8 helicopter are available from May–Oct on Sat and Sun between noon–5:30pm, taking off from Peter and Paul Fortress (www.baltairlines.ru; tel: 812-611-0956, ₽5,000).

St Petersburg Card

Holders of the St Petersburg Card (www.petersburgcard.com) have free entrance to more than 60 museums, parks and palaces – this however does not include the Hermitage, but does include boat and bus tours and a hydrofoil trip to Peterhof Palace. Some (albeit few) restaurants and shops offer discounts to card-holders. The card can also be topped up to buy public transport tickets electronically. Cards can be ordered online (and collected personally or sent at a fee to your hotel) or at 16 places in the city centre. Cards are valid for 2, 3, 5 and 7 days and cost ₽3,200–₽5,500. It is probably only worth buying a card if you stay a minimum of 5 days.

Finding Your Feet

■ **Guided tours of the city: Peterswalk** (www.peterswalk.com) is a 4-hour guided tour on foot, held in English and available from April–Oct daily at 10:30am; no advance booking necessary (₽1,500; meeting place: Café Small Double, Kasanskaya Ul. 26). Sat, Sun at 11am as well as during the White Nights. Guided tours of the city by bike are held in Russian and English on Tue, Thu at 10:30pm (₽2,200, meeitng place: Skatprokat, Gontsharnaya Ul. 7). Guided tours of the city for individual visitors can be booked, for example, with Lothar Deeg, the author of this book (e-mail: guide@infoburg.info).

Drawbridges
They are an attraction and a nuisance at the same time. From April to November all the bridges over the Neva (apart from the high motorway bridge) are opened every night between 1:25am and about 5am to let freight ships pass in convoy. If you don't get back to the right side of the river on time you will have to wait until around 3am when Palace Bridge, Blagoveshchensky Bridge and Exchange Bridge are let down again for about 30 mins. For a detailed timetable and up-to-date information on changes, see www.mostotrest-spb.ru.

Accommodation

The range of accommodation available in St Petersburg is vast with more than 300 hotels, 800 mini-hotels, some 1,000 hostels, plus apartments and holiday flats. The difference in quality and price is enormous as well. The spectrum ranges from exclusive hotels to simple hostels in back premises for backpackers on a low budget.

Location
Anyone wanting to explore the city on their own will want to stay in the city centre. The most important sights can then be reached without even having to take the metro and visiting bars, pubs or events in the evening is unproblematic. St Isaac's Square is surrounded by 4 and 5-star hotels and on and near Nevsky Prospekt, between Anichkov Bridge and Moscow Station, there are many hotels to choose from. If you want to enjoy everything the city has to offer then staying here is a perfect base.

Booking a Hotel Room
Accommodation is easy to book via such websites as www.hotels.com; www.booking.com or www.hostelworld.com. With a list of 4,500 addresses the greatest selection can be found under www.hotels.ru (in English).

Hotel Prices
Room prices depend very much on the time of year. In the low season from October to April, except for the time around New Year, a double room in a 3 or 4-star hotel will be around ₽3,500–₽5,000. Prices soar during the White Nights. If you want to save money, travel in May or August rather than in June and July.

Insider Tip

Apartments and Holiday Flats

Renting out holiday flats and rooms has something of a tradition in St Petersburg as, for many people, it is a source of additional income in the summer when they are at their dachas. This low-priced form of accommodation can best be found under www.airbnb.com or through the STN agency (www.saint-petersburg-apartments.com). Mini-hotels (guesthouses with 4–20 rooms) can also be booked on this website.

Hostels

The market for cheap accommodation is booming – which explains the range available. Most hostels are relatively new and unconventional (see also ► 43). Many only have multi-bed rooms (₽500–₽1,400), but cheap doubles and family rooms, sometimes with their own bathrooms (from around ₽3,500), can also be found.

Accommodation Prices
for a double room per night (incl. breakfast) in the high season:
£ under ₽5,000 ££ ₽5,000–₽10,000 £££ ₽10,000–₽20,000 ££££ over ₽20,000

HOTELS

3mostA ££
A small, friendly hotel (26 rooms) in an excellent location on the Moyka between the Church of the Resurrection of Christ and the Hermitage. The rooms are spacious and, from the glass-roofed terrace, the view extends over the rooftops to the brightly coloured church domes.
✚ 203 D1 ⊠ Nab. reki Moyki 3a
☎ 812-315-0200; www.3mosta.com
Ⓜ Nevsky Prospekt

Alexander House £££
Small but delightful and very individual in character: all 20 rooms are furnished in the style and spirit of a city that the hotel owners find particularly interesting. This carefully renovated merchant's house is located away from the hustle and bustle on a romantic canal. Just 10 mins. walk to the Mariinsky Theatre.
✚ 205 D2 ⊠ Nab. Kryukova kan. 27
☎ 812-575-3877; www.a-house.ru
Ⓔ Lermontovsky Pr. (tram 3, bus 49, 181)

Dinastia £
There are lots of places to eat on Ul. Rubinshteyna but hotels are scarce. The Dinastia was here long before the street became so hip. It has 62 plainly furnished rooms – it is not luxurious but provides plenty of space and everything one needs.
✚ 206 B3 ⊠ Ul. Rubinshteyna 29
☎ 812-644-5343; www.dynasty.eurasia-hotel.ru
Ⓜ Dostoyevskaya

DOM Boutique Hotel £££
This hotel, that opened in 2016, has the flair somewhere between a country house and a London club, created by British designers. The colourful mixture of styles that only a real dandy would dare to match up, is continued in the 60 rooms. The location in a side road behind the Summer Garden is very peaceful and yet central. The hotel has an Italian restaurant.
✚ 203 E2 ⊠ Gangutskaya Ul. 4
☎ 812-245-1040; www.domboutiquehotel.com
Ⓜ Gostiny Dvor

Dostoyevsky £££
As a hotel it merits a 3-star rating rather than four – but the location is well worth paying for. The 218 rooms occupy the top three floors of a shopping centre behind an historic façade on busy Vladimir Square. You will find a supermarket

Finding Your Feet

in the basement that is open 24 hours, two metro stations at the door and the nightspot Rubinshteyna behind the building.

🏠 206 B3 ✉ Vladimirsky Pr. 19
☎ 812-331-3200; www.dostoevsky-hotel.ru
🚇 Dostoyevskaya

Esperans £

With just 5 rooms (all en-suite) this is a typical mini-hotel except that it is not in an old apartment building but in an up-market new build right next to the Cabin of Peter the Great (also called Peter's Cottage). What is equally unusual is its location on the 8th floor, its stylish modern interior and the generously sized kitchen/lounge area.

🏠 203 D3 ✉ Michurinskaya Ul. 6
☎ 812-927-5720; www.esperanshotel.ru
🚇 Gorkovskaya

Grand Hotel Europe ££££

St Petersburg's classic, 140-year old hotel with its historical atmosphere, belongs to the Belmond chain. The hotel with its some 300 rooms offers state-of-the-art comfort and impeccable service. Russian Art Nouveau dominates the bar, the elegant Restaurant L'Europe in the atrium and one floor which has been furnished with period furniture in keeping with the style of the good old days.

🏠 206 A4 ✉ Mikhailovskaya Ul. 1–7
☎ 812-329-6000; www.belmond.com
🚇 Nevsky Prospekt

Ekaterina £

The rooms are small, the furnishing simple, breakfast is basic. But this is St Petersburg's only hotel in one of the imperial palaces! It is housed in one of the single-storeyed wings that form a semi-circle at the back of Catherine Palace. If you are lucky (or book one of the more luxurious rooms) you will be able to see the floodlit Baroque façade from your bed. A perfect place for a meditative time out and long walks in the park.

🏠 208 C3 ✉ Pushkin, Ul. Sadovaya 5
☎ 812-466-8042; www.hotelekaterina.ru
🚌 Dvortsovaya Ul. (bus 371, K-342)

Nevsky Hotel Grand ££

This flagship hotel of a small chain has 164 rooms. The best location in the city centre and the low price make up for its negative aspects: the standard rooms are tiny and do not have a fridge. The rooms in a separate block Nevsky Grand Energy are bigger but you always have to negotiate stairs.

🏠 205 F4 ✉ Bolshaya Konyushennaya Ul. 10,
☎ 812-312-1206; www.hon.ru
🚇 Gostiny Dvor

New Peterhof ££

A chic, modern, 4-star hotel with a number of top sights in the immediate vicinity – and all at a very reasonable price. Does such a place exist? Yes, it does – the New Peterhof Palace that lies between the Palace and Olgin Pond. And the bus-stop for the city centre is right outside the door.

🏠 208 B2
✉ Petergof, St Petersburgsky Pr. 34
☎ 812-319-1010; www.new-peterhof.com
🚌 Pravlenskaya Ul. (lines 200, 210, K-224, K-300, K-404, K-424 from Avtovo metro station)

Petersburg Hotel £

Two Swiss-run mini-hotels on Griboedov Canal each with 4 rooms like in a shared flat. One flat is close to the Nevsky on Bank Bridge, the other on the corner of the 'in' street Gorokhovaya. There is a kitchen for residents' use in each flat.

🏠 205 E3
✉ Griboedov Canal Embankment 29
☎ 812-913-9657; www.petersburg-hotel.com
🚇 Nevsky Prospekt

Peterville £

This clean, modern hotel with a pleasantly reserved beige-brown décor has 23 low-priced rooms with everything you need for a comfortable night's sleep.

Breakfast is served in the hotel's own bistro Philibert. Peterville is close to the metro and the cultural venues on Ligovsky Prospekt – and is at the heart of an area so typical of St Petersburg.

✚ 206 C2 ✉ Kolomenskaya Ul. 29
☎ 812-607-5747; www.peterville.ru
Ⓜ Ligovsky Prospekt

Solo Sokos Palace Bridge ££

This modern hotel close to the Strelka with 324 rooms belongs to the Finnish Sokos chain. It stands out due to its cool Nordic design and its spa area (8 saunas and a large pool) that is popular among locals too.

✚ 202 B2 ✉ Birzhevoi Per. 2–4
☎ 812-335-2200; www.sokoshotels.com; www.pbwellnessclub.ru Ⓜ sportivnaya

Happy Pushkin ££

This plush, retro hotel owes its name to the legendary poet who lived here just after he was married. There are 48 rooms, including singles, and several suites, some of which are huge. Prices are unusually reasonable. Peaceful location near New Holland.

✚ 205 D3 ✉ Galernaya Ul. 53
☎ 812-777-1799; www.happypushkin.ru
Ⓜ Pl. Truda (trolley 5, 22)

Taleon Imperial Hotel ££££

The epitome of elegance. The former city palace of the Swiss merchant family Elisseeff forms the heart of this 120-room hotel. Rooms are furnished in the typical Petersburg Empire Style – including those in the new extension that cannot be seen from the road. This has a spa with a generously sized pool under a glass roof.

✚ 205 F4 ✉ Nevsky Pr. 15
☎ 812-324-9911; www.taleonimperialhotel.com
Ⓜ Admiralteyskaya

Traditional Hotel £££

Several of the 16 rooms in this little deluxe hotel in the district

known as Petrograd Side have a wonderful view of the Neva. To the left is the fortress, in the centre the Winter Palace, to the right Strelka – and at night you can see the opened bridges. The one drawback is the traffic that crawls along all around the building.

✚ 202 C2 ✉ Pr. Dobrolyubova 2
☎ 812-405-8855; www.traditionhotel.ru
Ⓜ Sportivnaya

W ££££

This swanky but nevertheless homely designer hotel with 137 generously sized rooms attracts the style-conscious, dynamically minded with well-padded wallets. The open-air bar on the roof terrace – on level with St Isaac's Cathedral and the Admiralty – is equally impressive.

✚ 205 E4 ✉ Voznesensky Pr. 6
☎ 812-610-6161; www.wstpetersburg.com
Ⓜ Admiralteyskaya

Insider Tip

HOSTELS

Aqua Hostel £

Large hostel with 150 beds and one unique characteristic – it floats. It is moored right next to the old Petrovsky Stadium.

✚ 202 B3 ✉ Zhdanowskaya nab. 1
☎ 812-903-3215; www.aqua-hostel.ru
Ⓜ Sportivnaya

Location Hostel £

Trendy accommodation in the vibrant Etashi Creative Centre with three, ultra cool designer rooms with their own bathrooms.

✚ 206 C2 ✉ Ligovsky Pr. 74
☎ 812-329-1274; www.location-hostel.ru
Ⓜ Ligovsky Prospekt

Baby Lemonade Hostel £

Individually and cleverly designed rooms (some attic rooms) with a romantic rock 'n' roll flair. All beds have curtains. Top central location.

✚ 206 B4 ✉ Inzhenernaya Ul. 7
☎ 812-570-7943; www.vk.com/epoquehostels
Ⓜ Gostiny Dvor

Food and Drink

**The restaurant scene in St Petersburg is varied, imaginative, international –
and dynamic. Virtually no popular, traditional eateries were able to establish
themselves during the drab Soviet era which means that a 20-year old restaurant is considered a well-established, time-proven classic. Just let yourself
be pleasantly surprised!**

Traditional and International

■ Ukrainian cuisine is closely related to **Russian cuisine** although everything is a little bit more hearty, fattier and meat orientated. The people of
Georgia broadened the culinary horizon of the Russians many decades
ago with their juicy and spicy grilled dishes whereas, from Uzbekistan,
the first waft of exotic Asian cuisine whet the appetite of Russians in the
Soviet era. In the meantime Italian, French, German, Arabian, Japanese
and Chinese food has found a new home on the Neva.

■ Anyone who wants to try Russian fare does not necessarily have to seek
out a restaurant with explicitly local dishes. Some Russian classics such
as *borscht* (beetroot soup) or *pelmeni* (small dumplings filled with minced
meat) can be found on virtually every menu.

■ The Russians love a hearty **breakfast**. For this reason, *sosiski* (small
sausages) with *pyure* (mashed potato) or *grechikha* (buckwheat), *blini*
(pancakes), *syrniki* (quark cakes) and *pierogi* (dumplings/dough filled
with vegetables, fruit, meat or fish) may also appear on the table in hotels
frequented by locals.

■ **Snack stands** often sell *blini* and *pierogi* as well. The Georgian cheese-
filled bread *khachapuri* is also very popular. *Shawarma* is the name of
a variation of kebab found in St Petersburg. Imaginative burgers and
falafel are hot favourites in the popular streetfood bars.

■ In Russia, **soup** is not only a starter but a meal in its own right. This can
be seen on many menus as the weight of each helping is given. 500g of
solyanka (a slightly sour stew with gherkins, cabbage, olives, lemons and
meat) is very filling!

■ Russia's classic **salads** are the *salad olivye* made of beef, potatoes, carrots,
peas and egg as well as *selyodka pod shuboy* ('herring in a fur coat'). The
fish is covered with layers of pototo, carrot, beetroot and mayonnaise.

■ The good-value *bisnes-lantch* (business lunch), is a small, speedy full
meal available in almost all restaurants during the working week, generally from noon–3pm/4pm; a *shvedsky stol* ('Swedish table'), on the other
hand, is a self-service buffet.

■ In virtually 95 percent of all eateries **menus in English** are available – or
else the *menyu* is already in two languages.

Vegetarian Food

Russian gastronomy still holds fast to the notion that a fully-fledged meal can
only be created with meat. However, the number of vegetarian restaurants
or eateries that offer a range of vegetarian dishes is increasing from year
to year – and this has been taken into consideration in the restaurant tips
listed in this guide.

Meal Times

In St Petersburg the daily routine is one to two hours later than that in central
and western Europe. As a consequence, lunch is generally eaten between

1pm and 3pm and dinner between 8pm–10pm. As a tourist this doesn't really apply as hot food is served non-stop in restaurants and cafés during normal opening hours (from 11am or noon–11pm or later).

Restaurant Categories

- A *restoran* implies a more sophisticated gastronomic standard. There is a cloakroom, tables are set, cooking times are longer. In the evening there is often live music; in some places there is dancing.
- In a *kafe* things are less formal; you can also simply have a drink here when lunch or dinner is not being served. The choice of food is however often quite extensive, as is the range of prices, comfort and culinary skill. In simple *kafes* you do not order at the table but at the bar (where sometimes you also have to collect your meal yourself).
- The serving of *alkoholika* is the mainstay of a *bar* – although quite often the menu is surprisingly extensive too. Many bars are pub-like in character from their furnishings to the range of beers on offer.
- A *kofeynya* or *konditorskaya* is the equivalent of a western café with pastries, cakes and desserts. Sometimes, but not always, this is supplemented by a small number of hot snacks and alcoholic drinks. Many cafés are branches of a chain, such as the **Coffeeshop Company** (the best), **Coffee House, Idealnaya Chashka** or **Stolle** (prized for its *pierogi* – dumplings/buns).
- A *stolovaya* is a canteen; often nicely furnished places which operate along the lines of a self-service cafeteria. This market is also dominated by chains such as **Stolovaya No. 1** (very cheap) or **Tarelka** serving standard Russian fare. **Teremok** and **Chaynaya Lozhka** largely serve pancakes.
- A *rumochnaya* is a vodka bar; but, as no Russian drinks his 'little water' without a bite to eat, such 'bites' are served here too.

Tipping

When you pay your bill you will be given the exact change. If you were happy with the service leave 5–10 percent of the total sum in the folder in which the bill arrived. Barkeepers and cloakroom attendants are more than pleased to be given a small tip although this is not automatically expected.

Restaurant Prices
for a main course (without drinks):
£ under ₽450   ££ ₽450–₽900   £££ over ₽900

Shopping

Even though there is a lot on offer and the opening times are customer friendly, St Petersburg is not a shopping destination. Quality products in the fashion, design and accessories sectors are largely imported and cheaper in western European cities where the selection is also better. This metropolis, with a population of 5 million, is only a good spot for bargain hunters is you are explicitly on the look-out for Russian goods.

Finding Your Feet

Where to Shop

- **Nevsky Prospekt** (➤ 130) is St Petersburg's main shopping street *par excellence* – with two special areas of interest: firstly, the department store **Gostiny Dvor** (➤ 148) and the immediate vicinity – whereby all the shops here have a charming nostalgic aura. On the opposite side of the road there is a whole range of traditional shops such as the House of Books (**Dom Knigi;** ➤ 148), the shopping gallery **Passage** (➤ 148) and the delicatessen **Eliseyev** (➤ 148).
- The second popular area to shop on the Nevsky is **Uprising Square** (Ploshchad Vosstaniya; ➤ 130) around Moscow Station. The two shopping malls **Gallery** (➤ 149) and **Nevsky Centre** (➤ 149) attract masses of shoppers – together the two are home to more than 380 shops!
- **Hay Square** (Sennaya Ploshchad; ➤ 123) is a traditionally lively place – even if the city council ordered all the stands and kiosks on the square to be demolished in 2016. There are still two shopping centres left. The famously infamous **Apraksin Dvor** (➤ 148), the central market for everything non-edible, is virtually next-door. There is also a food market on Hay Square. More attractive however is **Kuznechny Rynok** (➤ 142) in the city centre. Market halls near tourist sights also exist in Petrograd Side, e.g. **Sytny Rynok** (➤ 98), and on Vasilyevsky Island (Bolshoi Pr. 16).

What to Buy

- **Classical Russian souvenirs** such as matryoshka dolls, lacquerware, fur hats and painted easter eggs are available in every souvenir shop that has set up business in and around Palace Square and on Nevsky Prospekt. These and other gifts (such as snow globes, t-shirts and mugs) can be found here and on the street market on Griboyedov Canal outside the Church of the Resurrection of Christ (➤ 61). The items in the souvenir department on the Nevsky side of the ground floor in **Gostiny Dvor** (➤ 148) are perhaps of greater artistic quality. These also include painted trays, birch-bark containers and carvings from the north of Russia.
- In the **textile** section, the colourful, artistically printed Pavlovo-Posad wool and silk scarves will keep any woman warm, unless of course she prefers the plain coloured – white or grey – Orenburg goat-down shawl which is as light as a feather.
- Men may like the warming quality of **vodka**, *konyak* or **brandy**! Any large food shop stocks a good selection and there are specialist shops for all sorts of alcoholic beverages. Apart from Russian *konyak* Armenian liquor is also quite rightly well represented.
- Jugs, vases and figures made of **Gzhel porcelain** that can be recognised by its white glaze with blue decoration are typically Russian souvenirs. Products made by the Imperial Porcelain Manufactory of St Petersburg, founded in 1744, are much more elegant. Tea and coffee sets as well as small porcelain works of art can be found in the company's main outlet (➤ 149) and in around 30 other branches in the city.
- As an art metropolis St Petersburg also has a matching range of **arts and crafts** for sale such as in the streetmarket outside the Catholic church (Nevsky Pr. 32–34). There are lots of galleries under one roof in **Perinniye Ryadi** (➤ 148), diagonally opposite Dumskaya Ulitsa.

Opening Times
Food shops, supermarkets, bureaux de change and chemists are generally open every day from 9am–11pm, if not around the clock. Specialist shops, department stores and shopping malls are mostly open from 10am–10pm every day, boutiques 11am–9pm. There are no general regulations governing opening times except for one: shops must display their opening hours and keep to them.

Entertainment

Even at times in the year other than the White Nights the evenings in St Petersburg can be long and the nights short. The range of concerts and performances of all types is huge and of a high standard – not just opera and ballet, for which the city is world famous. This also applies to classical music, jazz and rock. And it is not without reason that St Petersburg is also known as the capital of Russian rock. When concerts finish the night-life really gets going in the many bars and clubs.

Information
■ It's not easy to get a good overview of what's going on especially since the one magazine in English, the St Petersburg Times, is no longer being published. A good source of information on the Internet for those with a knowledge of Russian is *Afischa Plus* (http://calendar.fontanka.ru), which provides details about current exhibitions, book presentations and readings.
■ There is a summary of what's on in the local web magazine *Fontanka.ru* every week just before the start of the weekend.
■ The website www.afisha.ru lists the films being shown in local cinemas (films are generally with Russian synchronisation).
■ The Petersburg edition of *The Village* (www.the-village.ru) also has culture and lifestyle reports.

Tickets
■ Tickets for many events can be bought online under www.bileter.ru, the city's advance booking office on the web, which has more than 100 ticket points in the city. You can generally find a *teatralnaya kassa* in metro stations and in shopping centres.
■ The central office is located opposite Gostiny Dvor (➤ 148; Nevsky Pr. 42; daily 8am–midnight).
■ A list of events for the current month is displayed at theatre box offices; there are also flyers and posters that keep people informed as to what is happening when and where.
■ Tickets for the three prime venues for classical opera and ballet, the Opera House, the Mariinsky Theatre (➤ 111) and the Mikhailovsky Theatre (➤ 149), as well as the Philharmonia (➤ 149) for concerts, are only available at the respective box offices or on the institutions' own websites.

Festivals & Events
■ New Year, Christmas (on 7 January) and the *Maslenitsa* ('Butter/Pancake Week', end Feb/beginning March) are traditional **folk festivals**

Finding Your Feet

celebrated outside even in winterly temperatures. **Open-air concerts** are held and there are all sorts of magical winter markets set up on central spots such as on Palace Square, the Strelka, at the Peter and Paul Fortress and on Ostrovsky Square.

- The Mariinsky Theatre stages two major festivals every year. At the beginning of April there is the **Mariinsky Ballet Festival** with international guest stars and at least one premiere of its own; from the end of May to the end of July **Stars of the White Nights** is held with international figures from the worlds of ballet, opera and electronic music.

- 27 May is the city's official **anniversary celebration of its foundation**. On the following Sunday there are several classical open-air concerts and a huge fireworks display. The biggest party in the city, **Alye Parusa** (Scarlet Sails; www.parusaspb.ru), marking the end of the scholastic year, generally takes place on the last Saturday in June. A gigantic show with music, laser and firework displays transforms the Neva between the Winter Palace and the Fortress into a huge stage during the White Nights, watched by hundreds of thousands along the banks.

- The park on Yelagin Island (➤ 187) is host to two cultivated open-air festivals in July: the **Stereoleto** is more a rock festival, the **Usadba Jazz** a more relaxed affair.

Jazz

The best addresses for jazz are the **Jazz Music Philharmonia** (➤ 149), the **JFC Jazz Club** (Shpalernaya Ul. 33; www.jfc-club.spb.ru), where blues, funk and soul are played, and the more casual club **Dom 7** (➤ 74).

Bars & Clubs

Live gigs and concerts are more frequent in bars and clubs at the end of the week and at weekends. There's less on offer Mon–Wed and the venues are correspondingly less full.

- Rubinshteyna Ul. is totally 'in' at the moment as *the* place to go in the evening with at least 50 bars and clubs to suit everyone's taste – and that number is increasing fast (➤ 150).

- Spurred on and sparked off by a number of trashy bars in the vaulted basement of the semi-derelict Small Gostiny Dvor, the corner of Lomonossova Ul. and Dumskaya Ul. (➤ 150) has now become a real hotspot in the bar scene.

- On Stable Square (Konyushennaya Pl.; ➤ 74) there is also a whole phalanx of bars, music and nightclubs ranging from upmarket to underground.

- The short street Belinskogo Ul. (➤ 150) boasts a number of bars.

- Russia's largest disco is the three-storey **Metro Club** (daily 10pm–6am; www.metroclub.ru, Ligovsky Pr. 174; metro: Obvodny Canal). **Rossi's** (Zodchego Rossi Ul. 1; www.rossis.ru) is also a dance and party club of the classic variety.

- Anyone looking for where Petersburg rock started out will find what they are looking for in the above and below-ground **Club Griboyedov** (Voronezhskaya Ul. 2a; www.griboedovclub.ru) or in the **Fish Fabrique** (➤ 140).

- The museum club **Kamchatka** (Blochina Ul. 15; www.vk.com/club602338) has achieved cult status as the rock musician Viktor Tsoi once stoked the boilers here. In the USSR even rock stars had to have a decent job.

Between
Winter Palace &
Summer Garden

☀ Little Treats

The longest escalator in the world

Just be patient! The main escalator in
Admiralteyskaya metro station is 137m (450ft)
long and going down it takes 3 minutes
and 15 seconds.

How to have the Hermitage to yourself

Hardly anybody strays into the collections
of Ancient and Early History in the **Hermitage**
(►54). Which means that you can marvel
at the oldest carpet in the world, for example,
all on your own, in Room 26. It is some
2,400 years old!

Luck and charm

Anyone can throw a coin into a fountain –
but getting it to land on the projecting plinth
supporting the tiny bronze sculpture of the
Little Goldfinch outside **St Michael's Castle**
(►69) is much more difficult!

Getting Your Bearings

The founder of the city, Peter the Great, had his permanent seats, the Summer Palace and the Winter Palace, built on the southern bank of the Neva. As such he determined the development of this area. The palace riverbank became the face of the young Russian capital that was very much to be seen – and Palace Square the representative heart of the city.

This central district, that was most strongly influenced by St Petersburg's former role as a capital city, stretches for some two kilometres (1.2mi) along the Neva and the course of the River Moyka. In addition to the width of the Neva, expansive open areas ensure that dignified distances are kept between buildings. Elegant, classical European urban planning with Baroque and Classicist architecture meets the proverbial expanse of Russia. And there is not a single new building to spoil this planned, yet historical cityscape.

In the west, Alexander Column in the centre of the huge Palace Square, acts more or less as a hub from which the whole of St Petersburg radiates. The Winter Palace that faces this square is the magnificent former principal residence of the imperial Romanov family. Today, it is the main building of the State Hermitage Museum from which there are links to the Small, Old and New Hermitage buildings – annexes the tsar had built to house the extensive art collections. The branch of the Hermitage in the east wing of the massive General Staff Building on the south side of the square, on the other hand, is run as an independent art museum.

Further to the east are several other important sights, grouped around The Field of Mars, a former military drill ground: the Church of the Resurrection of Christ – completely covered with mosaics on the inside – adds a hint of old Russian architecture to the cityscape. St Michael's Castle was the stronghold of ostracised Tsar Paul I. The Summer Garden, Russia's oldest park, is a green museum. And, today, the Marble Palace also combines the most exquisite interior decoration with its new use as a museum.

Gorokhovaya ul.

Sightseeing with culinary treats: dinner cruise on the Neva

Neva

Troitskiy most

nab. Kutuzova

nab. reki Fontanki

Fontanka

Dvortsovaya nab.

Moshkov per.

Milionnaya ul.

Aptekarskiy per.

Marble Palace

14

Summer Garden

15

Marsovo Pole

Museum of Applied Art **17**

nab. Lebyazhey kanavki

1-y Inzhenernyy most

Panteley- monovskiy most

Bolshoy Konyushennyy most

nab. reki Moyki

Moyka

Saint Michael's Castle **16**

The Hermitage ⭐**1**

Milionnaya ul.

Pevcheskiy most

Konyushennaya pl.

Church of the Spilled Blood ⭐**10**

Mikhaylovskiy Sad

Palace Square **11**

Bol. Konyushennaya ul.

Shvedskiy per.

0   200 m
0   200 yd

General Staff Building **12**

Moyka

Peter the Great Aquatory **13**

Nevsky Prospekt

Ⓜ Admiralteyskaya

Alexander Column on Palace Square

Between Winter Palace & Summer Garden

The Perfect Day

Get to know the highlights in the city centre on this day tour, spending some time in the Hermitage as well as exploring the verdant parks and soaking in the views from a high vantage point.

🕘 9am

Take the metro to the Admiralteyskaya stop. There are several cafés here to choose from – such as **Bushé** (➤ 73) or **Bonch** (➤ 73) – where you can indulge in a hearty breakfast.

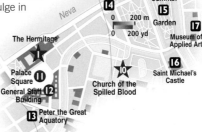

🕙 10am

Stroll along to ⓫ **Palace Square** (➤ 63) and take in the vast dimensions of the building ensemble around it. The ⭐ **Hermitage** (➤ 54) – both the main complex in the Winter Palace as gallery in the ⓬ **General Staff** open at 10:30am. If you are will be able to enjoy the splendid Impressionist collection without the crowds.

well as the new branch **Building** (➤ 65) opposite – among the first visitors of the day, you

🕐 1pm

Time for a lunch break: the twin restaurants **NEP** and **Rasputin** (➤ 72), right on Palace Square, for example, are two possibilities. Or the inviting restaurant **Jat** (nab. reki Moyki 16) opposite, on the other side of the canal.

🕝 2:30pm

Having regained your strength take a short detour on your way to the Winter Palace along the narrow and romantic **Winter Canal** and have a look at the **Atlas statues** (fig. left) in front of the **New Hermitage** (➤ 54).

🕒 3pm

Now it's time to visit the ⭐ **Hermitage** (➤ 54). If you need a break while there head for the museum café on the first floor for a snack and a cup of coffee.

🕕 6pm

To let all the impressions of the art treasures you have seen in the tsarist palace sink in and to give your feet time to recover, take a breath of fresh air on the relaxing roof terrace of the chic **PMI Bar** (➤ 74).

🕐 7pm

Having just admired the brightly coloured domes from above, now take the chance to see the inside of the ⭐**Church of the Spilled Blood** (fig. top; ➤ 61). During the high season it stays open longer.

🕐 8pm

In summer it stays light until late so take a walk through the parks in the city centre. Passing through **Michael Garden** and around **16 St Michael's Castle** (➤ 69) you will reach the corner of the canals Fontanka/Moyka. If you lean over the parapet you will see **St Petersburg's smallest statue**, the Little Goldfinch (fig. below). Cross over the road and go into the **15 Summer Garden** (➤ 68). Stroll around the oldest park in Russia, head for the Neva and cross the Field of Mars diagonally to reach the Church of the Resurrection of Christ.

🕐 9pm

By this time you will certainly have worked up an appetite for dinner in one of the good restaurants on Stable Square such as **Meat Head** (➤ 72), **Nachodka** or **Jamie's Italian** (➤ 71)!

🕐 11pm

Fancy another drink? Or a dance? Or a pint in nice surroundings? The adjoining block, which was where the royal carriages were once kept, is now home to a large number of bars, clubs and pubs, covering a wide spectrum from trashy to elegant.

★The Hermitage
(Gosudarstvenniy Ermitaz)

One of the largest art museums in the world in one of the most magnificent palaces in Europe – the Hermitage is a fascinating treasure trove waiting to be explored. Even for those not interested in painting, sculpture, furniture, coins and other exquisite works of art, the splendid rooms of the Winter Palace and the adjacent buildings are bound to impress. The main residence of the imperial Romanov family is a place one simply has to have seen.

The Hermitage is so typical of St Petersburg: it is enormous, rambling, cosmopolitan and bursting with a mixture of cultures; a place where history was written and which was not spared by history either. And it is a tourist attraction of the highest order. If you would like to take a closer look without the crowds then you should plan your visit in winter on a week day – or two, as it is hardly possible to do justice to the art treasures assembled here in one fell swoop.

Insider Tip

The Winter Palace
The Winter Palace, the principal residence of the Romanov dynasty, is in itself the most impressive exhibit to be seen. The largest palace in the city was built in 1754–62 by Bartolomeo Rastrelli. To be able to do this he had to demolish another residence he had built for the tsarist family 20 years earlier on the same site. The palace was one of many commissions for grandiose projects by the Tsaritsa Elizabeth who, however, did not live to see its completion. The first chatelaine to live here for any time was Catherine the Great – who also laid the foundation for the present art museum. 225 paintings, acquired in 1764 from an art dealer in Berlin, formed the core of her private collection. These works hung in an elongated wing – the **Small Hermitage** – that the ruler had built to her taste by Yuri Felten as her private apartments. This building had a roof garden that flanked the first picture gallery and could not be seen from elsewhere.

The Great Hermitage – which later acquired the name **Old Hermitage** – was soon built parallel to the Neva to house the rapidly growing imperial art collection. In 1842–51 the much larger **New Hermitage** was built behind it to the plans of the Munich architect Leo von Klenze. It was conceived as Russia's first museum open to the general public.

Shortly beforehand, the interior of the Baroque Winter Palace had

---

TREASURIES

The two treasuries in the Hermitage can only be visited as part of a guided tour (in Russian and English, ₽300). The **Gold Room** houses unbelievably filigree, artistic gold work made by the Scythians that is some 2,500 years old. The **Diamond Room** in the New Hermitage displays exquisite works incorporating these precious stones from several eras.

Today, the Winter Palace houses one of the most famous museums in the world

been remodelled largely in the Classicist style under the direction of Vasily Stasov, having been severely damaged by a fire in 1837 that raged for three days. On 25 October 1917 members of the Russian Provisional Government were arrested in the Winter Palace (in Room 188) by the Bolsheviks. After the October Revolution the then-nationalised museum expanded on the one hand through the incorporation of numerous private collections that had been confiscated and, on the other hand, the Communists exchanged several exceptional works of art abroad for foreign currency. During the Siege the building was severely damaged – but not the collections that had largely been evacuated to the Ural Mountains.

The most recent radical change in the history of the museum was in 2014 when a branch was opened in the General Staff Building (►65). This is where the magnificent collection of works by the French Impressionists and Post-Impressionists has been moved to.

Visits

Access to the Hermitage is from Palace Square – for tourists not part of a group it is via the large inner courtyard, for groups access is from the square itself. From the ticket area go to the right towards the magnificent **Jordan Staircase** to reach the upper floor. The ceremonial Baroque staircase is one of the few elements by Rastrelli inside the palace that has survived. After the fire of 1837 it was reconstructed largely according to the original plans.

If you are not heading for one of the temporary exhibitions in the state rooms facing the Neva that are straight in front of you, turn left at the top of the staircase into the **Field Marshals' Room** (Room 193). To see the most impressive rooms in the Winter Palace cross this room to reach the **Small Throne Room** (Room 194) with its walls hung in red velvet. It was designed as a Memorial Room to Peter the Great. You then arrive at the **Armorial Hall** (Room 195):

Between Winter Palace & Summer Garden

the suits of armour that give the room its
name hardly stand out against the shining
gold columns – and are actually concealed
in the chandeliers! Make a slight detour to
the left and cross the **Military Gallery of
1812** (Room 197) which boasts 300 portraits
of generals. This will bring you to the **Large
Throne Hall** or **St George Hall** (Room 198):
a special feature of this ceremonial room
clad in Carrara marble, the principal hall of
its kind in the Russian empire, is the perfect
symmetry of the exquisite parquet floor
with the decorative ceiling ornamentation
executed in copper.

A little further on you reach the **Grand
Church** (Room 271). Its restoration was
only completed in 2014. The church also
bears Rastrelli's Baroque handwriting.
The shredded military tunic worn by Tsar
Alexander II when he was assassinated in
1881 can be seen behind glass.

The next highlight is on the Palace
Square side: the **Alexander Hall** (Room 282)
where the silverware used in the tsarist
court is exhibited. The adjoining rooms to the right (283–289)
are devoted to 18th-century French art. On the corner with
the west wing of the palace the breathtakingly beautiful
Gold Drawing Room (Room 304) marks the start to the
extremely luxurious private apartments of the Tsaritsa
Maria Alexandrovna. The wife of Alexander II enjoyed the
use of an unusually exquisite boudoir (Room 306). The
West Wing also includes one of the most impressive rooms,
the **Library of Nicholas II** (Room 178), completed in 1895
in the medieval Gothic Revival style. Returning to the Neva
side of the building, do not miss the **Malachite Drawing Room**
(Room 189) which is one of the most elegant reception
rooms in the palace.

**The Jordan
Staircase
looks much
as it did when
Rastrelli first
built it**

The Small, Old and
New Hermitages

The Field Marshals' Room
is also the starting point for
a tour of the museum's
most important art treas-
ures. The corridor (Room
200), hung with gobelins,
leads to the beautiful
Pavilion Hall (Room 204) in
the **Small Hermitage**. From
this high-ceilinged room,
designed in the 1850s by
Andrei Stackenschneider
with Arab and Roman
stylistic elements, there is

HERMITAGE THEATRE
The Hermitage Theatre dating from the 1780s
is also part of the museum complex. Its foyer
is on a bridge over the Winter Canal. The
highly decorated theatre itself can only be
seen if you visit a performance. The theatre
stands on the site of the **first Winter Palace of
Peter the Great**. 30 years ago the inner courtyard and several rooms, once part of the palace
that was thought to have been demolished,
were found in the foundations below the stage
area and have skillfully been reconstructed
(Dvortsovaya nab. 32, opening times as for
the Hermitage, ₽300).

a view of both the Neva and the Hanging Gardens. The famous **Peacock Clock** from the 1770s in this room is in full working order but is only wound up once or twice a month. In the galleries to the left and right of the **roof garden**, i.e. in the original Hermitage building, decorative artworks from the Middle Ages can be seen (Room 259), as well as Dutch painting such as by the two Pieter Brueghels (Room 262) and Early German painting by Lucas Cranach the Elder among others (Room 255).

The Old Hermitage is reserved for the Italian Old Masters. Highlights include the formal **Da Vinci Room** (Room 214) with two madonnas by the great master, and the small **Titian Room** (Room 221). Passing the crossing to the **Hermitage Theatre** (Room 225), the **Raphael Loggias** (Room 227) are reached. Created in the 1780s, these copies of the loggia in the Apostolic Palace in the Vatican are equally elaborately painted in bold colours. The loggias lead into the **New Hermitage** that is 70 years younger. The central section of the building in the Neo-Renaissance style contains three high-ceilinged rooms for monumental works and is indirectly lit from overhead lights (Rooms 237–239). After the ⚔ **Kinghts' Hall** with collections of arms and armour (Room 243) the Flemish Masters are reached. This includes a room with 33 paintings by Rubens (Room 247). A tour of the upper floor finishes with Dutch works of art in the **Rembrandt Room** (Room 254) which boasts more than 20 works by the Old Master himself.

To complete the overall picture of the palace complex and its collections go down the stairs passing the Malachite Vase (Room 206) and pass through the marble-clad galleries of works from **Classical Antiquity** (Rooms 106–131) on the ground floor of the New Hermitage. The **Egyptian Collection** (Room 100) leads to the museum shop, cafés and the exit.

INSIDER INFO

- Make sure you **pick up an up-to-date plan** of the complex when you enter. It is otherwise very difficult to find your way around this labyrinth of rooms.
- **Audio guides** in English are available for P500. These can be hired after your tickets have been checked and at the top of the Jordan Staircase.
- Taking **photographs** for private use is permitted, but without using a flash. Photography is generally not allowed in temporary exhibitions.
- In the Rastrelli Gallery (ground floor, to the right in front of the Jordan Staircase) is a well stocked **museum shop**, with a good range of prints and art books.
- Large **bags and rucksacks** must be left in the cloakroom.
- The only **toilets** are on the ground floor!

Insider
Tip

Russian Baroque: The Winter Palace

The Winter Palace is a major work of the Russian Baroque and forms the heart of the Hermitage. Its unique collections provide an overview of the complete cultural and art history of the world with exhibits dating from prehistory to the present day.

❶ **Inner Courtyard** Access to the Winter Palace is from Palace Square (⓫) through the inner courtyard. There are ticket offices, an information desk and a cloakroom on the Neva side of the building.

❷ **Main Gallery** The Main Gallery, designed by Vasily Stasov in 1837–39, leads from the vestibule to the Jordan or Ambassadors' Staircase.

❸ **Jordan Staircase** The magnificent Jordan Staircase designed by Bartolomeo Rastrelli leads to the upper floor of the palace.

❹ **Armorial Hall** The Armorial Hall was where glittering balls and receptions were once held.

❺ **Large Throne Hall** The throne made in 1732 in London for Empress Anna Ivanovna can be seen on the dais in this elaborately decorated room. The relief above it depicts St George killing the dragon.

❻ **Grand Church** The interior of the church is largely the same as when Bartolomeo Rastrelli created it in 1754–1762. The ceiling painting depicts the Resurrection. Services were held here on special occasions. It was here that the last tsar, Nicholas II, married Princess Alix of Hesse and by Rhine, later Tsarina Alexandra Feodorovna, in 1894.

❼ **Gold Drawing Room** The White Hall forms the beginning of a series of rooms on the first floor designed by Alexander Brüllov which also takes in the Gold Drawing Room. These were the apartments used by the Tsarina Maria Alexandrovna in the 19th century.

❽ **Rotunda** The Rotunda forms the link between the private apartments of the tsar and the state rooms.

❾ **Concert Hall** The hall is one of the three state rooms on the side of the palace overlooking the Neva and is decorated with statues of muses and figures holding musical instruments.

❿ **Ballroom** This room is also known as the Nicholas Hall since a portrait of Nicholas I was hung here in 1856. The room is now used for temporary exhibitions.

⓫ **Palace Square** The southern façade of the Hermitage faces Palace Square.

The Hermitage

The wedding of Nicholas II and Alexandra Feodorovna, held in the Grand Church in November 1894, was a comparatively modest affair as the tsar's father had died suddenly just a few days beforehand

Between Winter Palace & Summer Garden

Art and history lovers can spend many more hours on the ground floor of the Winter Palace exploring the less frequented departments with exhibits from early Eurasian cultures. The only permanent displays on the 2nd floor at present are in the Indian, Japanese, Byzantium and Near East sections as well as numismatics.

TAKING A BREAK

The gastronomy in the Hermitage is very modest. In the **Rastrelli Gallery** there is a simple **cafeteria** which offers rather pricey sandwiches and pastries. A little bit further on is the slightly cheaper Internet Café with the same range of fare. Bearing this is mind, it makes good sense to have something to eat elsewhere before or after visiting the museum.

The Pavilion Hall in the Small Hermitage with its wonderful Roman mosaic

➕ 205 E/F4 ✉ Dvortsovaya pl. 2 ☎ 812-710-9079; www.hermitage.ru
🕐 Tue–Sun 10:30am–6pm, Wed, Fri until 9pm
Ⓜ Admiralteyskaya 🚋 Dvortsovaya pl. (trolley 1, 7, 10, 11; bus 7, 10, 24, 191)
✋ May–Sep P700, otherwise P600

INSIDER INFO

- During the summer season a **long queue** forms every day in front of the Hermitage. However, this is only for Russian citizens who want reduced admission (P400). Foreigners have to pay the full price of P600. Tickets are available from the green automatic ticket machines in the inner courtyard to the left and right of the entrance archway (cash or credit cards accepted). You can then go to the front of the queue and wait to be let in with the next batch of visitors. In addition, during the summer, there is also a separate entrance on the left in the courtyard for ticket holders. However there is no cloakroom here.

Insider Tip

- Using the **ticket machines** is much cheaper than pre-booking tickets on the Internet. The online price of US$17.95 is just about 100 percent more expensive! A ticket valid for two consecutive days is available online for US$22.95.

- Entrance to the museum is **free of charge** for children and students (incl. foreigners with any form of student ID). However you then have to join the queue at the back.

- Tickets to the Hermitage also provide entrance to the branch galleries in the **General Staff Building** (▶ 65), the **Menshikov Palace** (▶ 92) and the **Winter Palace of Peter the Great** (▶ 56), albeit they are only valid for one day.

- On the first Thursday of the month and on 7 December entrance to the Hermitage is **free of charge**. However, a free ticket still has to be collected from a ticket machine. From May to August and also in January the queues on such days are enormous and the museum consequently jam packed. Instead of queuing for hours on end it makes

Insider Tip

more sense to visit the much less frequented General Staff Building instead – as the branch galleries are also free of charge.

⑩ Church of the Spilled Blood
(Tserkov' Spasa na Krovi)

So times change: A commemorative building to the victim of a terror act that, stylistically, does not match the architecture of the city at all, has in the course of a century become one of St Petersburg's most famous landmarks. The church is not just an eye-opener on the outside – the interior is a mosaic wonderland.

The **Church of the Resurrection of Christ**, another of its many names, was erected on the very site where Tsar Alexander II was fatally wounded in 1881 after a bomb exploded. That explains why – unusually in St Petersburg's generally linear street system – the church protrudes so photogenically from the uniform row of façades on Griboyedov Canal. The tower with the golden dome marks the exact spot where the assassination took place on the bank of the canal. Inside the church, a jasper ciborium (baldachin) forms a

The prototype for the Church of the Resurrection of Christ is in Moscow

canopy over a section of the original bank-side balustrade and cobblestones where the fatally wounded emperor lay bleeding heavily – hence the church's name.

The Church of the Resurrection of Christ is modelled on St Basil's Cathedral on Red Square in Moscow. While the latter is already 450 years old, the St Petersburg version is a modern construction. Completed in 1907 it was even planned with electric lighting from the outset. The Old Russian architectural style represents a break with that otherwise found in St Petersburg with its uniform streets of Baroque and Classicist buildings in the city centre. The architect, Alfred Parland, was actually born in St Petersburg. His father was Scottish and his mother was from Swabia in southern Germany.

As in all old Orthodox churches, the interior looks as if frescos of icons have been painted on the walls right up to the dome. In this case, however, all ornamental work and

all the pictures of saints are actually **mosaics**. The surface area of the walls, more than 7,000m² (75,350ft²) in total, is covered in tiny, brightly coloured mosaic tiles – a traditional technique used in Russia – that took ten years to complete. Only if you look more closely will you be able to detect the influence of Art Nouveau in some of the figures of angels. The floor, on the other hand, with 45 different mosaic patterns, was prefabricated in Genoa.

More than 20 types of stone were used in the Church of the Resurrection of Christ

TAKING A BREAK

The chic Italian restaurant **Park Giuseppe** is located in a pavilion on the edge of Michael Garden (nab. kan. Griboedov 2w; www.park-restaurant.ru; daily 11am–midnight, Fri, Sat until 1am).

✚ 203 D1 ✉ Nab. kan. Griboedov 2 ☎ 812-315-1636; www.cathedral.ru, 🕐 Thu–Tue 10:30am–6pm, May–Sep until 10:30pm; service daily 7:30am 🚇 Gostiny Dvor 💵 P250, from 6pm P400

INSIDER INFO

Insider Tip

The wonderfully ornamental gate that separates the church from **Michael Garden** next to St Michael's Castle (➤ 135) was created at the same time as the church and is an open invitation to take a walk around the most beautiful of the parks in the city centre (daily 10am–8pm, May–Sep until 10pm, closed in April, free entrance).

⑪ Palace Square
(Dvortsovaya Ploshchad)

The vast square in front of the Winter Palace is both a visiting card and the city's 'best parlour': a jewel of urban planning that met the tsar's representational requirements just as much as the need today for a generously proportioned inner-city space.

Even if it means a little detour, the first time you visit Palace Square, coming from Nevsky Prospekt, you should approach it via Bolshaya Morskaya Ulitsa. A huge double arch and a bend in the street hide the view of the square until the last moment – only to reveal its architectural perfection all of a sudden. Facing you, on the opposite side of the square, is the 220m (720ft)-long Baroque façade of the **Winter Palace** (► 54). The lively rhythm of columns and projections on the façade and the many figures and urns on the roof create an elegant and inviting impression despite the sheer dimensions of the palace. And even if you do not intend visiting the Hermitage just yet, pass under the triple arches into the inner courtyard.

Insider Tip

Alexander Column, plum in the middle of the square, was designed by **Auguste de Montferrand** who also built St Isaac's Cathedral (► 106). It rises 47.5m (156ft) into the air like a vast sceptre and is very much a statement of the Russian emperor's claim to power. It is in fact one single granite monolith weighing 600 tons. Using a massive scaffold and winching devices it was manoeuvred into position on 30 August 1832 in less than two hours using the muscle power of 2,400 men alone. Since then the column has stood upright without wobbling and without being fixed in any way on its 400-ton pedestal. The people of St Petersburg never trusted the monument's stability. Montferrand, however, demonstratively walked his dog around the column for years on end. The column is crowned by an allegorical figure of an angel that, irrespective of any gesture of humbleness, is crushing a serpent with a cross.

INSIDER INFO

- The third building on the square is the Guard Corps Headquarters. It is well worthwhile going just a little bit further to the left into **Millionaya Ulitsa** to reach St Petersburg's perhaps most photogenic spot: the **former entrance to the New Hermitage** flanked by ten massive statues of Atlas and the narrow **Winter Canal** – where St Petersburg really does look like Venice.

Insider Tip

- Come to Palace Square late in the evening when it is evocatively lit up and the hoards of tourists, horse-drawn carriages, photographers and hawkers have gone. And if one of the buskers is still playing at the base of Alexander Column you can hear how amazing the acoustics are!

Between Winter Palace & Summer Garden

Not coincidentally, the angel has the facial features of Emperor **Alexander I**, to whom this monument is dedicated. This is, however, also a victory column celebrating Russia's triumph over Napoleon in 1812–14.

The sculpture the architect **Carlo Rossi** placed opposite the Winter Palace on the triumphal arch of the massive **General Staff Building** (➤65), built in 1819–29, marks the same victory. It shows Nike, the goddess of victory, in a carriage drawn by six horses. Through the addition of the General Staff Building, with its 500m (1640ft)-long, concave façade, the former Admiralty Ground was turned into one of the most impressive squares in the world. Its harmonious façade corresponds with the **Admiralty** (➤118) of similar dimensions diagonally opposite and provides a visual anchor within this 12½ acre space.

The west wing still houses the High Command for the St Petersburg military district. The east wing used to be occupied by ministerial offices but is now part of the Hermitage (➤54).

A number of different events are held on Palace Square in swift succession between May and July – concerts, sports competitions, festivals and parades. During this time there are almost always stages or stands of some kind being put up or taken down – that rather ruins the aura conjured up at other times.

View through the triumphal arch of the General Staff Building and Alexander Column as well as the southern front of the Winter Palace

TAKING A BREAK

There are no cafés or restaurants on the square itself so head towards Moyka instead – for the vegetarian café **Troitsky Most** (nab. reki Moyki 30; daily 8:30am–10:30pm), for example, which bakes its own cakes and pastries.

➕ 205 E/F4
✉ Dvortsovaya pl.
🚇 Admiralteyskaya
🚌 Dvortsovaya pl. (trolley bus 1, 7, 10, 11; bus 7, 10, 24, 191)

⑫ General Staff Building
(Zdanie Glavnovo Shtaba)

In 2014 the Hermitage opened a long-overdue new museum building right on Palace Square. An extremely skillful remodelling of the historical General Staff Building is now home to the sensational collection of pictures by great French artists such as Monet, Manet, Renoir, Gauguin, Cezanne, Picasso and Matisse. But not only to them...

The extensive revamping of the east wing of the General Staff Building – with bold architectural interventions by St Petersburg's standards – has liberated the museum from the shackles of its wonderful but antiquated former

A huge glass roof has been built over the inner courtyards in the General Staff Building

home, bearing the technological requirements of a modern museum in mind. To create space for events, installations and old and new, large-format works of art, five inner courtyards have been covered with glass roofs. Huge portals open into these atria forming a wide link for visitors to follow from one atrium to the next. Several rooms on the top floor have also been fitted with funnel-like overhead lights. Of these changes to the General Staff Building, however, very little can be detected from the outside.

You may want to start your visit by walking through the atria, painted a neutral but dignified grey, to get an impression of the remodelling scheme. Then take the lift up to the 4th floor which is largely occupied by the **Sergey Shchukin and the Morozov Brothers Memorial Gallery**. The gallery with this rather clumsy sounding name honours these men of independent means from Moscow who specifically collected French Impressionist and Post-Impressionist

Insider Tip

Between Winter Palace & Summer Garden

works before the October Revolution. Their collections, which became state-owned property in 1918, initially formed the State Museum for New Western Art. This was dissolved in 1948 and the masterpieces – slandered as being decadent and bourgeois – divided between the Pushkin Museum in Moscow and the Hermitage. The decision-makers in Leningrad were bolder and secured the lion's share. This display was supplemented by looted art, captured by Russia in 1945 and stored in the Hermitage's secret depots until 1995.

Insider Tip
One of the best places to start your visit is Room 403 that is devoted to **Claude Monet**. Impressionist masterpieces by Manet, Degas, Sisley, Pissarro and van Gogh then follow. Renoir, Cézanne and Gauguin take up two rooms (407, 412). These are also interspersed with pictures by other artists but the great names are always represented by at least a dozen works.

A link from the tip of the inner-most courtyard does not just mark the entrance to the other side of the building but also to works of 20th-century modern art. 30 works by Pablo Picasso are presented here in four rooms (431–435). A total of 36 pictures by Henri Matisse are on display in three further rooms (from 437). After this flight into the realms of works of art that would fetch billions of pounds on the open market, it is a little bit difficult to do full justice to the third floor. This largely houses 19th-century art – with many works from France and a few less from Holland, Belgium and Germany. In Room 352, however, you can delight in a total of eight works by Caspar David Friedrich. The interior of the former finance and foreign ministries, that has retained its original magnificence in parts, is the setting for a comprehensive presentation on the Empire style (317–330). You may want to finish off your visit with a look in Room 303 where works by Kandinsky and Malevich are displayed that mark the beginning of abstract painting.

TAKING A BREAK

A **cafeteria** on the ground floor – also used by museum staff – offers a wide variety of food. It is located before the area for which valid tickets are required which means that it is freely accessible during museum opening times.

✚ 205 F4 ✉ Dvortsovaya pl. 6–8 ☎ 812-710-9079; www.hermitage.ru
🕑 Tue–Sun 10:30am–6pm, Wed, Fri until 9pm 🚇 Admiralteyskaya
🚌 Dvortsovaya pl. (trolley bus 1, 7, 10, 11; bus 7, 10, 24, 191) 🎫 P300

INSIDER INFO

- As in the main Hermitage building opposite it is advisable to pick up a **floor plan** at the ticket desk as it is easy to lose your orientation.

Insider Tip
- If you want to visit the **Fabergé Museum** (➤ 138) but can't fit it in timewise there is a also a small exhibition of works by the court jeweller in the General Staff Building, albeit with only one of the famous eggs.

At Your Leisure

13 Peter the Great Aquatory (Petrovskaya Akvatoria)

On the 6th floor of a business centre, right above the entrance to Admiralteyskaya metro station, visitors can marvel at **St Petersburg at the time of its foundation** – as models to the scale of 1:87. Some 25,000 tiny figures from all walks of life people the cityscape that covers 500m² (5,400ft²) and the 20t of water that swishes about in the middle – giving the model its name. The models include the city centre with the Peter and Paul Fortress, the Strelka and the Admiralty district, as well as the palaces Peterhof and Oranienbaum, and Kronstadt docks.

The model that depicts various scenes from the 18th century is packed with state-of-the-art technology. Ships drawn along magnetic lines seem to sail around as if by magic, carriages bump over the cobbles and thousands of mini

diodes bring the street lanterns and other light sources to life. In addition, the meticulously made model, based on historical evidence, includes several buildings that have long since disappeared, such as parts of Peter the Great's Winter Palace and the warehouses built on stilts in the Neva. And while Peter the Great – shrunk to just 2.5cm (1in) – puffs away at his pipe during a lavish party on the roof terrace of Menshikov Palace, his subjects' modest farmsteads struggle to survive in

Winterly, 18th-century St Petersburg reflected in the Neva

the face of a storm tide just beyond
New Holland.

🕂 205 E4 ✉ Malaya Morskaya Ul. 4
☎ 812-933-4152; www.peteraqua.ru
🕓 Daily 10am–10pm 🚇 Admiralteyskaya
💰 P400 (Sat, Sun P450)

14 Marble Palace (Mramorny Dvorez)

The Marble Palace, completed in
1785, is the most impressive
building in St Petersburg's most
beautiful row of façades along the
palace embankment. It was a
present from Catherine the Great
to her companion and lover Count
Grigory Orlov who, however, did not
live to see the completion of this
magnificent building. The early
Classicist palace was the first of
its kind in the city. The complete
façade is of natural stone – grey
and brown granite – with pink
marble being used for the columns
and pilasters. The palace owes its
name to the grand staircase made
of Italian and Russian marble as
well as the **marble hall** with walls
clad in marble of various shades
and deep-blue lazurite.

**The equestrian statue of Alexander III
outside the Marble Palace**

Today, the palace houses a
branch of the **Russian Museum**
(► 135). Outside the entrance is the
equestrian statue to Alexander III.
From 1909 until 1937 it stood on a
high plinth outside Moscow Station.
Even during the tsarist era this
statue was disliked and criticised
as having the elegance of a bull-
dozer. Locally it was known as the
statue of a 'bonehead on a hippo
on a chest of drawers'!

The main attraction among the   *Insider Tip*
exhibitions in the Marble Palace
is the **Museum Ludwig** that was
opened in 1995. The collectors
Peter and Irene Ludwig from
Aachen, Germany, presented
their extensive collection of
Russian and international art from
the second half of the 20th century
to the Russian Museum. It includes icons of Pop Art by Andy
Warhol and Roy Lichtenstein, as
well as works by Anselm Kiefer,
Jörg Immendorf, Georg Baselitz
and Jeff Koons.

🕂 203 D2 ✉ Millionaya Ul. 5a
🕓 812-595-4248; www.rusmuseum.ru
🕓 Mon, Wed, Fri–Sun 10am–6pm,
Thu 1pm–9pm 🚇 Suvorovskaya pl.
(bus 46, 49, tram 3) 💰 P300

15 Summer Garden (Letniy Sad)

Russia's oldest park is a green
island in the middle of the city –
literally, as the Summer Garden
is surrounded on all four sides
by water. Peter the Great already
ordered the park to be laid out
from 1704 onwards; in 1710
building work on the **Summer
Palace** in the northeastern corner
of the park was commenced.

Peter the Great's Summer Palace is quite modest in size

This 'tsarist dacha' is the **oldest stone house in St Petersburg** and has survived unaltered for three centuries. From outside the two-storey, hipped-roofed building looks quite plain; its interior however is finished in solid oak and walnut and fitted with state-of-the-art technology. There are six flushing lavatories and a weather station to keep the keen sailor informed with up-to-the-minute data on the speed and direction of the wind.

The park has largely been re-stored to the strict rules applied to landscape gardening in the early 18th century with trellises lining most paths and forming a screen. There are, however, numerous openings leading to groves where hidden surprises include aviaries and quiet corners for intimate tête-à-têtes. The elegant marble statues and fountains the tsar had placed at certain points can still be seen. Peter also kept porcupines here too – and organised his *assemblées* in the park – extravagant feasts where alcohol flowed freely.

Floods destroyed much of the park's fixtures in 1777. However, at the same time, Yury Felten – Catherine II's court architect – created another jewel on the Neva

side of the park: 36 pink marble columns support a cast-iron railing. Its elegance and symmetry were praised as an aesthetic 'wonder of the world' and a brilliant combina-tion of architecture and nature in its day. The Summer Garden, with its 90 sculptures (mostly of Greek gods, philosophers and allegorical figures) and two nostalgic garden cafés, is still a place of elegant, cultivated recreation – very much as the tsar intended when he first opened his private garden to a 'respectably dressed public' in 1755.

🚼 203 E2
✉ Island between the Neva, Fontanka, Moyka and the Swan Canal – Lebyazhya Kanavka
☎ 812-595-4248; www.rusmuseum.ru
🕐 May–Sep daily 10am–10pm, Oct–March 10am–8pm; Summer Palace closed for renovation until 2018
🚌 Letniy sad (bus 46, 49, K76, K212, tram 3)
🎫 Free

🔟 Saint Michael's Castle (Mikhailovsky Zamok)

It is not by chance that this is the only tsarist residence in the city that is not called a *dvorets* (palace), but a *samok* (castle). Paul I's fairy-tale castle was to be representative but also defensive as, since his coronation, the son of Catherine

Between Winter Palace & Summer Garden

the Great feared nothing more than a palace revolt. This formidable castle, complete with moats and drawbridges, was ready for occupation in 1801. Isolating himself from the world, however, did not help him much: 40 days after moving in, Paul I was strangled in his bed chamber by conspirators.

The royal residence, which had not been completely finished by that time, was abandoned after the tsar's assassination. An engineering college was established in the building in 1823 which is why it is also known as the 'engineers' castle'. It now houses a branch of the Russian Museum which includes a portrait gallery and is also used for temporary exhibitions. A look inside the – freely accessible – octagonal inner courtyard with one of the few monuments to Paul I (2003) is well worthwhile. Paul I also had an equestrian statue of Peter I erected outside the castle that he had had cast 50 years previously.

✚ 203 E1 ✉ Sadovaya Ul. 2
☎ 812-595-4248; www.rusmuseum.ru
🕓 Mon, Wed, Fri–Sun 10am–6pm, Thu 1pm–9pm
🚇 Nevsky Pr. 💷 P300

🔟 Museum of Applied Art (Musey Prikladnogo Isskustva)

The museum that forms part of the **Alexander Stieglitz Academy of Applied Art** is obviously not keen on attracting lots of visitors as notices on the two main entrances each refer to the other as the correct entrance to the museum! The left-hand one, however, is the door you need. On the other side of the Solart galley there is in fact a ticket office. The Academy's **design collection** is

presented in 14 rather gloomy rooms on the ground floor. Glass showcases display artistically forged old keys and a large collection of tiled stoves as well as providing an overview of the history of ceramics, cabinet making and glass with a wide variety of objects.

The building itself that was constructed in 1888–98 is an architectural primer. In the spirit of historicism that was very popular then, individual rooms have been designed in the Byzantine, Roman and Gothic styles. In the space of just a few yards you can move from the Early Middle Ages in Russia to the Baroque and the ultimately dominant Italian Renaissance. At the end of your tour you will find yourself in the most holy of places: the breathtakingly beautiful, two-storeyed **atrium**. A plaster copy of the Pergamon Altar frieze, now in Berlin, surrounds the balcony.

✚ 203 E1 ✉ Solyanoy per. 15
☎ 812-273-3258; www.stieglitzmuseum.ru
🕓 Sep–July Tue–Sat 11am–5pm
🚌 Letniy sad (bus 46, 49, K76, K212, tram 3)
💷 P300

The Atrium in the Museum for Applied Art

Where to…
Eat and Drink

Prices
for a main course (without drinks):
£ under P450   ££ P450–P900   £££ over P900

RESTAURANTS

Botanika ££
This pleasant organic café/bistro next to the Academy of Applied Art (➤70) serves vegetarian food only with dishes from Italy, India, Japan and Russia. ⚇ Small children will love the play area with its nooks and crannies.
➕ 206 B4 ✉ Ul. Pestelya 7
☎ 812-272-7091; www.cafebotanika.ru
🕐 Mon–Sat 11am–1am, Sun until midnight
🚇 Letniy sad (bus 46, 49, K76, K212)

Gogol £££
Excellent restaurant serving Russian fare with an atmosphere reminiscent of a living room from Gogol's day.
➕ 205 E4 ✉ Malaya Morskaya Ul. 8
☎ 812-312-6097; www.restaurant-gogol.ru
🕐 Daily noon–11pm
🚇 Admiralteyskaya

Gosti ££
At first you might think this is a quaint cake shop. The restaurant is on the floor above – and is charming. It has an incredibly cosy, somewhat rambling interior in the old fashioned, country-house style. It's very easy to stay here a bit longer than planned! And the cooking is convincing too, finding a delicate balance between the rustic and the refined. The range of desserts is impressive and is certain to tempt the ⚇ children back from the playroom. **Insider Tip**
➕ 205 E4 ✉ Malaya Morskaya Ul. 13
☎ 812-312-5820; www.gdegosti.ru
🕐 9–11pm 🚇 Admiralteyskaya

Jamie's Italian £££
The high vaulted ceiling of this former carriage house to the Winter Palace gives the restaurant a market hall look. The British TV star chef Jamie Oliver – as the licence owner – ensures the high level of cuisine from afar, and choice suppliers provide fresh ingredients from the region. This is the modern and sophisticated Italian-style restaurant's recipe for success.
➕ 205 F4 ✉ Konyushennaya pl. 2
☎ 812-600-2570; www.ginza.ru
🕐 Mon–Fri from 9:30am, Sat, Sun from noon until the last guest leaves
🚇 Gostiny Dvor

Literaturnoje Kafe £££
A very elegant, nostalgic coffee-house which is not surprising considering its long tradition. The former Swiss confectionery Wolf and Béranger was once a meeting place for the intellectual and bohemian. The great poet Alexander Pushkin was a regular visitor and it was here that the met up with his seconds on 27 January 1837 before heading off for the duel that was to cost him his young life. A wax figure of Pushkin stands at the entrance next to the large menu with classical Russian dishes. Dinner is accompanied with music every evening from 7pm onwards; at lunch time prices are 20% cheaper. **Insider Tip**
➕ 205 F4 ✉ Nevsky Pr. 18
☎ 812-312-6057; www.litcafe.su
🕐 Sun–Thu 11am–11pm, Fri, Sat until 1am
🚇 Admiralteyskaya

Between Winter Palace & Summer Garden

Meat Head £££

If, after a visit to the Church of the Spilled Blood (➤ 61), you are hankering after a hearty meal, you don't have to go very far. Right opposite you will find this respectable, large steakhouse which has lots of tables in the windows under huge brick arches. Should you prefer fish – no problem! One door further down the road is the seafood restaurant **Nachodka** under the same management (tel: 812-926-4343).

🞧 205 F4
✉ Nab. kanala Griboedov 3
☎ 812-923-0044; www.meat-head.ru
🕓 Sun–Wed noon–11pm, Thu–Sat until 1am
Ⓠ Gostiny Dvor

Rasputin £

Rasputin is very close to Palace Square. Instead of charging for its location, this charmingly nostalgic place offers down-to-earth food at reasonable prices. It shares a kitchen with the restaurant **NEP** (Mon and Tue noon–11:30pm, Wed–Sun until 1am), located in the same building, that is about 25 percent more expensive and whose interior and cabaret programme (Wed–Sun 8:30pm; ₽340) has revived the 1920s.

🞧 205 F4 ✉ Nab. reki Moyki 37
☎ 812-571-7591; www.rasputin-cafe.ru
🕓 Daily 10am–11pm
Ⓠ Admiralteyskaya

Rustaveli ££

A provincial Georgian idyll among St Petersburg's palaces. This little, single-storey, village-like building, lying on the quiet banks of the Moyka, houses a traditional restaurant serving correspondingly juicy/hearty Caucasian fare.

🞧 206 A4
✉ Nab. reki Moyki 9
☎ 812-598-1622
🕓 Daily 10am–10:30pm
Ⓠ Gostiny Dvor

Sac voyage ££

'The Pregnant Spy's Travel Bag' is the full name of this place – and the inside is similarly bizarre too with its mixture of steam punk and military, junk room and torture chamber that just falls short of an X-rating. Serious partying takes place here on Fridays and Saturdays. The food, on the other hand, is more conventional.

Insider Tip

🞧 205 F4
✉ Bolshaya Konyushennaya Ul. 17
☎ 812-495-9796
🕓 Sun–Thu 11am–1am, Fri, Sat until 2am
Ⓠ Gostiny Dvor

Treska £

You have to duck to enter this little gastro bar through a window. It features the cod in both its name and its logo without actually being a fish restaurant as such. In fact, there's quite a lot here that is unusual – after all, we are in the **Golitsyn Loft** (➤ 32) creative complex. If you order a salad with smoked cod, this is served together with the smoke. And the landlord brews his own craft beer. Live music from Thu–Sun from 9pm onwards.

🞧 203 E1
✉ Nab. reki Fontanki 20 ☎ 929-106-6835; www.facebook.com/treskabar
🕓 Sun–Thu 1pm–1am, Fri, Sat until 5am
Ⓠ Gostiny Dvor 🚌 Letniy sad (bus 46, 49)

1001 notsch ££

Uzbek cuisine has quite an influence on Russian eating habits. Everyone here knows the large dough-wrap *manti* or the rice dish *plov* (pilaf). This long-established restaurant does not just take its guests on a culinary trip down the Silk Road but invites them to enjoy a belly dance with their pud or a puff on a hookah.

🞧 203 D1 ✉ Millionaya Ul. 21
☎ 812-570-1703; www.1001night.org
🕓 Sun–Thu noon–11pm, Fri, Sat until 2am
Ⓠ Gostiny Dvor

CAFÉS

Bonch

This modern, bright corner café offers either a good breakfast, one of 40 desserts, or something more substantial from its pretty extensive menu, all washed down with a wide variety of personally concocted pick-me-ups. Anyone who likes the food here and its cool chic will also fall for the Asia restaurant **King Pong** next door, under the same management.

➕ 205 F4
✉ Bolshaya Morskaya Ul. 16
☎ 812-740-7083; www.bonchcoffee.ru
🕐 Mon–Fri 8:30am–11pm, Sat 10am–11pm, Sun 10am–9pm
Ⓜ Admiralteyskaya

Bushé

Appealing bakery-cum-cake shop. Its range of snacks and salads makes it equally suitable for a small lunch. Another, centrally-located branch of this chain (where wine is also served after 5pm) can be found at Griboyedov Canal 18.

➕ 205 E4 ✉ Malaya Morskaya Ul. 7
☎ 812-640-5151; www.bushe.ru
🕐 Daily 8am–10pm
Ⓜ Admiralteyskaya

Double-B

One of the best places in the city for coffee fans. This small, minimalistic café belongs to an aspiring Russian chain entirely committed to achieving perfection in its preparation of teas and coffees. For this reason only snacks are available as accompaniments to beverages. *Insider Tip*

➕ 203 D1 ✉ Millionaya Ul. 18
☎ 812-928-0818; www.double-b.ru
🕐 Mon–Fri 9am–9pm, Sat, Sun 11am–9pm
Ⓜ Gostiny Dvor

Where to...
Shop

Ignoring the omnipresent souvenir trade, the area around the Winter Palace is not a shopping district.

AMBER & JEWELLERY

If you are looking for something beautiful and authentic then how about a bit of 'Baltic Gold'. *Insider Tip*
The largest amber reserves are, after all, to be found on the Sambia Peninsula northwest of Kaliningrad. Thanks to the Amber Room, St Petersburg is particularly closely associated with this wonderful material used in jewellery. For this reason there are several large amber boutiques around here: **Amber Palace** (nab. reki Moyki 35; www.amberpalace.ru), near Palace Square;

Amber of Russia (Konyushennaya pl. 2), huge, over two floors; **Amber & Art** (nab. reki Moyki 1; www.belugadeluxe.com), very superior.

Traditional jewellery as well as silverware can be found at a location that, historically speaking, was destined for this purpose: the jewellery's **Jachont** (Bolshaya Morskaya Ul. 24; www.juvelirtorg.spb.ru) is in the building which once housed the court jeweller Fabergé.

SOUVENIRS

A visit to the permanent **souvenir market** on Griboyedov Canal, between the Church of the Resurrection and the Benois Wing of the Russian Museum, is more interesting than the average souvenir shop. You will find an exhaustive selection of matryoshka dolls, wooden Easter eggs and Putin T-shirts (to name just three of the most popular products). You can even haggle a little here too.

Where to...
Go Out

CLASSICAL MUSIC

There are two classical music venues near the Winter Palace. One is the noble **Hermitage Theatre** (►56) that, however, does not have an ensemble or orchestra of its own. During the summer season it is nearly always host to the same old ballet performances of *Swan Lake* aimed at the package tourist.

On the other hand, a richly varied number of events, especially for choral and chamber music, is held at **Kapella** (nab. reki Moyki 20; tel: 812-314-1058; www.capella.spb.ru), a beautiful concert hall that was once the home of the tsarist court choir and orchestra.

BARS, PUBS & CLUBS

The rest of the evening can be spent 'going around the block' – in the true sense of the phrase – as the carriage park that belonged to the tsarist court occupied a whole district of its own. The area between Griboyedov Canal, Shvedski per., Bolshaya Konyushennaya Ul. and Stable Square (Konyushennaya pl.) has now become a nightlife hotspot. There is something here for every taste and budget – just go off and explore!

On the eastern and western sides you will find **48 Chairs** (daily noon–midnight) and **Dom 7** (Mon–Fri noon–midnight, Sat, Sun until 5am) respectively – two jazz venues. One is more a restaurant, the other more a pub.

Four nightlife hotspots have set themselves up in a rather run-down courtyard that can be accessed from the Griboyedov Canal side: the music club **Mod** with a pizzeria

and roof terrace (daily 6pm–6am; www.modclub.info) and **Akakao** (Sun, Tue–Thu 6pm–3am, Fri until 6am, Sat until 8am), the **Tiger** bar (Wed–Sun 6pm–6am) and the house dance club **LUX** (Fri, Sat from 11pm). The popular jazz and funk bar **Saigon** (Sun–Thu 11am–2am, Fri, Sat until 6am) where you can also eat well and the rave club **Stackenschneider** (Fri, Sat from 11:55pm) lie tucked away in the large main courtyard (best accessed from the north).

On the south side, in the pedestrian precinct, is the more up-market pub, the **James Cook** (Sun–Thu noon–2am, Fri, Sat until 4am) and, on the west side, a lovely, whacky cellar bar, the **Krolik Bar** (Mon–Fri from 11am, Sat, Sun from 12, Sun–Thu until midnight, Fri, Sat until 5am) and the minimalistic winebar **Vinostudio** (Mon–Thu noon–2am, Fri noon–5am, Sat 2pm–5am, Sun 2pm–2am).

The evening can of course be very pleasantly spent in one of the superior restaurants on Stable Square such as **Jamie's Italian** (►71), **Meat Head** (►72) or **Nachodka**.

If you are looking for a cocktail bar you'll have to walk a little, heading for Moyka. **Daiquiri Bar** (Konyushennya per. 1; daily 4pm–4am) is a classic in the booming St Petersburg bar scene. And a highlight (literally) on a summer's evening is no doubt a visit to the noble **PMI Bar** (nab. reki Moyki 7, Sun–Thu noon–11pm, Fri, Sat until 1am; http://pmibar.com) with its roof terrace on the 9th floor offering a panoramic view all around – the perfect place for a midnight sundowner on a White Night!

However, if you prefer something more unusual, let yourself be surprised by the wide variety of drinks and the inspirational creativity of the start-up bar scene in **Golitsyn Loft** (►32; www.luna-info.ru/spaces/golitsyn-loft).

Petrograd Side & Vasilyevsky Island

 Little Treats

Café in the Grotto
Anyone on their way from Gorkovskaya metro station to Peter and Paul Fortress (▶82) passes a **man-made grotto** in a park where superb coffee is brewed.

Open-air Tango
At weekends during the summer you can dance to the sound of Latin American music in the evenings on **Strelka** (▶80) when the dance schools invite everyone to join in!

A 'Total Art' Experience
In chamber-like rooms called **U-Spaces** in the art museum **Erarta** (▶89) try out a 'total installation' experience, each lasting 15 mins. (at an extra cost of ₽200).

Getting Your Bearings

Two historical districts are located on islands in the Neva delta, surrounded by arms of the river. To the southwest is Vasilyevsky Island and, to the northeast, Petrograd Side. It was here that the history of St Petersburg all started.

Tiny Hare Island, where the fortress named St Peter's Castle (*burg*) was built in 1703, is also part of Petrograd Side. It is now called the Peter and Paul Fortress after the cathedral dedicated to Peter and Paul built within its walls where the tombs of the imperial Romanov family can be found. The settlement that grew up around it took on the name of the fortress. The first and oldest house in the city still exists. It was built for the personal use of Tsar Peter I. Petrograd Side however is characterised by its attractive family houses from the Art Nouveau period.

The eastern tip of Vasilyevsky Island is particularly interesting. The temple-like Old Stock Exchange and the two prominent Rostral Columns have become architectural landmarks of St Petersburg. In the 18th century the centre of the perfectly designed capital city was to be here on the Strelka and along the nearby banks of the Neva. The idea was only partially put into practice with the 'Kunstkamera', the Twelve Colleges building, Menshikov Palace and the Academy of Art forming a highly representative line of façades along the waterfront to this day. The old residential areas on Vasilyevsky Island are situated on the 'Lines', as the streets are called that run strictly parallel to one another, each with a number of its own. Peter the Great actually wanted these to be canals but nothing became of this plan.

By the way, there is a Bolshoi Prospekt and a Maliy Prospekt in both districts. Addresses need to have the letters V.O (Vasilyevsky Ostrov) or P.S. (Petrogradskaya Storona) on them to avoid any confusion!

TOP 10

⭐ Strelka ➤ 80
⭐ Peter and Paul Fortress
(Petropavlovskaya Krepost) ➤ 82

Don't Miss

⓲ Cabin of Peter the Great (Domik Petra I) ➤ 87
⓳ Erarta ➤ 89

At Your Leisure

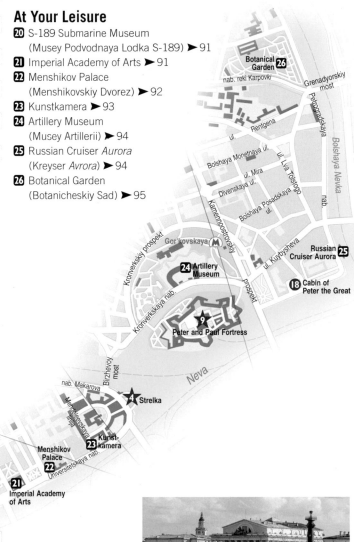

**Motorboats heading for the
Peter and Paul Fortress from
the Strelka with the temple-
like Old Stock Exchange and
the Rostral Columns**

The Perfect Day

This day tour guides you across three islands on the north bank of the Neva and takes you back to St Petersburg's historical roots: Peter and Paul Fortress and the Strelka once formed the heart of the city. Now they are geared to pedestrians and provide a breath of fresh air. You can then spend the evening well away from the normal tourist playground.

🕐 10am

Make sure you have a hearty breakfast – a 6.5-km (4mi)-hike lies ahead of you – before taking the metro to **Gorkovskaya station**. Passing the mosque (fig. left) and the **Kschessinskaya Villa** (► 185) on the way, take a look at the ⑱ **Cabin of Peter the Great** (► 87) on the banks of the Neva.

🕐 11am

While exploring traces from the time the city was founded go across Trinity Square to ⭐ **Peter and Paul Fortress** (► 82). Entering the fortress through **Peter's Gate** (► 83) walk straight ahead, passing the controversial **Peter Memorial** (► 86), to **Peter and Paul Cathedral** (► 83) where the tombs of the tsarist family are located. Before visiting the prison in **Trubetskoy Bastion** (► 86) take a stroll through the Neva Gate to the river for a breath of fresh air and to take in the incredible view of the palaces lining the river bank opposite.

🕐 1pm

Leave the fortified island by taking the bridge to the west and you will reach ⭐ **Strelka** (► 80) on Vasilyevsky Island, via the so-called Exchange Bridge nearby. Enjoy the peace that this wide stretch of water exudes even though this is really the very centre of St Petersburg! Pass the **Old Stock Exchange** (► 80) to reach the **Twelve Colleges building** (► 81) on Mendeleevskaya Liniya. A good place to stop for lunch is **Grad Petrov**, a brewery restaurant on the riverbank right next to the Lomonossov Memorial.

🕐 3pm

Now feeling invigorated how about heading for one of the museums to find out more about Peter the Great and his time? Depending on your personal interest you could walk a little further to the left to the

23 **Kunstkamera** (►93) or to the right to **22** **Menshikov Palace** (fig. above; ►92), which you have to pass anyway on this tour of the city.

🕔 5pm

Take a break and enjoy the view over the Neva at the **21** **sphinxes in front of the Academy of Art** (fig. left below; ►91) with an espresso in your hand from one of the omnipresent vending machines. Our route takes you past the memorial to St Petersburg's first architect, Domenico Trezzini, and turns away from the bank to reach Lines 6 or 7 that lead to **Vasileostrovskaya metro station** 800m (2,600ft) further on.

🕕 6pm

As it will still be a little early to head back to your hotel we suggest a stroll along Line 6 and 7 between Bolshoi Prospekt and Srednij Prospekt – a **pedestrianised area** that has a pleasantly provincial air. There are a large number of places to eat to suit every taste, many of them with terraces outside, ranging from cafés and bars to pizzerias and the family-friendly restaurant **Prianosti i radosti** (►96). Far from the madding tourist crowd you can spend a lovely evening here side by side with the residents of St Petersburg. And don't forget to toast the founder of the city and his mad idea of building an elegant capital city in the windy and swampy Neva delta!

26 Botanical Garden

Gor'kovskaja Ⓜ

Russian Cruiser Aurora **25**

24 Artillery Museum

18 Cabin of Peter the Great

Peter and Paul Fortress

Neva

Strelka

Menshikov Palace **22**

Kunst-kamera **23**

21 Imperial Academy of Arts

0 — 500 m
0 — 500 yd

19 Erarta

S-189 Submarine Museum **20**

Strelka

Nowhere else in the city centre does St Petersburg's highly representative architecture blend so harmoniously with the Neva's vast expanse of water as on the eastern tip of Vasilyevsky Island. This is a place that is simply too lovely to leave just to the tourists so many locals come here in the evenings too to marvel at the city where they live.

Everyone in St Petersburg knows where Strelka is. But the name hardly ever appears on street maps although it is very appropriate, meaning 'arrow' or 'point' in Russian. The tip of Vasilyevsky Island divides the waters of the Neva on its way to the Baltic for a second time. Officially, this promontory is called Exchange Square – which is also fully justified as the **Old Stock Exchange**, built in the style of a classical Greek temple with 44 Doric columns, dominates the scene. From 1939 until 2014 the Old Stock Exchange was home to the Naval Museum. At present, the building is empty. After its renovation, the heraldry collection from the Hermitage will be presented here.

Dancing in the summer at the base of the Rostral Columns set against the floodlit Old Stock Exchange

The Old Stock Exchange and the two prominent, rust-red **Rostral Columns** erected around 1810 are the work of the French architect Thomas de Thomon. Despite the extremely elegant appearance of the Strelka ensemble, the buildings in fact all served a functional purpose, even if this is no longer obvious. For 150 years this was the site of St Petersburg's port. The Old Stock Exchange's raised base was once used for storage. And the Rostral Columns, decorated with the prows of ships (Latin: *rostrum*) and allegorical figures of four Russian rivers – the Neva and Volkhov as well as the Volga and Dnieper – were once beacons. There are still powerful gas-fired torches at the top of each column which are however only lit on special occasions. The symmetrical building complexes that flank the Old Stock Exchange on either side were formerly warehouses. Adjacent to these are two other buildings with central towers: to the south is the **Kunstkamera** (➤ 93), to the right the former customs office.

A wide semicircular embankment with massive stone spheres wraps around the tip itself, dropping down to the water. It is a popular place for wedding photos with palaces, the bridge and fortress forming an impressive backdrop. The local motorbike scene gathers on Exchange Square (under the north column) on balmy summer evenings but it is equally popular among hawkers and those out for a stroll or to admire the White Nights. The goings-on can also be watched from a few small street cafés.

Twelve Colleges Building

According to plans drawn up in the early 18th century it was originally intended that the representative centre of the future city be built on the Strelka. However, its somewhat isolated island location thwarted this. Nevertheless, a large space behind the Old Stock Exchange was not built on until 1900, when a gynaecological clinic was erected. The almost 400m (1,300ft)-long façade of the **Twelve Colleges Building** (1722–42) once overlooked this open space. Domenico Trezzini intended this ensemble of terraced buildings, built in Peter the Great's lifetime, to house Russia's parliament offices. Each of the ten ministries, as well as the Senate and the Synod, was given an identical building. A two-storey open walkway linking the buildings ensured easy access to all offices. Since the early 19th century, the Twelve Colleges have been used as the main building of the **St Petersburg State University**. Unfortunately, it is not accessible to the general public – a great shame, as the open walkway at the back was later glazed in. Its incredible length has made it the most famous corridor in St Petersburg.

TAKING A BREAK

The only restaurants in this area are quite exclusive and correspondingly expensive. One exception is the **Grand Kafe Neva** (daily 10am–midnight) on the corner of Universitetskaya nab /Tamoshenniy per. with a terrace open throughout the summer.

✚ 205 E5 ✉ Birshevaya Ploshchad
🚊 Birshevaya Ploshchad (trolley bus 7; bus 10, 191 from Nevsky Pr.)

INSIDER INFO

The southern-most of the two warehouses boasts a display run by the 🏛 **Zoological Museum** of almost the whole animal kingdom – albeit stuffed. The collection of mammoths is unique – the museum having three animals that lay mummified in the permafrost in Siberia for 40,000 years (Universitetskaya nab. 1; tel: 812-328-0112; www.zin.ru, Wed–Mon 11am–6pm, entrance fee: ₽200).

Insider Tip

★Peter and Paul Fortress
(Petropavlovskaya Krepost)

The bastion on Hare Island formed the nucleus of St Petersburg, its construction in 1703 marking the beginning of the city's history. However, the fortress never had to fend off enemies of any kind. The city's highest church tower stretches into the sky above the thick walls that protect the tombs of the imperial Romanovs and now house a museum complex.

The golden needle on Peter and Paul Cathedral is visible from afar but is not necessary quite so easy to get to. There are only two wooden bridges connecting Petrograd Side with **Hare Island**. This small island, some 870m (2,850ft) long, was picked out by the Russians in 1703 as the perfect site for a fortress to be able to defend the mouth of the Neva. The island was right on the main shipping channel and so small as to be fortified in its entirety. No enemy forces were to be able to dig beneath its walls.

A hexagonal bastion comprising earth ramparts and wooden palisades was quickly raised. In 1703, Domenico Trezzini – a young architect from Ticino – took on the planning and management of the large building site. The ramparts were strengthened by solid brick walls encasing casemates (fortified chambers). In the 1730s so-called ravelins – detached triangular fortifications – were added

The nucleus of the city: Peter and Paul Fortress

Peter and Paul Fortress

to the west and east. This explains why **St Peter's Gate** (1714–18) on the eastern side, bearing the ornamentation of a triumphal arch, is in an inner courtyard, to the left of which is the central information and ticket area. Around 1775 the walls facing the Neva were clad in granite. A **viewing platform** on the top of the wall offers what is probably the most beautiful panorama of the city.

Insider Tip

The construction of a cathedral in the middle of the fortress began in 1712. It was completed in 1733. The towering golden spire that can be seen for miles around, with the figure of an angel on the top, was originally 112m (367ft) high. In 1858 it was extended to 122.5m (402ft), when the tip was replaced by a metal construction. Up until 2013 the Baroque **Peter and Paul Cathedral** was the tallest building in the city. Unlike churches built before and after the time of Peter I, this is a hall church with a central nave and, in keeping with western architecture, even has a pulpit. To the right, in front of the exceptional golden iconostasis, are six tsars' tombs including those of the two 'Greats' – Peter I and Catherine II. Russia's last monarch, Nicholas II, who was murdered with the rest of his family, was laid to rest in 1998 in a side chapel to the right of the entrance. As the cathedral was not considered grand enough to house the family tombs of the Romanovs, a large burial chapel was added in 1900 where members of the former tsarist family are still buried today. The fortress is St Petersburg's most extensive pedestrianised area and, at the same time, a museum complex with a variety of different displays.

INSIDER INFO

- If you can understand Russian well enough the guided tour of the **bell-tower** in Peter and Paul Cathedral is really worth the small fee. Lightning strikes, technical details and a number of historical and heroic climbing actions up the golden spire are described in vivid detail. If you buy a ticket just for the cathedral you can climb up to 43m (141ft) on your own for an additional payement of ₽150. The view is, however, spoilt by bells, walls and wire mesh. From the colonnade of St Isaac's Cathedral (▶ 107), that is at the same height, you get a much better view of the city.
- **Sightseeing flights** (▶ 39) take off from just north of the fortress at weekends. You can watch Mi-8 helicopters taking off and landing too. But stand well back – things can get pretty breezy!
- There are a number of commercial exhibitions in the fortress. Regardless of whether they feature dragons, wax figures or instruments of torture, a visit cannot really be recommended. However, what the **Siberian left-handed man** (*Sibiriski lewscha*) does in his shows (daily 10am–7pm; entrance fee: ₽300) in the coach house is truly amazing: the miniature artist Anatoli Kovenko from Omsk makes camal caravans pass through the eye of a needle and mosquitos play chess – which is all only visible through a microscope.

Insider Tip

The Nucleus of the City

The history of St Petersburg began with the very first structure erected on the site of Peter and Paul Fortress in May 1703. Earth ramparts and wooden buildings were initially constructed but, by 1706, a stone fortification wall in the shape of an irregular hexagon had already been begun. The cathedral and adjoining burial chapel is the final resting place of several members of the imperial family.

❶ Ticket office The ticket office for entry to the museums, the cathedral and the prison is on the left after passing through St John's Gate.

❷ St Peter's Gate St Peter's Gate leads into the actual fortification itself. The Russian double-headed eagle hovers over the archway.

❸ Engineers' House The Engineers' House of 1748/49 is now a branch of the Museum of the History of St Petersburg.

❹ Burial Chapel The burial chapel, built around 1900, is linked to the Peter and Paul Cathedral by a corridor.

❺ Peter and Paul Cathedral The cathedral, where the tombs of Peter I and Catherine II can be found, is the burial place of many members of the tsarist family.

❻ Commander's House The Commander's House was built in 1743–46 and now houses the Museum of the History of St Petersburg.

Peter and Paul Fortress

7 Tsars' Bastion Tours of the bastion walls start here.

8 Neva Gate The entrance to the fortress from the water is through the Neva Gate. The high water marks of the Neva during various floods are recorded inside.

9 Trubetskoy Bastion This bastion was used from 1872 until 1921 as a high-security prison. The cells, recreated down to the last detail, can now be visited.

10 Aleksei Ravelin Served as a preliminary fortification.

A last look at St Petersburg at its best before going down again onto the bastion walls

Petrograd Side & Vasilyevsky Island

The **State Museum of the History of St Petersburg** (up until 1918), located in the former commander's house, is well worth seeing and rich in variety. To the left of it is the controversial **statue** commemorating the city's founding father – sculpted by Mihail Chemiakin, Peter the Great is depicted as a monstrous giant with tentacle-like fingers and a disproportionately small head.

The strangely proportioned bronze statue of Peter the Great

A high-security prison created in the **Trubetskoy Bastion** in 1872 can also be visited. Political prisoners in particular were kept in solitary confinement here to await their trials. The oppressively bare cells have been reconstructed down to the last detail. From 1917 onwards, the victorious revolutionary leaders imprisoned and executed many of their chief opponents here. The prison was closed in 1921.

A walk along the very popular **sandy beach** on the southern side of the complex will dispel any gloomy thoughts. Even though swimming is officially not allowed, many locals do so anyway – and the Neva is actually relatively clean.

Insider Tip

TAKING A BREAK

Koryushka (daily noon–1am; www.ginza.ru) is a good and nicely decorated restaurant with large windows on the western tip of Hare Island, guaranteeing you a magnificent view of the Strelka and Winter Palace. By the way: *koryushka* is a popular type of fish served in restaurants that has a certain cult following in St Petersburg.

Insider Tip

✚ 205 E/F5 ✉ Sayachiy Ostrov
☎ 812-230-6431,www.spbmuseum.ru
🕐 Island: daily 6am–10pm. Fortress: daily 9am–9pm. Peter and Paul Cathedral: May–Sep daily 10am–7pm, Tue until 6pm, Sun from 11am.
Guided tours of the bell-tower: Thu–Tue 11:30am, 1pm, 2:30pm, 4pm. Prison: daily 10am–7pm, Tue until 6pm (Cathedral and Prison Oct–April, closed Wed).
Other museums and exhibitions: Thu–Tue 11am–7pm.
Poterna and Neva Panorama: May–Sep daily 10am–9pm, Oct–April daily 11am–6pm
🚇 Gorkovskaya
💵 Fortress: free; Cathedral: P450, Bell-tower: P150, Prison: P200, Museum of the History of St Petersburg 1703–1918: P200, Poterna and Neva Panorama: P250

SPORTS ON HARE ISLAND

Hare Island is a unique playground for leisure activities. In winter, the 'walruses' (hard-core health fanatics) take a dip in the water through a hole in the ice in the southeast corner of the island. To the east of the Neva Gate is a corner in the fortifications that is sheltered from the wind and is a perfect sun-trap in the afternoon. Even when those out for a walk are well wrapped up against the cold, sun worshippers can be seen here up against the wall in their bathing costumes. On the west side there is an area for playing *gorodki*. This now national sport had almost been completely forgotten. It is a kind of skittles played by throwing bat-like sticks and making them spin.

⑱ Cabin of Peter the Great
(Domik Petra I)

Exactly ten days after work started on Peter and Paul Fortress in May 1703 Peter I asked for a log cabin to be built for him nearby. No sooner said than done. The little hut erected on the building site on the bank of the Neva – then proudly called the 'very first palace' – still stands to this day. This relict from the days the city was first founded is encased within an outer building.

The Cabin of Peter the Great (or Peter's Cottage) is not only the oldest building to be seen in the city but actually the very first building completed – a rarity indeed! It has survived so long thanks to the tsar's request in 1723 that a protective roof be built over the log cabin. It was the first building in Russia to be given heritage status and listed as a building of special historical interest. In the middle of the 19th century the building encasing it was completely rebuilt. The cabin is now run as a **branch of the Russian Museum** (➤ 135).

Like a **Russian doll** – a *matryoshka* – the brick building surrounded by old trees encases the tsar's cabin inside as well as a small exhibition on the founding of the city. This includes a model that shows the cabin in its less urban setting in 1706. A rowing boat built by the skilled tsar Peter himself is also on display.

This simple log cabin was the first place where Peter the Great lived in St Petersburg

You cannot actually go into the cabin itself which has a floor area of just 65m² (670ft²). Instead you can look through the open windows at everything inside. Note the remains of the painted brick pattern that originally covered the outer walls. This was an attempt to make the 'temporary' structure look more permanent and give it a solid, more urban appearance. Peter's first abode was, after all, erected in just four days. There was no heating. The doors that are only 1.82m (6ft) high and came from Swedish ships that had

Insider Tip

MEMORIAL FOR THE VICTIMS OF STALINISM
Trinity Square (Troitskaya Ploshchad) was originally the centre of the young city. This was where the port, Gostiny Dvor, the church, the parliamentary buildings and the city's first tavern were located. None of these have survived. The square has the first – and only – memorial to the victims of the Stalin era in the form of a glacial boulder from the Solovetsky Islands in the White Sea where the Soviets established their first large forced-labour camp in 1923.

A view through
the window
into the city
founder's study
in the 'very
first palace'

been captured. How often Peter the Great – who was
2.04m (6.7ft) tall – hit his head on the door frames of his
new house with their carefully painted floral decoration,
has not been passed down!

He only actually lived here during the summer in 1703.
The cottage has two main rooms and a small bedroom of just
7m² (75ft²). The desk chair in the study deserves a closer
look too – it was also made by the tsar himself.

Insider Tip

In Peter's day the cabin stood on a spot closer to the water
than today. The road along the river bank reinforced with
granite was only built at the beginning of the 20th century.
Two frog-liked **lion statues** flank steps down into the water
opposite the cabin. They were brought to the Russian capital
in 1907 from Manchuria which, at that time, was under
Russian control. Immediately opposite, on the other bank
of the Neva, is Peter's **Summer Palace** (1710–14) (▶ 68) –
the first and oldest stone building in the city.

TAKING A BREAK

In the residential block just behind Peter's cabin, built in
1964 to house the Soviet elite, is the popular sushi restaurant
Jakitoriya. In summer you can sit outside on the terrace
under sunshades (daily 11am–6am; tel: 812-970-4858;
www.yakitoriya.spb.ru).

✚ 203 E3 ✉ Petrovskaya nab. 6 ☎ 812-595-4248; www.rusmuseum.ru
🕐 Wed, Fri–Mon 10am–6pm, Thu 1pm–9pm (closed last Mon in the month)
🚇 Gorkovskaya 🚋 Troitskaya pl. (bus 49; tram 3, 6, 40) 🗺 P200

⑲ Erarta

The two major museums, the Hermitage and the Russian Museum, have little to offer in the way of contemporary art. During the Soviet era they were barely allowed to acquire new works and, later, this was not possible due to empty coffers and high prices on the art market. Thanks to a private initiative this gap in art history was closed in 2010. Erarta is the largest private museum for modern art in the country.

Museums of modern art are usually instantly recognisable. Erarta is different. It is housed in a representative but not exactly aesthetically outstanding administration building from the Stalin era, once occupied by a rubber research institute. And its location in the last row on the far side of Vasilyevsky Island is neither exquisite nor central.

But it is well worth a visit – especially if you are interested in art and want to get a thorough and representative overview of the work of contemporary Russian artists sponsored by the private Erarta foundation. A pragmatic approach has been adopted. The works of the 250 protégés are not only on show but can also be bought. Apart from a really interestingly stocked souvenir and art shop, the museum also has a gallery selling original works of art with branches in London and Hong Kong.

The entrance to the art museum is flanked by Time ('era') and Art ('arta')

Insider Tip

Petrograd Side & Vasilyevsky Island

Visitors are welcomed by two monumental sculptures outside the entrance that symbolise **'era'** and **'arta'** – time and art. 2,300 works form the core of the permanent exhibition that covers the period from the 1950s up to the present day. It extends over all five floors in the left wing of the cleverly revamped building. Apart from painting and sculpture, objets d'art and several large installations are displayed. The gallery occupies the first floor of the right wing with a room above used for temporary exhibitions. The central section is used for concerts and plays.

KURYOKHIN CENTER

This other important modern art institution is almost next door to Erarta. The Kuryokhin Center building is however being completely renovated and will not be open again before 2019. Until that time the **Sergei Kuryokhin Museum** can be found at Ligovsky Prospekt 73 (www.kuryokhin.net).

Unlike many other museums in the city, all works in Erarta are labelled in English throughout. Texts about many of the exhibits in both English and Russian that have been written by visitors and put on the museum website are also on view.

Insider Tip

TAKING A BREAK

The catering in Erarta is also exemplary. **Erarta Café** is a chic eatery on the lower floor with a terrace open in the summer. If you just want a snack, try the cafeteria on the 3rd floor with tables on the balcony.

Russian art from the mid 20th century presented in spacious exhibition rooms

🚇 204 A3 ✉ 29. Liniya 2
☎ 812-324-0809; www.erarta.com
🕐 Wed–Mon 10am–10pm
🚌 28. i 29 linii (bus 6, 128, tram 6 from Vasileostrovskaya metro station)
💰 P500

At Your Leisure

The museum submarine was still in service up until 1990

🔟 S-189 Submarine Museum (Musey Podvodnaya Lodka S-189)

Unlike the *Aurora* (➤94) and the icebreaker *Krassin* (➤see below) the third museum ship in the city open to visitors is not historically important as such. The diesel submarine S-189 was launched in Leningrad in 1954 and formed part of the Soviet Union's Baltic Fleet until 1990. After rusting away for ten years in Kronstadt and then sinking, an initiative founded by

Russian submarine enthusiasts organised the salvage and restoration of this 76m (250ft)-long vessel. Visitors can try to imagine what it must have been like for the crew of 54 to have had to live and work in such cramped surroundings.

➕ 204 C4 ✉ Nab. Lieutenant Schmidt, on a level with Line 16
☎ 904-613-7099; www.s-189.ru
🕐 Wed–Sun 11am–7pm, guided tours in Russian every 30 mins. until 6pm
🚌 14. i 15. linii (bus 1 from Vasileostrovskaya metro station) 💰 ₽400

🔟 Imperial Academy of Arts (Akademiya Chudoshestv)

The massive, Neoclassical building erected in 1764–88 that dominates the river bank by the university, demonstrates to this day the importance attached to the state-funded training of painters, sculptors and architects at that time. The exhibits in the Academy Museum, however, are largely copies made for teaching purposes and the interesting architecture section with historical models is, unfortunately, not open to the public at the moment. Unless there is a particularly good temporary exhibition on show, even art lovers can save themselves the not inexpensive entrance fee.

The Neva embankment outside the Academy is impressive. A broad flight of steps down to the water is flanked by two **sphinxes** that once guarded the entrance to a temple

ICEBREAKER *KRASSIN*

Some 600m (2,000ft) further down the river the museum icebreaker, the *Krassin*, awaits old seasalts! Built in 1916 in England the ship came to world fame in 1928 when it rescued the survivors of an airship that had crashed during an expedition led by Umberto Nobile. The deck structures date from the 1950s (www.krassin.ru; guided tours in Russian every hour, Wed–Sun 11am–5pm; ₽400).

PHOTOGENIC GRIFFINS
The four chubby-cheeked but stern-looking bronze griffins that flank the semicircular stone benches below the sphinxes are particularly photogenic. These are replicas made in 1960 of the originals that have been lost.

in the Valley of the Kings in Upper Egypt. The inscription on the pedestal includes the date 1832 when the huge sculptures that each weigh 23t were transported to 'the city of St Peter'. The sphinxes bear the face of the pharaoh Amenhotep III, frequently found on stone carvings, who died around 1350BC. Being some 3,400 years old, these statues are not only the oldest monuments in St Petersburg but are roughly as old as the Neva itself! It was around this time that the waters of Lake Ladoga broke through a ridge of land to the east of St Petersburg, creating the present course of the river.

✚ 205 D4 ✉ Universitetskaya nab. 17
☎ 812-323-6496; www.nimrah.ru
🕐 Wed–Sun 11am–7pm
🚇 Vasileostrovskaya 🚌 1-ya i Kadetskaya linii (bus 7, 24 and trolley 1, 10, 11 from Nevsky Pr.)
📖 P500

22 Menshikov Palace (Menshikovskiy Dvorez)

In 1711 the first palace building in the new city was ready for occupation. However, it was not Peter the Great who moved in, but his friend Alexander Menshikov (1673–1729) who had been appointed governor of the city. While the ruler himself lived in understated modesty, Menshikov loved pomp and luxury. His Early Baroque palace on the waterside on Vasilyevsky Island was the premier address for state receptions and glittering parties.

As a **branch of the Hermitage** the palace houses an exhibition with the clumsy title

Decorative tiles can also be found in the bedrooms in Menshikov Palace

'Russian Culture in the 1st Third of the 18th Century' – a journey back in time that takes visitors into the private apartments of Russia's former *éminence grise*. As one will see, a small anteroom panelled in walnut from floor to ceiling or a bedroom with walls covered in hand-painted Dutch tiles were the height of fashion.

✚ 205 D4 ✉ Universitetskaya nab. 15
☎ 812-323-1112; www.hermitage.ru
🕐 Tue–Sun 10:30am–6pm, Wed, Fri until 9pm
🚇 Universitet (trolley bus 1, 10, 11; bus 7, 24 from Nevsky Prospekt)
📖 P300

The Globe of Gottorf in the room in the tower at the Kunstkamera

🔢 Kunstkamera

The Kunstkamera, built in 1718, is not only the **oldest museum in Russia** but – according to the institution's own website – reputedly the first purpose-built museum in the world. In those days a *Kunstkamera* was seen not just as an art collection but as a grand cabinet of curiosities with rare and unusual objects especially from the fields of zoology and anatomy. It was founded in 1714 when Tsar Peter I in his quest for knowledge had his collections

transferred from Moscow to his new capital city.

The almost 100m (328ft)-long building, completed in 1727, was erected to accommodate the Academy of Science that was founded in 1724. It includes a library as well as an anatomy theatre for lectures in medicine and an observatory in a characteristic tower. It now houses the **Museum for Anthropology and Ethnography**.

The presentation of the artefacts, idols and the traditional costumes of East Asian, North American and African tribes, largely collected during the tsarist era, is quaintly antiquated. The main attraction is the room with 'The Kunstkamera's First Natural History Collection'. This is where animal and human foetuses, spliced skulls, organs and all sorts of monstrosities, preserved in spiritus more than 300 years ago, are on display. With their help Peter the Great hoped to assist young Russian scientists in their quest for knowledge into life's secrets. Small children and anyone who can't sleep after watching a horror film is best advised to avoid these exhibits.

➕ 205 E4 ✉ Universitetskaya nab. 3
☎ 812-328-1412; www.kunstkamera.ru
🕐 Tue–Sun 11am–6pm, June–Aug until 7pm (closed last Tue in the month)
🚇 Universitetskaya nab.
(trolley bus 1, 10, 11; bus 7, 24, 191 from Nevsky Prospekt)
📖 P250

GLOBE OF GOTTORF

A literally world-shattering exhibit is right at the top of the tower in the Kunstkamera – and can only be seen as part of a guided tour for groups (available in several languages; book one week in advance; group fee: P6,700) – the Globe of Gottorf, made around 1660 for the Duke of Holstein-Gottorf. Peter the Great was fascinated by it and acquired it as a diplomatic gift. What makes this historically unique globe with a diameter of 3.10m (10ft) so very interesting is that it is also a planetarium with a bench inside. When the globe is turned, the firmament painted on the inside moves too. Peter the Great is reputed to have spent many an hour here where he could ponder on the ways of the world.

Insider Tip

Petrograd Side & Vasilyevsky Island

24 Artillery Museum (Musey Artillerii)

The museum is as vast and sabre-rattling as its official name suggests: 'Military-Historical Museum of the Artillery, Pioneering and Communications Forces of the Defence Ministry of the Russian Federation'. For almost 150 years it has been housed in the crownwork fortification – a horseshoe-shaped armoury built on the bastions once used to defend Peter and Paul Fortress on the landward side.

The courtyard area is filled with a large open-air presentation of Russian military engineering. Inside this somewhat bleak building there are large exhibition areas principally devoted to World War II seen from a patriotic, Soviet point of view. On the other hand, a room on the ground floor where the transition from the sword and lance to guns is documented, exudes the aura of an historical arsenal.

✚ 203 D3 ✉ Kronwerkskaya nab.
☎ 812-232-0296; www.artillery-museum.ru
🕐 Wed–Sun 11am–6pm (closed last Thu in the month) Ⓜ Gorkovskaya 💷 P400

25 The Cruiser *Aurora* (Kreyser *Avrora*)

Old warships, spruced up to serve as floating museums, can be found in many harbour cities in the world. However, during the Soviet era, the *Aurora* that was launched in 1900 was considered a sight worth seeing, certainly on a par with the Hermitage. On 25 October 1917 a blank shot was fired from the bows of the cruiser. It was reputedly a signal to the Bolsheviks to storm the Winter Palace. Today, however, talk is of just one shot intended as a test of vigilance. The legend of the shot from the *Aurora* marking the start of the 'Great Socialist October Revolution' has nevertheless found its way into Soviet history books – and turned the ship into an icon of the Revolution in steel. And thanks to this myth,

A signal shot from the *Aurora* supposedly marked the beginning of the October Revolution

the ship has survived to this day. Its history is actually not exactly one of fame and glory: in 1905 the cruiser was involved in the naval Battle of Tsushima that ended catastrophically for Russia. Only a handful of Russian ships, including the badly damaged *Aurora*, managed to escape the Japanese. In World War I it served in the Baltic as a training and guard ship and supported infantry operations. During the Siege of Leningrad in World War II its guns were removed and used on land. In 1944 it was decided to raise the Aurora that had been

26 Botanical Garden (Botanicheskiy Sad)

St Petersburg's botanical garden is one of the institutions that belong the first generation in the city. In 1713 Peter the Great had an 'Apothecaries' Garden' laid out on the site with the principal aim of providing the army and navy with medicinal plants. Since then, the isle that lies beyond the small River Karpovka has been known as 'Apothecary Island'. In 1823 the herbal garden became a scientific botanical institute.

Not far from the 326m (1,070ft)-high television tower (open to visitors) the well-maintained and extensive garden now boasts more than 80,000 different species of plant and covers an area of more than 17ha (42 acres). The glass-houses known as the **Orangeries** form the heart of the botanical garden. They can only be visited as part of a 50-min. guided tour in groups of max. 15 people whereby one has to choose between either tropical flora, subtropical or water plants (incl. the large palm house). When and which tour takes place is only displayed at the cash desk. Children under 4 years of age may not be taken inside due to the hot temperature and the humidity.

🚩 203 D/E4 ✉ Ul. Professora Popova 2 (entrance in summer: corner nab. reki Karpovki/Aptekarskiy Pr.)
☎ 812-372-5464; www.botsad-spb.com
🕙 Park: daily 10am–7pm; glasshouses: Tue–Sun 10am–5:30pm (only as part of guided tours in Russian)
🚇 Petrogradskaya
💰 Park: ₽100; guided tour: ₽300

sunk by shelling in the harbour of Oranienbaum and to turn it into a museum ship. Since 1948 the armoured cruiser that was restored in 2014–2016 has been at its 'eternal mooring' outside the Nakhimov Naval School.

Today, the *Aurora* is a **branch of the Naval Museum** (➤ 119). Visitors can stroll across the spick and span teak deck and admire the numerous nostalgic brass and steel pieces of maritime equipment. Below deck there is an exhibition on the ship's history.

🚩 203 E3 ✉ Petrogradskaya nab., opposite No. 2 ☎ 812-303-8513; www.navalmuseum.ru 🕙 Wed–Sun 11am–6pm
🚇 Gorkovskaya 🚊 Ul. Chapayeva (tram 3, 6, 40; bus 49) 💰 ₽600

INSIDER INFO

Throughout the year it is hot and humid in the glasshouses in the botanical garden. There is nowhere to hand in coats and jackets as guided tours end at exits that are several hundred yards from the entrance. As a consequence, it is better only to take a light jacket or similar with you that you can carry under your arm in the tropical forest.

Insider Tip

Where to...
Eat and Drink

Prices
for a main course (without drinks):
£ under ₽450   ££ ₽450–₽900   £££ over ₽900

Barvinok £

This eatery, housed in a building rather like a farm hut, may be small but the choice of down-to-earth Ukrainian dishes is huge. The only disadvantage is that there is no menu in English but the landlady knows how to help people out. And like at a village gathering, guests sit on long, solid wooden benches and eat and drink and drink and… And it isn't even expensive.

➕ 202 C3   ✉ Ul. Mira 7
☎ 812-237-1494
🕐 Daily 11am–11pm   🚇 Gorkovkaya

Pryanosti i radosti ££

The building dates from the 1720s and is therefore ancient by local standards. This charming restaurant is however bright and new. It is designed to attract 👫 young families in particular. You can wine and dine in the large courtyard at the back as well as play, dig, go on a swing and stroke rabbits. There is another branch (without a garden) in Petrograd Side: Malaya Posadskaya Ul. 3

➕ 204 C4   ✉ 6. Liniya 13
☎ 812-640-1616; www.ginza.ru
🕐 Daily 9am–1am
🚇 Vasileostrovskaya

Suliko £

A small basement café with tasty authentic Georgian food at low prices. Even if the open barbecue in the dining room itself tickles the taste buds, go for the dishes served piping hot in clay pots. These are easy to pick out on the menu. Branches in the city centre:

Kasanskaya Ul. 6 and Ul. Vosstaniya 7.

➕ 203 D3   ✉ Kamennoostrovskiy Pr. 14
☎ 812-232-8807
🕐 Daily 11am–11:30pm   🚇 Gorkovskaya

Tolsty Frayer £

The success of this St Petersburg chain of pubs is based on several factors: a tasty home brewed beer, old-fashioned traditional décor with dated Soviet propaganda material – and a free plate of nibbles with the first beer (you don't have to eat the dried fish!). The food is down-to-earth, filling and tasty. Other branches: Line 8, no 43 on Vasilyevsky Island and Ul. Belinskogo 13 and Dumskaya Ul. 3 in the city centre.

➕ 202 C3   ✉ Ul. Mira 11
☎ 812-232-3056; www.tolstiy-fraer.ru
🕐 Daily 10am–1am, Fri, Sat until 3am
🚇 Gorkovskaya

Troizky most £

This quiet, alcohol and meat-free cafeteria was opened more than 20 years ago. The portions may be a little small but then so are the prices so it makes good sense to combine a couple of dishes and then choose something from the salad or cake bars that are continuously freshly made on the spot. This is were vegans can really tuck in! On Vasilyevsky Island there is a branch on Line 6, no. 27 (in the courtyard).

➕ 203 D3   ✉ Kamennoostrovskiy Pr. 9 (entrance on Malaya Posadkaya Ul.)
☎ 812-942-2397; www.vegetarian-cafe.com
🕐 Daily 9am–10pm   🚇 Gorkovskaya

Restoran £££

As laconic as the name, so are both the severe but elegant interior in the early St Petersburg style and the menu itself. The classically Russian dishes here are simply listed as 'salmon', 'zander' or 'beef'. Good food doesn't need a long explanation!

🚩 202 C1 ✉ Tamoshenniy Per. 2
☎ 812-327-8977; www.russkiyrestaurant-spb.ru
🕐 Daily noon–midnight
🚌 Universitetskaya nab. (trolley bus 1, 10, 11; bus 7, 24, 191 from Nevsky Pr.)

Volga-Volga £££

The Ginza Project restaurant holding owns more than 40 different restaurants in the city (and has now expanded to Moscow, Baku, London and New York as well). This is its flagship – literally.

Insider Tip
Four times a day the modern and elegantly furnished restaurant departs from its mooring with its guests on board for a one-hour round trip on the Neva. Visits have to be correspondingly timed. The emphasis on the extensive menu of this, the only restaurant ship in the city, is – as you would expect –

on seafood of the very best quality. Entrées include wickedly expensive delicacies such as oysters and red king (Kamchatka) crab. Plain seaman's fare is available too, such as 'maritime macaroni' served with minced meat. Italian and Asian dishes round off the choice. If the weather permits, there are a few tables on the open upper deck that are (relatively) well protected from the wind. A 10% service charge is made – that is not normally levied in this area – on top of the already pretty hefty price. This probably doesn't worry the majority of the obviously well-heeled diners. Nothing now hints at the origin of this luxury liner, the *Dunayevsky*. As part of the St Petersburg tourist boat fleet, it was actually built in 1962 in Magdeburg as a simple cargo vessel, the *ST-750*, operating on rivers in the Soviet Union.

🚩 203 E3 ✉ Petrovskaya nab. opposite No. 8
☎ 812-640-1616, https://ginza.ru/spb/restaurant/Volga-Volga
🕐 April–Sep daily noon–2am.
Departure times: 3pm, 7pm, 10pm, midnight
🚇 Gorkovskaya
🚌 Ul. Chapayeva (bus 49, tram 3, 6, 40)

Where to...
Shop

The districts on the Neva Islands are, generally speaking, not particularly attractive for shoppers. The businesses and shops primarily meet the everyday needs of those living there.

BOLSHOI PROSPEKT

Bolshoi Prospekt on Petrograd Side is the only street for shopping of any renown beyond the boundaries of the district itself. Unlike Nevsky

Prospekt, however, there are neither any department stores nor malls here and only a few branches of larger chains and luxury labels of world fame. Having said that, the street between the metro stations Petrogradskaya and Sportivnaya is actually the best address for fans of expensive shoes and fashion boutiques, jewellery and perfume.

Insider Tip

The **Boutique Gallery Apriori** (Bolshoi Pr. 58) with a selection of exclusive shops on three floors is the starting point for any window-shopping tour along this attractive road. Most of the clothes are from France or Italy but the Siberian fashion designer Alexander Bogdanov also has a boutique here – **BGD.**

MARKETS

Some 500m (1,640ft) to the west of Gorkovskaya metro station is **Sytny Rynok**, St Petersburg's oldest market. It comprises a lovely market building dating from 1913 where food is sold and an outside area with a colourful assortment of stands and stalls. Dacha gardeners sell there vegetables, fruit, berries and mushrooms here too together with professional traders and producers. Treat yourself to some fresh raspberries or cherries in the summer or, in the autumn, vitamin-rich bilberries and cranberries which grow profusely in the forests and swamps around the city. In the halls you will find wonderfully presented stands of fruit and eager stallholders from southern regions as well as stalls of honey, dried fruit and nuts – products that make perfect little gifts too.

If you are on the lookout for stylish Russian opera glasses for your visit to the Mariinsky Theatre, make a detour into the narrow roads (by St Petersburg standards) behind the market where you will find a good selection in the specialist shop **Galilei** (Sablinskaya Ul. 10; www.veber.ru).

There is also a typically Russian **market on Vasilyevsky Island** at Bolshoi Prospekt 14 on the corner of Line 5.

Where to...
Go Out

BARS

With the exception of theatres and cinemas, culture in general and nightlife on Petrograd Side still leaves something to be de-sired. The music is being played on the other side of the river…

On Vasilyevsky Island things are similar except for some slightly more lively corners such as in the pedestrian precinct on Lines 6 and 7 and at the southern exit of Sportivnaya metro station where the **Helsinkibar** (Kadetskaya Linya 31; daily from 6pm) fuses Finnish design with craft beer and with DJs who create a real party mood.

In the same corner building – but on the front facing the bank – competition can be found in the form of the quieter gastro-pub **Brugge** (nab. Makarova 22; daily noon–2am), run by a Belgian brewery.

A few doors down is the **Buterbrodsky Bar** (nab. Makarova 16; daily noon–midnight) – designed like an incompleted renovation – serving its own speciality of *smörrebrod* and a liqueur brewed to a secret recipe.

BEER GARDEN

The only real beer garden in the whole city is near the brand-new football stadium in which several World Cup matches are to be held in summer 2018. Pretzels, sausages and Oktoberfest chicken, not to mention **Karl & Friedrich's** self-brewed beer, go down a treat even with ultra-critical, true-to-heart Bavarians. The only difference here is that you don't sit under chestnut trees but under birches instead (we are in Russia, after all!). There is also a lovely 🧒 **children's playground** and a mini zoo behind the brewery with ostriches, raccoons, goats and other animals that are not on the menu on the other side of the building.

🚍 202 to the west A5
✉ Yuschnaya Doroga 15
☎ 812-320-7978; www.k-f.ru
🕐 Sun–Thu noon–midnight, Fri, Sat until 1am.
Mini zoo: daily until 9pm 🚇 Krestovsky ostrov

Admiralteysky District

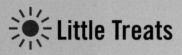 **Little Treats**

Mixing culture and sport

Since sport is also culture: When on **New Holland** (➤ 119) – the 'culture island' – why not hire badminton rackets or table-tennis bats, frisbees or pétanque balls for a quick break?

Coffee on the roof

Walking up the dark stairs might be a little scary but then light pours in and you can enjoy the panoramic view in **Solaris Lab** (Per. Pirogova 18; daily 1pm–midnight, Sat, Sun until 2am), an artists' café near the Mariinsky Theatre (➤ 111).

Service with a song

In **Sadko** (➤ 122) there are many music students and young choir and opera singers who work as waiters. On Saturday and Sunday evenings the sound of arias often fills the restaurant.

Getting Your Bearings

Of all the districts in St Petersburg this is the most maritime, not only thanks to its proximity to the harbour but also because of the network of canals that is the most dense here. Besides the four stretches of water – the Moyka, Griboyedov Canal, Fontanka and Obvodny Canal – surrounding the city centre like the rings of a tree, there is Kyukov Canal that passes through the middle connecting them all. The two bends in Griboyedov Canal also set it apart from the otherwise straight lines found in St Petersburg.

The Admiralteysky administrative district occupies the western half of the inner city south of the Neva. The boundary to the Central District (▶ 125) runs along Gorokhovaya Ulitsa, the middle one of three axes that form part of the overall urban plan, radiating out from the Admiralty's Golden Needle.

The massive, highly representative buildings at the district's most northerly point, Senate Square, catch the eye and attract visitors. The Admiralty embodies Russia's sometime aspiration to naval supremacy and the gigantic St Isaac's Cathedral underlines the country's deep religious roots, the linked buildings of the Senate and the Synod symbolising the symbiosis of the state and the church. The 'Bronze Horseman' at its centre is an exceptionally beautiful and impressive statue to the founder of the city, Peter the Great.

The contrasts found in this district are great too. Just a few streets away a network of small roads can be found where ordinary seamen and shipbuilders once lived. Even today, the Kolomna district to the west of Kyukov Canal, that prosperity and the modern age seem to have passed by, is the most romantic area in the inner city. Nevertheless one of the jewels in St Petersburg's cultural crown gleams away here, far from the next metro station –

namely the Mariinsky Theatre on Theatre Square. Steeped in tradition it boasts three stages, one old and two new. And St Nicholas Naval Cathedral, arguably St Petersburg's most beautiful church, deserves to be explored more closely rather than just *en passant* on board a boat touring the canals.

St Nicholas Naval Cathedral is dedicated to the patron saint of mariners

TOP 10

Don't Miss

At Your Leisure

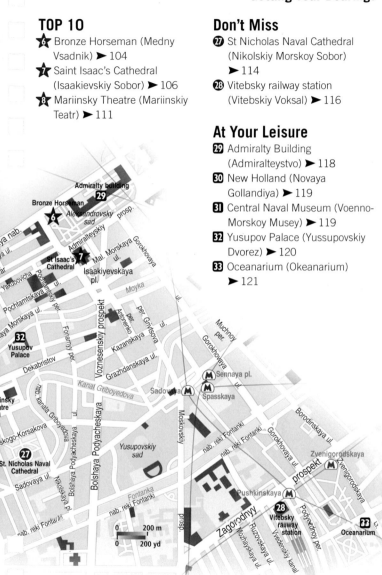

The Perfect Day

This inner-city tour is full of variety. It leads you down a number of romantic canals, taking in St Petersburg's imperial highlights – the Bronze Horseman and St Isaac's Cathedral – to the cultural heart, Theatre Square, and a magically beautiful station. And you will have a chance to do some shopping too.

🕘 9am
The café-restaurant **Schastye** in the traditional Hotel Angleterre opened recently. It offers a good and varied breakfast with a view of St Isaac's Square. Afterwards take a stroll to the ⭐**Bronze Horseman** (► 104) to pay your regards to the founder of the city, Peter I.

🕙 10:30am
Enjoy exploring ⭐**St Isaac's Cathedral** (fig. above; ► 106) as one of the first visitors of the day. Then climb up to the colonnade below the dome. A wonderful view in all directions over the city's rooftops well makes up for the effort.

🕛 Noon
Walk along quiet Pochtamtskaya Ulitsa and have a peek inside the huge and nostalgic main hall of the **Central Post Office** (fig. right). Depending on the weather and your interests you may want to visit the **31 Central Naval Museum** (► 119) or the cultural centre **30 New Holland Island** (► 119) that is in the process of being built.

🕑 2pm
Theatre Square is not only home to the venerable **Mariinsky Theatre** (► 111) but also to a number of restaurants that are perfect for a lunch break – such as **Sadko** (► 122) or the **Shamrock Pub**. (► 113). If you haven't already done so in advance, this would be a good opportunity to buy tickets at the booking office for a performance at the opera house or a ballet during your stay in the city.

⏰ 4pm

Soak in the relaxing atmosphere around **㉗ St Nicholas Naval Cathedral** (➤ 114) and count all the bridges you can see from nearby Pikalov Bridge where the Kyukov and Griboyedov canals meet!

⏰ 5pm

Following Griboyedov Canal, which is surprisingly quiet and romantic considering you are in the middle of a large city, you come to all-the-more-hectic **Hay Square** (Sennaya Ploshchad; fig. right; ➤ 123). Bang in the middle of everday life in St Petersburg you now have the chance to do some shopping, visit the market or enjoy a cup of tea in one of the countless cafés and snack bars.

⏰ 7pm

Ulitsa Yefimova between the two shopping malls **Pik** and **Sennaya** (➤ 123) leads to a pedestrian bridge over the Fontanka. Some 100m (328ft) further on to the left, turn right into the Little Cossack Lane (Maly Kasatshy Pereulok), right into Great Cossack Lane and then again into Sagorodny Prospekt. Passing through this typical Old Town district that has hardly changed for decades, you reach perfectly restored **㉘ Vitebsky Station** (➤ 116).

⏰ 8pm

After having had a good look around this Art Deco station it will be time for dinner. The relaxing **Dickens Pub** (➤ 122) can be reached easily from here on foot or take a metro from no less elegant Pushkinskaya Station to the restaurant **Tandoor** (➤ 123) near the **㉙ Admiralty**.

⭐6 Bronze Horseman
(Medny Vsadnik)

This, the most famous statue commemorating the founder of the city, Peter I, has also become one of the city's most easily recognised landmarks. On the back of an eager, rearing horse the great tsar and reformer has been pointing to the future since 1782. And the statue's ginormous pedestal is almost as interesting as the equestrian statue itself.

Shortly after her ascension to the throne Empress Catherine II commissioned an exceptional statue to be made to honour Tsar Peter the Great whom she greatly admired. The French sculptor Étienne Falconet was summoned to Russia to carry out this commission and spent 15 years in all in St Petersburg. He was accompanied by his pupil Marie-Anne Collot who was largely responsible for the statue's head, a plaster model of which can now be seen in the Russian Museum (► 135). The statue was unveiled in 1782. The laconic inscription on either side of the pedestal, one in Latin and the other in Russian, simply indicates the names 'Peter the First' and 'Catherine the Second' and the date.

Falconet went to great lengths to depict the tsar less as a field marshal in a victory pose and more as the dynamic ruler and innovative visionary, clad in a Roman toga and crowned with a laurel wreath. As an allegory to the taming of his own land, the rider is not sitting on a saddle but on a bearskin. The serpent that his steed is trampling stands for internal as well as external resistance that had duly been crushed. The reptile however also plays an important role with regard to the statics. Through the connecting horse's tail and the serpent a third point has been created to support the statue's artistically daring balancing act.

The expressiveness of this composition that reaches a height of 10.1m (33ft) is due to a large extent to its pedestal in the form of a breaking wave. It was carved from one single glacial boulder that also provided the material for the pieces added in front and behind. It was found in a forest some 15km (9.3mi) to the northwest after a search for such a stone was announced. The farmer was given the princely reward of 100 roubles for the tip.

The transport of this huge monolith, known as the **Thunder**

IRON, COPPER OR BRONZE

The English name of the statue – the 'Bronze Horseman' – tells us implicitly what it is made of. In many other languages, however, this is not the case, implying the work is made of iron or copper. Even the Russian name 'Medny Vsadnik' is misleading as this actually means 'Copper Horseman'. This is due to a certain artistic licence (and poetic translations), influenced most probably by Alexander Pushkin's poem 'Medny Vsadnik' whose tragic hero is chased through the streets by the statue that has come to life.

Bronze Horseman

Statue of Peter the Great on Senate Square

Stone, turned into an epic task and took two years. The unearthed stone was drawn on a wooden platform that rolled along wooden tracks on copper ball-bearings. In winter 1769/70 the stone was moved a distance of 8km (5mi) down the coast over the frozen ground by manpower alone. At the same time stonemasons clambered onto this colossal stone to chip away any unneeded material. Weighing 1250 tons, the stone reached its final location on a pontoon flanked by sailing ships. Never before – or since – has such a mighty monolith been moved in the history of mankind!

Senate Square

Senate Square, on which the statue is located, was the scene of a revolt by aristocratic officers in December 1825 against the newly crowned emperor Nicholas I. The latter's troops, however, quashed this first attempted Russian revolution. After the revolt the square was called Decembrist Square for a long time. It is now laid out as a park between the Neva, the **Admiralty** (➤ 118), **St Isaac's Cathedral** (➤ 106) and a distinctive double building by the architect Carlo Rossi erected in 1829–34 for the parliamentary Senate and the church leaders in the Synod. It now houses the Boris Yeltsin Presidential Library as well as the **Constitutional Court** of the Russian Federation.

TAKING A BREAK

If the weather is nice try one of the street cafés on the river-side promenade in front of the Admiralty – or the **Bridge Bar** (Admiralteyskaya nab. 12; www.bridgebar.ru; daily noon–4am) on the other side of the street.

➕ 205 E4

⭐Saint Isaac's Cathedral
(Isaakievskiy Sobor)

St Isaac's Cathedral, with its golden dome towering over the city centre, cannot really be missed. Rising to a height of 101.5m (333ft) it is not actually the highest but nevertheless one of the largest buildings in the historical centre of St Petersburg. The interior is equally impressive not simply on account of its sheer size but due to its magnificent decoration. The cathedral is also the only place in the city centre from which you can enjoy a 360 degree panoramic view.

St Isaac's Cathedral was constructed between 1818 and 1858 – and the blueprint was clear: to build a representative cathedral worthy of an imperial capital city. This leading role was not achieved by any of the three churches that were consecrated before St Isaac's was built, the first two of which were on this site where the Bronze Horseman (► 104) now stands.

St Isaac's Cathedral is one of the largest domed buildings in the world

Tsar Alexander I commissioned the previously unknown French architect **Auguste de Montferrand** with its design. The talented draughtsman had only arrived in St Petersburg in 1816. The cathedral would be his lifetime's achievement as he died just one month after its consecration. His wish to be buried there, however, was not met as Montferrand was a Catholic. During his career he also built the **Alexander Column** on **Palace Square** (➤63) and one other building: the triangular 'House with Lions', now the 'Lion Palace' hotel right next to the cathedral.

When building the cathedral, use was made of the foundations and walls of the previous churches on the site in the chancel area. However, wooden piles in the form of 10,762 tree trunks had to be driven into the soft ground to bear the additional load. To achieve an absolutely flat foundation a trick was used. The area excavated for the building was flooded as winter set in and, when ice formed, it acted like a spirit level, showing exactly where the tree trunks had to be cut. There were other unconventional phases during the building's construction too. The sixteen red granite columns that decorate both the north and south portals and the eight on the west and east side were erected before the outer walls were built, for instance, because vast wooden scaffolding was needed to raise each of these 17m (56ft) tall and 114t monoliths. The construction designed by the engineer **Agustín de Betancourt** from the island of Tenerife was so perfect that it did not even creak once, so Montferrand noted with some pride. It only took 45 minutes per column until they were standing upright – and this was all done with pure manpower.

The **dome**, supported on a tholobate and twenty-four polished granite columns from a quarry near Vyborg, is made of metal. From the **colonnade**, 41m (135ft) above ground level that is reached via a spiral staircase, a panoramic view of the city can be enjoyed. Warning: the opening at the top of the spiral staircase onto the roof is very narrow and this is followed by a climb up cantilevered steps.

The completion of the opulent decorative work in the **interior** of the cathedral took another sixteen years. The 150 large-format mosaics and paintings, as well as 300 sculptures, provide a stark contrast to the severity of the Classicist exterior. The walls are clad with a beige-yellow marble. Unusual accents of colour in the white and golden

INSIDER INFO

You can gaze at the pastel colours of the northern sky, watch the bridges being raised and enjoy the parade of cargo boats sailing in and out from a particularly good vantage point during the White Nights. From 1 June until 20 August (except Wed) the colonnade of St Isaac's Cathedral is also open at night from 10:30pm–4:30am. The entrance fee is, however, ₽400 and you cannot of course see that much of the rest of the city in the semi-dark.

Insider Tip

A Massive Dome

400,000 workers – a quarter of whom died of sickness or in accidents during the construction period – built this huge domed cathedral over 40 years. It measures 101m (331ft) long, 97m (318ft) wide and 101m (331ft) high. Under a dome with an internal diameter of 21.8m (71.5ft), this heavily decorated church, that was formerly the principal one in the city, can seat a congregation of some 12,000.

❶ **Figures of Angels** Angels holding torches can be seen at the corners of the cathedral. The torches are lit on high church festivals.

❷ **Porticoes** Each façade has a portico with columns of red Finnish granite, each of which weights 114 tons. The bases are made of bronze. The east and west façades have porticoes each with eight columns.

❸ **Ground Plan** The cathedral is built in the shape of a cross with the main dome rising above the intersection in the middle.

❹ **Smaller Domes** The four smaller domes lie above the columns integrated in the walls of the two longest walls.

❺ **Reliefs on the Tympanum** The high reliefs are made of bronze; the one on the south façade was cast by the sculptor Ivan Vitali of St Petersburg and depicts the Adoration of the Magi.

❻ **Bronze Doors** The bronze door reliefs are also by Vitali. They depict various saints and scenes from the life of Christ.

The uninterrupted view from the colonnade of St Isaac's Cathedral is exceptional

Saint Isaac's Cathedral

Admiralteysky District

iconostasis are provided by four vivid green columns made of malachite and two blue ones of lapis lazuli. From the central door you look directly at a stained-glass window with an image of Christ made in Munich. This was an absolute first in Russia at that time.

The bust of the architect, Montferrand, made with all the forty-three different types of stone used in the building of the cathedral, is correspondingly colourful. A model of the scaffolding used to erect the columns of the porticoes, one of the cathedral itself and of the three previous churches on the site – all to scale – are also on display as, since 1928, the cathedral has been used as a **state museum**. In 2017, however, its transfer from the City of St Petersburg back to the Church was agreed. This means that the entrance fee will disappear at due course; how quickly this will happen remains to be seen.

> **BLOCKADE TRACES**
> There are deep scars on the otherwise so smooth columns on the western façade of the cathedral. These were caused by granades that exploded during the blockade in World War II and have consciously been left as a reminder.

TAKING A BREAK

The restaurant landscape around the cathedral is dominated by 5-star hotels. While, of course, you can also have a cup of coffee there, the cake shop **Bise** (daily 8:30am–11pm, Sat, Sun from 10am, Pochtamtskaya Ul. 1) is somewhat cosier and also calls itself a restaurant – and not without good reason.

✚ 205 E3 ✉ Isaakievskaya pl. ☎ 812-315-9732; www.cathedral.ru
🕐 Cathedral: Thu–Tue 10:30am–6pm, May–Sep until 10:30pm;
colonnade: daily 10:30am–6pm, May–Sep until 10:30pm
(closed Nov–April on the 3rd Wed in each month)
🚇 Admiralteyskaya
💰 Cathedral: ₽250; evenings: ₽400. Colonnade: ₽150, evenings ₽300

INSIDER INFO

Insider Tip

The generally quiet **Museum District** (as the locals like to call this area) lies to the west of St Isaac's Cathedral between Moyka and broad Konnogvardeyskiy Bulvar. And there are indeed a surprising lot of things to do and see here.
- The **Manege**, an exhibition space for modern art (tel: 812-611-1100; www.manege. spb.ru, Fri–Wed 10am–6pm, entrance fees vary depending on exhibitions) is at Konnogvardeyskiy Bulvar 2 while No. 4 houses the private **Vodka Museum** (tel: 812-943-1431; www.vodkamuseum.su; daily noon–7pm; entrance fee: ₽170)
- The **Post and Telegraph Museum** (tel: 812-571-0060; www.rustelecom-museum.ru, Tue–Sat 10:30am–6pm, closed on last Thu in the month, entrance fee: ₽200) is located at Pochtamtskaya Ul. 7; no. 14 is home to the **Religious History Museum** (tel: 812-315-3080; www.gmir.ru, Thu–Tue 10am–6pm, Tue until 9pm, Sat until 8pm; entrance fee: ₽400)
- The house where the novelist Vladimir Nabokov was born, Bolshaya Morskaya Ul. 47, is now the **Nabokov Museum** (tel: 812-315-4713; http://nabokov.museums. spbu.ru; Tue–Fri 11am–6pm, Sat noon–5pm; free entrance)
- The **Central Naval Museum** (➤ 119) lies on Kyukov Canal

⭐8 Mariinsky Theatre
(Mariinskiy Teatr)

What the Hermitage is for fine art in the cultural metropolis of St Petersburg, the Mariinsky Theatre is for opera and ballet – the very best of its kind. Classical ballet is extremely popular even if the long-standing general director and star conductor Valery Gergiev also encourages modern and experimental performances in carefully portioned doses, too. The Mariinsky is so successful and famous that it now performs on several stages in the meantime. The sublime, classical principal company has two other venues right next door and a third one in Vladivostok.

Together with its outstanding orchestra, the opera house and ballet ensemble were famous throughout the world back in the Soviet era when it was known as the Kirov Theatre from Leningrad. Since 1992 it has been operating under its historical name meaning 'Maria's Theatre' – in 1860 the theatre building was named after Maria Alexandrovna, the wife of tsar Alexander II. The theatre itself was, however, founded back in 1783. Even then it occupied a building on **Theatre Square** between the Moyka and Griboyedov Canal and Kyukov Canal. The Mariinsky Theatre building itself is reason enough to buy a ticket for a performance. The auditorium that seats 1,625 has gleaming golden balconies and magnificent Baroque boxes as well as regal foyers, making a visit to the theatre an experience not to be missed – even before the curtain is raised.

Almost all the great Russian operas were first performed at the Mariinsky Theatre

The conductor **Valery Gergiev** took over as artistic director in 1988 and was appointed general director soon afterwards. The creative and energetic artist with connections right up into the higher echelons of the Kremlin, has since turned

Admiralteysky District

Contemporary luxury in the lobby of Mariinsky II

the theatre into the flagship of Russian culture. However, it soon came to light that the magnificent, traditional old building could not meet the demands of the ambitious maestro – who has been the chief conductor of the Philharmonic Orchestra in Munich since 2015, too.

This led to the idea of building a new theatre right behind the main building on the other side of Kyukov Canal – to be paid for by the state. The French star architect Dominique Perrault won the first international architecture competition in post-Soviet Russia soon after the turn of the millennium. However, after much to-ing and fro-ing, his bold design was ultimately thrown overboard.

Mariinsky II, designed by the Canadian architects Diamond & Schmitt and opened in 2013, looks like a plain, functional building. Inside the concrete block, however, that swallowed up 550 million euros in the end, the most exacting demands have been met. While a back-lit onyx-clad wall and Swarowski chandeliers exude an element of cool luxury, the auditorium that seats 2,000 has been finished in a laconic, Nordic 'organic' style – that has actually worked out well. Visibility, space and the acoustics are optimal for all members of the audience. And behind and under the stage the most modern technology that could be needed has been installed to guarantee a state-of-the-art theatre experience and the most varied repertoire possible.

And as if that were not enough. While the completion of Mariinsky II seemed to take an eternity, Gergiev saw that a third stage for his theatre was built in just four years a little further down the road on the other side. On the site of a warehouse that burnt down in 2003, where props were once stored, a **concert hall** seating 1,100 was built. Seemingly non-descript on the outside, the quality of its acoustics has been highly praised. The stage for performers and the orchestra is in the middle

'SWAN LAKE'

The repertoire at the Mariinsky also includes the Tchaikovsky classic 'Swan Lake'. Churned out in conveyor-belt fashion with performances every day during August, when traditionally there are no other performances, it is an external troupe that appears here – put on purely for the tourists.

Valery Gergiev conducting the inaugural concert in Mariinsky II in April 2013

with tiered seating on two sides. Narrow balconies on the sides conjure up the impression of an amphitheatre. Although not really suitable for the performance of plays, music lovers who come to a concert in this, the smallest of the three Mariinsky theatres, can enjoy the very best the arts have to offer.

Insider Tip

TAKING A BREAK

The traditional Irish **Shamrock Pub** (Ul. Dekabristov 27) right opposite the old Mariinsky Theatre was already the 'in' place to be even before a bar scene existed in the city at all. Both theatre-goers and actors alike make a bee-line for this pub to enjoy a pint of Guinness after a performance.

✚ 205 D2 ✉ Mariinsky I: Teatralnaya pl. 1; Mariinsky II: Ul. Dekabristov 34; concert hall: Ul. Dekabristov 37 ☎ 812-326-4141; www.mariinsky.ru
🕐 Performances begin: Oct–July daily 7pm/8pm; Sat, Sun also noon–2pm
Ⓜ Sennaya Ploshchad, Sadovaya, Spasskaya 🚌 from Nevsky Pr.: Teatralnaya pl. (bus 3, 27), Mariinsky teatr (bus 22) 💰 P1,000–P6,000

INSIDER INFO

■ Tickets for the Mariinsky are not available in the regular box-offices found all over the city but only through the Mariinsky itself and its two box-offices in the city centre. The larger one is halfway up the steps on the northwestern corner of the Gostiny Dvor (Nevsky Pr. 35; daily 11am–2:30pm, 4pm–9pm); the smaller one on the ground floor of the central railway booking office (nab. kan. Griboedov 24; daily 10:30am–1pm, 2pm–8pm, Sun until 4pm).

■ Tickets for the Mariinsky are otherwise also available online on the company's own website (with a good English version). It is advisable to buy tickets well in advance as the demand is huge, especially in summer. Not only will you be able to choose your seat but you will also save a lot of money, especially compared to tickets bought through a hotel reception or a travel company.

■ From October to July **a free concert** is given at 2pm by resident musicians in the Stravinsky Foyer (4th floor in Mariinsky II). Seat numbers are given out at the entrance as numbers are limited to 170.

Insider Tip

㉗ St Nicholas Naval Cathedral
(Nikolskiy Morskoy Sobor)

Perhaps the most beautiful ecclesiastical building in the city is in a quiet backwater of the Old City district at the picturesque intersection of two canals. This is where St Petersburg's label as the 'Venice of the North' really rings true.

Pikalov Bridge with its four ornamental obelisks was first built in 1785 to cross Griboyedov Canal at the point where it bends. The bridge is – by St Petersburg's standards – not only very old but it is also a special place. From here you can see eight other bridges if you turn around in a full circle.

The uncontested eye-catcher of this panoramic view is the **Baroque bell-tower** of St Nicholas Naval Cathedral, 100m (328ft) further north on Kyukov Canal. Of the cathedral itself you can see only the five golden domes that rise above the public buildings in front of it. The complex itself has the air of a peaceful monastery surrounded by greenery but it was in fact always the city's principal place of worship for the marines and shipbuilders who made up a large part of the local population. The cathedral was given the naval attribute in its name at the behest of Catherine II who had only come to the throne after a coup three weeks before its inauguration in 1762. From that time onwards this church, dedicated to the Russian navy, was to be where the glorious deeds of the Russian fleet – and the souls of sailors who had died at sea – were to be celebrated. This tradition is still upheld today. Commemorative plaques and services for the crew of the nuclear submarines *Komsomolez* (1989) and *Kursk* (2000) who perished can be found here.

Although the cathedral could be the work of the famous Rastrelli, bearing the date of its construction and its Baroque blue-and-white decoration in mind, it was in fact designed by the lesser-known **Savva Chevakinsky**, an architect in the service of the navy. At the time of its construction in 1753, its design marked the shift away from the western influence during the era of Peter the Great and a return to the fundamental principals of Russian Orthodox church architecture. The ground plan of the church is in the shape of a cross with four small domes surrounding one larger one in the middle. The bell-tower is separate. The building actually comprises two churches one above the other – the **lower church** with a low ceiling that can be easily heated in winter and the bright **upper church** with a high ceiling. A heating system was first installed in 1901.

The only major visible change during the cathedral's history was the replacement of wooden steps with ones

The bell-tower is some 100m (328ft) from St Nicholas Naval Cathedral itself

made of stone. Although plundered during the Soviet era it did, however, remain open. The elaborate white, gold and ultramarine decoration in the festive upper church can only be appreciated during services held at the weekends. But there is no need to feel awkward as the section open to tourists is separated from that of devout church-goers.

Insider Tip

TAKING A BREAK

Romeo's (Pr. Rimskogo-Korsakogo 43; daily 9am–midnight, Sat, Sun from 10am; www.romeosbarandkitchen.ru), right on Kyukov Canal, is a cake shop, bar and pizzeria rolled into one – and all very Italian at the same time!

➕ 205 D2 ✉ Nikolskaya pl. 1/3
☎ 812-714-7085; www.nikolskiysobor.ru
🕐 Lower church: daily 6:45am–9pm. Upper church (only open for services):
Sat from 6pm, Sun 9:30am–noon
🚇 Sennaya Ploshchad, Sadovaya, Spasskaya
🚌 Pr. Rimskogo-Korsakowa 39 (bus 3, 27 from Nevsky Pr.)
💰 Free

㉘ Vitebsky Station
(Vitebskiy Voksal)

This elegant station is a 'must-see' both for architecture fans and railway enthusiasts. The present building, erected in 1904 to replace an earlier stone structure, is a perfectly preserved – and carefully restored – Art Nouveau masterpiece down to the last detail, both inside and out. And that despite the fact that the architect Stanislav Brzhozovsk, who worked for the railways, was not regarded as a distinguished connoisseur of this style.

The building's asymmetrical façade with a clock tower on the left hand side and the large expanses of window are typical of the Art Nouveau style. The entrance is through the tower. The doors to the right that actually lead directly into the 20m (66ft)-high foyer area with its grand staircase, are locked. The waiting rooms and ticket halls, the chandeliers, tiled floors and playful banisters, as well as the thoroughly nostalgic platform hall with its wrought ironwork are not less noteworthy. The later is also on the upper level as trains would otherwise not be able to cross the bridge over Obvodny Canal just 600m (1,970ft) beyond the station. More than 100 years ago travellers' luggage reached the platform via lifts – today, you have to lug your bags up the stairs yourself. The station that looks like a stage set for 'Doctor Zhivago' is no longer a hive of activity. There are only some seven trains that arrive or depart from here destined for White Russia and the Ukraine.

Vitebsky is not only the most beautiful it is also the **oldest station in Russia**. However, nothing remains of the wooden building that existed when Russia's first stretch of railway was opened on 30 October 1837. At that time the line extended 24km (15mi) as far as Tsarskoye Selo

The Art Nouveau main hall at Vitebsky Station

Vitebsky Station – an Art Nouveau gem and Russia's oldest station

(► 162) where many members of the nobility had summer residences. The railway pioneer Franz Anton Ritter von Gerstner from Vienna, who built this stretch of railway, drove the train himself and took 35 minutes for the journey – only five minutes longer that the district line trains take today! One year later the line was extended as far as Pavlovsk (► 169) to the 'concert station' – so called because the station building was also used as a concert hall. A replica of the first locomotive, the **Provorny** ('The Swift') is displayed in a glazed 'sarcophagus' on the platform now used by local trains. This area, however, can only be accessed with a valid ticket available on the right-hand side of the building.

TAKING A BREAK

Various snack-bars can be found in the station. The cake shop **Sladkoyechka** (Sagorodny Pr. 45; daily 8:30am–10pm, Sat, Sun from 9:30am) diagonally opposite, is a little more up-market.

✚ 205 F2 ✉ BSagorodny Pr. 52
☎ 800-775-0000; www.vitebskiy-vokzal.ru
🔉 Open 24 hrs, every day 🚇 Pushkinskaya 🎫 Free

INSIDER INFO

■ The **wall paintings** on the first floor in the wonderfully nostalgic former first-class waiting room depict the **history of the station** and the first railway line.

■ About 200m (650ft) behind the station, to the right, is an **Art Nouveau pavilion** built in 1902. Now deserted and somewhat dilapidated it was originally reserved exclusively for the arrival and departure of Tsar Nicholas II's private train.

■ A new **railway museum** opened in 2017 adjoining the Baltic Station (www.railway-museum.ru; metro station Baltiyskaya) combines an old engine shed with a generously sized new-build. This has replaced the previous open-air museum alongside the tracks behind what was formerly known as Warsaw Station.

At Your Leisure

29 Admiralty Building (Admiralteystvo)

Three boulevards, including Nevsky Prospekt, intersect here. The Admiralty's 72m (236ft)-high golden needle marks the very hub of urban St Petersburg. At its top is a weather vane with a three-masted ship that has long since become a symbol of the city. The building, that has returned to being used as the headquarters of the Russian Fleet since 2012, is one of the city's giants with a length of 407m (1,335ft). The first Admiralty that was built of wood from 1704 onwards also reached such dimensions. Like a square bracket it wraps itself around the dockyard where Tsar Peter had his fleet built to be able to ward off the Swedes. The shipyard was protected by bastions and no other buildings were allowed to be built nearby to ensure an open field of fire. The open spaces were later used to create Palace Square, Senate Square and Alexander Garden. The spire dates from 1738. The

naval headquarters gained the representative, Classicist appearance it has today in 1823. The Admiralty can only be admired from the outside. On the inland side there are two impressive groups of figures on each side of the main entrance, each comprising three nymphs supporting the world on their shoulders.

On the side facing the Neva the Admiralty has two enormous wings. A canal once flowed through their gateways along which building material was transported to the shipyard. In the middle of the 19th century it was closed due to the emergence of steamers and steel ships. From 1880 onwards, extremely elegant houses were built here together with a pretty promenade along the bank.

A statue erected in 1910 (replica from 1996) opposite no. 6 is the only reminder now of the former maritime importance of this site. It shows the young Peter the Great making a boat himself out of wood. The depiction is actually totally

The spire on the Admiralty is one of St Petersburg's best-known landmarks

realistic as the tsar had both a thirst for knowledge and was skilled with his hands. During what is referred to as the 'Grand Embassy', the tsar completed an apprenticeship as a shipbuilder in Zaandam in Holland in 1697.

🚇 205 E4 ✉ Admiralteysky Prospekt 1
🚇 Admiralteyskaya

30 🚹 New Holland (Novaya Gollandiya)

The triangular-shaped island between the Moyka, Kyukov Canal and Admiralty Canal is a new attraction for the local residents of St Petersburg, too. The former naval site, listed as being of historical importance, is being transformed little by little into a cultural and leisure facility with an urban, organic touch.

Darya Zhukova's Moscow-based art museum **Garage** is involved behind the scenes, as the company that manages the site is part of the corporate empire established by her husband, the oligarch Roman Abramovich. New Holland Island was originally part of the shipyard near the Admiralty where wood needed in shipbuilding was dried in huge warehouses. The grand entrance arch, designed by Vallin de la Mothes in 1765, through which boats passed to reach the inner basin from the south, demonstrates the importance of the site to this day. Later, the navy established an engineering office and research laboratory here and, in 1830, a

naval prison was built on this island which, until now, had been out of bounds to civilians for almost 300 years.

In summer 2016 the first phase was completed and opened to the general public as a permanent attraction. Since this time the big pull on New Holland has been an imaginatively designed children's playground which includes a copy of the hull of a frigate which Peter the Great himself helped make in Holland. Although reduced in scale to 80 percent of its original size it still measures 6m (20ft) high and 26m (85ft) long. Parents can explore a herb garden or soak up the sun from a deckchair on the lawn, visit an exhibition pavilion or enjoy a cup of coffee in the snack-bar while letting their children play. A variety of different art and theatre events are also held here. In 2017, the old smithy and the circular naval prison became the first large buildings to open in their new functions that range from gastronomy, art, fashion, theatre, sport and youth work. It will, however, probably take until 2025 until all three of the large, 250-year-old warehouses have been restored and given a new lease of life.

🚇 205 D3 ✉ Nab. Admiralteyskogo kanala 2 (entrance opposite no. 31)
ℹ️ www.newhollandsp.ru
🕐 Daily 11am–10pm, Fri–Sun until 11pm
🚌 Pl. Truda (bus 3, 22, 27; trolley 5, 22)
🎟 Free

31 Central Naval Museum (Voenno-Morskoy Musey)

The Naval Museum, housed in a completely revamped former barracks on Kyukov Canal, opened in 2013. Previously it was in the Old Stock Exchange on the Strelka. The move has been very much for the better as it now has bright, spacious rooms with state-of-the-art technology. The elongated inner courtyard has been glazed over and looks rather like the hull of a

Admiralteysky District

ship. Between the many impressively large and detailed models of ships is the 'St Nicholas' – a boat that the young Tsar Peter I used to teach himself how to sail while living near Moscow from 1688 onwards. This sailing boat that was made in England was later nicknamed the 'grandfather of the Russian Fleet' and worshipped like a reliquary. A boathouse was originally built to preserve it right in front of Peter and Paul Cathedral (➤83).

The more than 300-year-old history of the Russian Fleet is brought to life again in dioramas, paintings, video documentations and through the many military artefacts. Peace-loving seafaring fans should be aware that this is primarily a military museum – displays of firearms and the history of naval battles are dominant elements in the museum.

🕂 205 D3 ✉ Pl. Truda 5 (entrance on the side facing Kyukov Canal)
☎ 812-303-8513; www.navalmuseum.ru
🕒 Wed–Sun 11am–6pm
🚇 Pl. Truda (bus 3, 22, 27; trolley 5, 22)
🍴 P500

🔢 Yusupov Palace (Yussupovskiy Dvorez)

From the outside, this Classicist town palace erected in 1770 is unspectacular. But after the Yusupovs – one of the most eminent and wealthy aristocratic families in Russia – bought the palace in 1830 and remodelled it several times, there was definitely nothing of the building's understatement left! There is hardly any other building, including the

imperial palaces, that has such a sumptuous yet stylish interior. Five generations of the princely Yusupov family amassed an extensive collection of art while living there. Since the palace was turned into a museum and a 'cultural palace for educationalists' soon after the Revolution, much of the breathtaking opulence has in fact been preserved in its original condition. One highlight of the palace interior is the private theatre built around 1860 in the Rococo style with seating for around 190 guests. Plays and ballet performances were held here frequently. On such occasions visi-

tors also had the opportunity of seeing the state rooms.

The palace is, however, best known as the scene of an historic crime, as it was here, in a basement room, that **Rasputin** was murdered in December 1916. The (in)famous faith healer fell victim to a plot devised by members of the nobility who feared the enormous influence he exerted on the tsarist family. The British intelligence service is reputed to have been involved in this, too. Whatever the case, the man of the house, Felix Yusupov, certainly

---

ART NOUVEAU POST OFFICE BUILDING

Just a few minutes walk from the Central Naval Museum in Pochtamtskaya Ulitsa is St Petersburg's **main post office**. The Art Nouveau main hall with a glazed roof, built in 1903, is wonderfully antiquated. But that also goes for the speed of the service here too! It's better not to try to hand in your postcards here (Pochtamtskaya Ulitsa 9; open 24 hours daily).

Most of the original furnishings in Yusupov Palace have been preserved

played a key role, having lured Rasputin into the trap. Rasputin was offered cakes poisoned with cyanide and was later shot several times in the stomach. His body was dumped in a side arm of the Neva. In the basement room in the palace wax figures have been used to create a re-enactment of the murder scene in its original setting. Admission to this is separate (entrance fee: ₽350) and is only open Fri–Mon 5pm–7:15pm.

🔲 205 D3 ☒ Nab. reki Moyki 94
☎ 812-314-9833; www.yusupov-palace.ru
🕐 Daily11–5pm 🚇 Ploshchad Truda
(trolley bus 5, 22; bus 3, 22, 27) 💲 ₽700

🟦 🏠 Oceanarium (Okeanarium)

Planeta Neptun is the name of this whole shopping and leisure centre opened in 2006 – and not without good reason as it also houses a professionally planned underwater world. Divided into 48 aquariums ranging in size from 300 litres to a huge 750m³ (26,500ft³), the most varied inhabitants of our lakes and seas – from the indigenous fish of

northwest Russia to tropical coral reefs – can be viewed.

The highlight is a 35m (115ft)-long glass tunnel through a large basin occupied by a couple of dozen sharks. At feeding time on Tue–Sun at 7pm divers show how well such predatory fish can be trained.

That this can be done with seals is familiar to all (show: Tue–Sun 11:30am and 4pm) – but take a look as what stingrays can do, too (daily 1pm).

The complex also has other 🏠 entertainments for children. For the very young there is a **dino park** with model beasts, an 'ultra' multimedia 7D cinema and the **Uschasy Peterburga** 'horror labyrinth' (min. age: 12 years) that passes through 13 rooms and in which the myths and bloody history of St Petersburg are brought to life.

🔲 206 B2 ☒ Ul. Marata 86 ☎ 812-448-0077;
www.planeta-neptun.ru/ocean
🕐 Daily 10am–8pm, June–Aug until 10pm
🚇 Svenigorodskaya 💲 ₽550–₽750

Insider Tip

Where to...
Eat and Drink

Prices
for a main course (without drinks):
£ under ₽450   ££ ₽450–₽900   £££ over ₽900

Dickens Pub ££

Insider Tip
This is St Petersburg's most beautiful pub as its seemingly authentic Victorian interior has gained a certain patina over the past 15 years. 40 different types of beer – including good and good-value Russian craft beer – a wide choice of whiskies and a menu that is a cut way above usual pub food with its burgers and fish and chips. The big plus point in summer is the beer garden outside the main entrance with high bushes separating visitors from the traffic along the river bank.

➕ 205 F2 ✉ Nab. reki Fontanki 108
☎ 812-380-7888; www.dickenspubs.ru
🕐 Daily noon–1am, Fri, Sat until 3am
Ⓜ Tekhnologichesky Institut

Est!Café £

Kolomna, the handworkers' district to the west of Kyukov Canal is not really known as a culinary eldorado. However, in this *kafe* with a Mediterranean flair you can enjoy a good meal. And it's lovely sitting at tables on the pavement as the riverside street has little traffic and is in the shade!

➕ 205 D2 ✉ Nab. Kryukova kanala 11
☎ 812-946-5388; www.estcafe.ru
🕐 Daily 11am–11pm 🚌 Pr. Rimskogo-Korsakowa 39 (bus 3, 27 from Nevsky Pr.)

Idiot ££

The name alludes to Dostoyevsky's novel and is arguably the place most frequented by the city's intellectuals. Indulge in Russian cuisine and chat quietly amid slightly shabby, 19th-century surroundings, to soft music and without flickering television screens. The food is equally lightly spiced and the number of vegetarian dishes extensive. Other plus points: the waitresses speak very good English and every guest gets a free vodka! However, a 10 percent service charge is automatically added to the already pretty substantial prices.

Insider Tip

➕ 205 E3 ✉ Nab. reki Moyki 82
☎ 812-315-1675; www.idiot-spb.com
🕐 Daily 11am–1am Ⓜ Admiralteyskaya

Russkaya Rumochnaya No.1 £££

The vodka museum (₽100 entrance fee for restaurant guests, otherwise ₽170; ➤ 110) owned by the same proprietors sets the tone. Furnished in the style of a traditional restaurant of the tsarist era, traditional Russian fare and values are to be found here. Nostalgic, yes, but without the rustic folklore. The plain dishes are not expensive but prices can shoot up astronomically if you go for black caviar and *polugar* – the virtually forgotten vodka made of rye.

➕ 205 E3 ✉ Konnogvardeyskiy Bulvar 4
☎ 812-570-6420; www.vodkaroom.ru
🕐 Daily noon–midnight 🚌 Pochtamtskaya Per. (trolley bus 5, 22) Ⓜ Admiralteyskaya

Sadko ££

The menu with mouth-watering pictures is just as inviting as the elegant, steel-grey interior that has, however, been 'enhanced' with Russian floral motifs. The food covers the very classical culinary spectrum from *pelmeni* and *beef stroganoff* to a variety of different fish dishes. Vegetarians, however, have to limit their choice to starters. The perfect place either before or after a visit to the Mariinsky as you only have to cross Theatre Square.

🚩 205 D3 ✉ Ul. Glinki 2
☎ 812-570-0831; www.sadko-rst.ru
🕐 Daily noon–1am 🚉 Teatralnaya pl.
(bus 3, 27), Mariinsky Teatr (bus 22)

Severyanin ££

This small, cosy restaurant furnished in the style of the turn of the 19th/20th century specialises in North Russian food. Fish, pork and poultry dominate but reindeer meat has also found its way onto the menu.

🚩 205 E3 ✉ Stolyarny per. 18
☎ 921-951-6396; www.severyanin.me
🕐 Daily noon–midnight
🚉 Sennaya pl./Sadovaya/Spasskaya

Tandoor ££

When this Indian restaurant first opened in 1994 it was considered somewhat exotic. Thanks to its tasty, authentic food and the relaxed and peaceful atmosphere it is still a popular place for fans of Asian and Indian cuisine more than twenty years later. And vegetarians appreciate the wide selection of dishes.

🚩 205 E4 ✉ Admiralteyskiy Pr. 10
☎ 812-312-3886; www.tandoor-spb.ru
🕐 Daily noon–11pm
🚉 Admiralteyskaya

Where to...
Shop

The Admiralteysky District does not have a main shopping street as such but it does have a shopping hotspot: Hay Square.

Sennaya Square (Sennaya Ploshchad), where three metro lines intersect, was known as 'the stomach of St Petersburg' back in Dostoyevsky's day. This is where the city's largest market and distribution centre is located.

The entrance to **Sennoi Rynok**, the large food market (daily 8am–8pm), is on Moskovskiy Prospekt between numbers 4 and 6. Go through the entrance into the courtyard and the market building is on the right. The fruit and vegetable stands are beautifully presented with much of the produce coming from the Caucasus and Central Asia. Melons, pomegranates, peaches, persimmons (kakis) and lychees may well look different from what westerners are used to. And Russian honey – which the charming vendors will want you to try – turns a pretty souvenir into a tasty one!

The large three-storey shopping mall **Sennaya** is immediately behind the market. The main entrance is at Ul. Yefimova 3. On the opposite side of the same road is **Pik** – another large shopping centre with specialist shops and boutiques (both daily 10am–10pm).

Gorokhovaya Ulitsa is tipped at becoming the next 'in' place to shop. Several **organic shops** – still something of a rarity in Russia – have started a new trend along this road. Although fresh vegetables are hardly to be found here, Russian manufacturers have been successful with non-perishable articles such as vegetarian sausages, vegan biscuits and fruit chips – with a wide variety of each.

Adi and **Organica** are located on Gorokhovaya (nos. 36 and 45, respectively) while **Dshagannat** and its beautifully presented wares can be found a few yards further on at nab. reki Fontanki 83.

Where to...
Go Out

Scattered around the west of the city centre are a number of bars and pubs. The only nightlife district in this part of the city is neither as turbulent as that behind Gostiny Dvor (➤ 148) nor as tightly packed as on Ulitsa Rubinsteyna (➤ 134) in the Central District. However, a dynamic and experimental gastro scene is emerging in the middle part of Gorokhovaya Ulitsa.

Right then: back to the bridge that crosses Griboyedov Canal with its perfect view of the Admiralty. In summer the windows of two trendy places right on the canal are wide open. To the right is the small and permanently packed café **I'm thankful for today** (no. 24; Mon–Thu 10am–1am, Fri, Sat 10am–2am, Sun 11am–1am); to the left **Mickey & Monkeys** (no. 27; Sun–Thu 10am–11pm, Fri, Sat until 1am) that is much bigger and, by the way, is run by the coffee expert of the same name. This restaurant-bar that achieved cult status among St Petersburg's 'in' crowd from the word go, boasts an extensive restaurant menu. However, you can equally well drop by in the evening just for a drink. Plain wooden ceilings and brick walls in the colonial style, loft-design furnishings and lighting, full-height arched windows extending over two floors, areas with a little louder or a little less music and fresh air on three sides in the summer.

That may be cool but perhaps you're looking for something a bit less swish? No problem. Just round the corner is **Stirka 40°** (Kasanskaya Ul. 26; http://40gradusov.ru, Sun–Thu 11am–midnight, Fri, Sat until 4am),

St Petersburg's only laundrette-cum-whacky DJ bar. Popular **Borodabar** (Kasanskaya Ul. 11; daily 5pm–3pm) on the same side road is, on the other hand, more of a cool place for hungry rock fans to hang out.

If you then walk down Gorokhovaya on the other side of Griboyedov Canal you will reach **Rocket & Bishop** (no. 26; www.bakuningroup.com; Mon–Fri 1pm–midnight, Sat, Sun until 2am) which serves craft beer and organic burgers.

One door down is **Cuba Space** (no. 28; daily noon–3am) with a Caribbean feel and corresponding rhythms and drinks.

The bar **Laboratoria 31** (no. 31; daily 3pm–8am) opposite is not for the faint of heart. Drinks are served in test tubes and conical flasks in keeping with the garish, chemistry-lab neon design.

Enough experiments for one day. Fancy a more up-market, down-to-earth 'place for lovers of the bar culture and homemade drinks'? Then the **Moonshine Bar** (nab. reki Moyki 56; tel: 931-964-8246; Sun–Thu 6pm–2am, Fri, Sat until 6am) is the perfect place for you. The only crux is that you have to ring up just beforehand to be let in by the pro barkeepers.

Of course each of the exclusive hotels around St Isaac's Square also has a bar. The **Wine Terrace** (open May–Sep), located on the 9th floor of the designer hotel **W** (➤ 43), however, rises above the rather boring and sedate mass of others in the true sense of the word. The clientele is young, chic and international; the music loud and the prices high. St Isaac's Cathedral (➤ 106) seems within an arm's reach and, looking to the side over the rim of your wine glass, your eye will fall on the Admiralty (➤ 118) and St Isaac's Square. On a balmy summer's evening this place will leave a lasting impression.

Central District

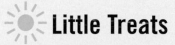 ## Little Treats

Sightseeing tour on a Harley

Cruise down the **Nevsky Prospekt** (➤ 130) to
that distinctive V-twin sound. Bikers often
gather in front of the Lutheran Church of
Saint Peter and Saint Paul and take paying
pillion passengers for a ride.

Far from the madding crowd

Hardly a soul strays onto the top floor of the
400m (1,312ft) long arcade in **Gostiny Dvor**
(➤ 148) – even though this is right in the
city centre!

Orient meets Wild West

All things exotic are to be expected in
Apraksin Dvor (➤ 148) – but not a rock 'n' roll
club, the **Money Honey** (Sadovaya Ul. 28/30,
korp.13; daily 9am–5:30am), in the style
of a Western saloon!

Getting Your Bearings

Cathedrals, palaces and large museums – no city centre can be made up of just these! This district also embraces the busy everyday activities of any modern city but without faceless glass temples and concrete bunkers. The heart of St Petersburg's city centre beats exclusively behind historical façades.

The Central District – as the administrative area of the city is called – actually covers much more than the city centre itself. The whole eastern half of the original city south of the Neva with its old buildings belongs to it as well, totalling 17km² (10.5mi²) in all. The backbone of this maxi-Old Town is the sheer endless Nevsky Prospekt that is not only a magnificent boulevard for strolls but, unfortunately, also a main artery with heavy traffic, day and night. However, thanks to the four intersections of the metro system virtually every part of this district can easily be reached while avoiding notorious traffic jams.

The Nevsky section between the stretches of the rivers Moyka and Fontanka is particularly rich in historical sights. This is where you will be able to explore the Russian Museum and Kazan Cathedral, the huge block taken up by the department store Gostiny Dvor and the Eliseyev brothers' delicatessen emporium – as well as the recently restored, exquisite nobleman's palace now occupied by the new Fabergé Museum.

On the one hand this area of St Petersburg is a lively city centre that has evolved over the centuries; on the other it is characterised by carefully planned architectural ensembles such as Arts Square, elegant Rossi Street and the area in front of Kazan Cathedral that, with its colonnades, emulates St Peter's in Rome.

Nevertheless, despite all the highly representative buildings, you only need to turn a couple of corners and move away from the main thoroughfares to discover areas which will provide several generations to come with enough restoration projects to keep them busy. These range from extensive mazes of interconnected courtyards to warehouse complexes such as that at Ligovsky Prospekt 50, or the huge bazaar site, Apraksin Dvor, with its narrow cobbled streets.

TOP 10

Don't Miss

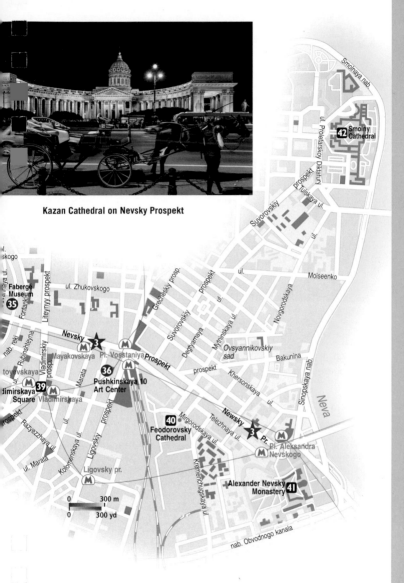

Kazan Cathedral on Nevsky Prospekt

At Your Leisure

The Perfect Day

This stroll around the centre criss-crosses the liveliest areas of the city centre, passing architectural highlights and famous museums while giving you time to shop, gain an insight into everyday life in St Petersburg and take a boat trip on the canal.

🕘 9:30am

There are lots of cafés on ⭐**Nevsky Prospekt** (➤ 130) near Mayakovskaya metro station where you can enjoy a hearty breakfast – the day is going to be a long one! Follow the Prospekt as far as **Anichkov Bridge** (➤ 133) over the Fontanka. Beyond the bridge on the right is a quay where boat tours start. Book a tour (ticket office opens at 10am) with an English-speaking guide or live electronic music in the evening! A few yards further on is the splendid ㉟**Fabergé-Museum** (➤ 138).

🕛 Noon

Pay a quick visit to the delicatessen **Eliseyev** (➤ 148) on the right-hand side of Nevsky. Then, passing the **memorial to Catherine the Great** (fig. above; ➤ 133) on the opposite side and rounding the vast **Alexandra Theatre**, turn into grand ㊳**Rossi Street** (➤ 142). Crossing the circular Lomonossov Square, Torgovy Pereulok leads right into a completely different world. Keeping slightly to the right you pass through the rabbit warren of little streets that make up the **Apraksin Dvor** open-air market (➤ 148). On reaching Sadovaya Ulitsa keep right as far as **Gostiny Dvor** (➤ 148). After exploring the traditional arcade on the first floor (fig. below) carry on down Ulitsa Lomonossova to Griboyedov Canal which is crossed by romantic ㊲**Bank Bridge** (➤ 142). Step inside **Kazan Cathedral** (➤ 131) and then have a look at the bookshop in the **Singer House** (➤ 148) on the other side of the Nevsky.

🕑 2pm

Following Griboyedov Canal head towards the Church of the Resurrection of Christ (➤ 61). On the corner of Italianskaya Ulitsa you will find somewhere to have lunch – either in the Georgian restaurant **ChaCha**, the cafeteria **Frikadelki** or the cool

Café Berlin. Having regained your strength you could then visit the **34 Russian Museum** (➤ 135) on Arts Square.

🕐 4:30pm

It may not be cheap, but on the short way back to Nevsky treat yourself to a coffee in the elegant period lobby bar in the **Grand Hotel Europe** (fig. below; ➤ 42).

🕐 5pm

Now head for **Gostiny Dvor** (➤ 148) for a bit of shopping before taking the metro – the entrance to Line 3 is in the department store. Travel two stops to Pl. Aleksandra Nevskogo.

🕐 6pm

The peace and quiet of **41 Alexander Nevsky Monastery** (➤ 143) is balsam for the soul after the noise of the city. Right at the end of Nevsky take a trolleybus 1, 22, bus 24, 27 or 191 and go as far as Pl. Vosstaniya – 'Uprising Square' – where you can visit the artists' commune **36 Pushkinskaya 10** (➤ 140).

🕐 8pm

From where you got out, take any line you like just one stop along the Nevsky to be able to start the **boat trip** you booked in the morning.

🕐 10pm

It's not too late for a snack supper, either in **Aragvi** (➤ 146) or in one of the many eateries along Ulitsa Rubinsteyna (➤ 134).

🕐 Midnight

If you happen to be in St Petersburg during the White Nights, take a stroll along the Fontanka. And if it happens to be dark, enjoy the brightly lit Nevsky Prospekt!

Central District

⭐Nevsky Prospekt

Nevsky Prospekt is the main artery in the centre of St Petersburg. Extending over a length of 4.5km (2.8mi), it runs straight through the middle with only one bend. The central section between the Moyka and Fontanka is particularly wide and this historical urban space is dominated by a well-balanced mixture of churches, cultural institutions and commerce.

Nevsky Prospekt is not only the most important and famous streets in St Petersburg but also the oldest. In 1711 it was decided to link all the major institutions on the southern bank of the Neva with one another. The construction of the road was started simultaneously at the **Admiralty** (► 118) at one end and **Alexander Nevsky Monastery** (► 143) at the other. However, the workers did not manage to keep to a straight line, resulting in the one bend in the 'Great Perspective Road', as Nevsky Prospekt was initially called.

The dead straight, three kilometre (1.8mi) main stretch is lined without interruption by historical buildings with the Admiralty's 'golden needle' always in view as a point of reference. The other end of the boulevard is marked by a 34m (112ft)-tall obelisk that was erected in 1985 on **Uprising Square** (Pl. Vosstaniya) to mark the 40th anniversary of the victory won in World War II.

Insider Tip Start your stroll down Nevsky on **Green Bridge** where the Prospekt crosses the first of the three ring-shaped

During the White Nights the stream of passers-by doesn't stop even in the early hours of the morning

A ROAD WITH A VIEW

Prospekt was the name given in Russia to long, straight roads. The name implies a distant view, a vista. St Petersburg's main street is therefore the 'Neva Prospect'. That is doubly true as, at both ends, the artery runs virtually right up to the bank of the Neva while the river itself between Alexander Nevsky Bridge and Palace Bridge creates a 9km (5.5mi)-long bow.

watercourses in the city centre – the **Moyka**. From here, the full magnificence of the Prospekt unfurls in front of you. The pale pink Baroque **Stroganov Palace** (Stroganovsky Dvorez, no. 17) was built in 1754 by Bartolomeo Rastrelli. Today, it houses a branch of the **Russian Museum** which includes an historic collection of minerals and an exhibition on exquisite hand-crafted items.

Churches of all Denominations

The building opposite (no. 20) is the former Dutch church that can only be distinguished as such by its dome. However, it is well worth having a look inside the Lutheran **Church of Saint Peter and Saint Paul** (Zerkov Sv. Petra) – between nos. 22 and 24 – built in the neo-Romanesque style. Once the church of a wealthy foreign congregation it now bears the traces of the vagaries of history. In 1962 an indoor swimming pool was installed in the nave with a diving platform on the site of the altar. 30 years later it was returned to the congregation but removing the concrete pool would have resulted in the building collapsing. A new floor was inserted instead which means that the pews are now one level higher than before.

The **Catholic** and **Armenian churches** (nos. 32–34 and 40–42, respectively) are also situated on the same side of the street – giving rise to Alexandre Dumas naming the Nevsky the 'street of religious tolerance'.

Of course a large Russian Orthodox church can't go missing. Before reaching the next bridge – this time over Griboyedov Canal – **Kazan Cathedral** (Kazansky Sobor; 1801–11) appears on the right, flanked by colonnades of 96 Corinthian columns. This way the architect Andrey Voronikhin concealed the fact that the cathedral only actually has a side entrance facing Nevsky. It is traditional for Orthodox churches to have the altar in the east and the main entrance in the west. From the outset the cathedral was conceived to house the St Petersburg copy of the miraculous icon of Our Lady of Kazan. It hangs on the right of the iconostasis and is the focal point of this church's intensive religious life. When Russia triumphed over Napoleon's armies in 1812 the recently completed church was turned into a Hall of Fame displaying a plethora of trophies.

ART CRYPT IN A SWIMMING POOL Insider Tip

One of the most unusual places in the city centre is the crypt in the **Church of Saint Peter and Saint Paul.** The pool area under the floor of the church as well as the catacombs painted by the artists Matt Lamb (USA) and Adam Schmidt (Russia) are sometimes opened for exhibitions and events.

Central District

Immediately to the right of the entrance is the key to the city, with those of Lübeck and Bremen hanging below. In front of the cathedral are two monuments to Field Marshals of the Russian Empire – to the left, Mikhail Kutuzov, to the right, Michael Barclay de Tolly, the 'Conqueror of Paris'.

The **Singer House** (Dom Singera, no. 28) immediately opposite is *the* most eye-catching building *par excellence* on the central stretch of the Nevsky. For almost 100 years the people of St Petersburg have known this building with its extravagantly high glass dome as the **House of Books** – as this once housed a large bookshop. Its elegant Art Nouveau interior alone merits a visit. But why does the female on the right in each of the three couples of valkyrie figures high up on the façade have a sewing machine under her arm? The building was originally the Russian headquarters of the US Singer Corporation, the leading manufacturer of sewing machines, and perfectly mirrored the company's innovative image. It was the first structure in St Petersburg to be built around a steel frame in 1904 – like a skyscraper. Conspicuous drainpipes, so typical of buildings in St Petersburg, cannot be seen here either as they have been integrated in the walls.

At the next crossroads take a look inside the legendary **Grand Hotel Europe** (➤ 42). The elegant lobby bar and the dining room in the decorative Art Nouveau style also exude the flair of 'the good old days'. On the opposite side of the street is the unmistakable pentagonal **tower of the *Duma***, the municipal assembly (no. 33), erected in 1804. The strange metal construction at the very top is an optical telegraph from the 1830s. In good weather, news could be transmitted to Warsaw, over a distance of 1,200km (745mi), within 15 minutes.

Yesteryear
Next to this is **Gostiny Dvor** (➤ 148) which boasts a sheer endless, two-storey arcaded walkway open to the public –

Nevsky Prospekt with the Singer House and its distinctive glass dome

Insider Tip

an unusual feature for a large department store. The building complex takes up the whole block and was designed by the architect Jean-Baptiste de la Mothe 250 years ago. At one point some 170 merchants did business in different sections of the building. After the Revolution this early version of a shopping mall fell into decline until the partitions inside were taken out in the 1950s to create the largest department store in the city.

The **Passage** (➤ 148), a shopping gallery on the opposite side of the Nevsky, is beautifully old-fashioned. Its long glass roof is reminiscent of the GUM department store in Moscow that was also built at the end of the 19th century.

A few doors down is the unmissable retail complex with its famous food hall established by the **Eliseyev brothers** (➤ 148). This gourmet temple opened in 1903 and extends over five floors with tall windows and elaborate Art Nouveau décor. The magnificent albeit somewhat kitschy interior incorporates massive floral light 'compositions'. Everything has now been carefully restored and attracts more customers than the range of items proffered in the delicatessen itself.

Immediately opposite is the park locally referred to as Katkin Sad (Little Kate's Garden) from where you have an unrestricted view of imposing **Alexandra Theatre** built in 1832. 'Little Kate' is none other than Catherine the Great to whom a 15m (49ft)-high **monument was erected** in 1873. At the feet of the empress, born Princess Sophie of Anhalt-Zerbst, are eight gentlemen (a select few of her reputed twenty-one favourites) as well as one lady, obviously a chaperone.

A further 250m (820ft) down the road is the **Anichkov Bridge** over the **Fontanka**. Between 1840 and 1850 Peter Klodt, a German-Baltic sculptor who specialised in figures of horses, created his famous composition for the bridge. The four bronze statues depict naked young men restraining horses – an allegory to the taming of natural forces by

The food hall at Eliseyev has been around since 1903

mankind. During the Siege of Leningrad these master-pieces were buried to protect them but the north-western-most pedestal was slightly damaged by shelling. These marks have been left for all to see.

On the far side of the Fontanka the chic Prospekt is entirely in the hands of commerce. Shops, cafés and hotels rub shoulders with each other all the way down to hectic **Uprising Square** outside **Moscow Station.**

TAKING A BREAK

Turn into Dumskaya Ulitsa at the Duma tower. No. 3, **Tolsty Frayer** (daily 10am–1am, Fri, Sat until 3am; www.tolstiy-fraer.ru), is an unspoilt pub; no. 5 is the Art Nouveau tearoom **Chainy Dom** (daily noon–3am, Fri, Sat until 5am; www.modern-cafe.ru).

Anichkov Bridge's fame comes from its 'horse tamers'

➕ 205 E/F4, 206 A4–C3, 207 D3/E2
Ⓐ Admiralteyskaya, Nevsky Prospekt, Gostiny Dvor

Stroganov Palace
✉ Nevsky Pr. 17 ☎ 812-595-4248; www.rusmuseum.ru
🕐 Wed, Fri–Mon 10am–6pm, Thu 1pm–9pm Ⓐ Admiralteyskaya 🎫 P300

Kazan Cathedral
✉ Nevsky Pr. 25/27 ℹ www.kazansky-sobor.ru
🕐 Service: daily 7am, 10am and 6pm Ⓐ Gostiny Dvor 🎫 Free

INSIDER INFO

Insider Tip ■ At night the grand boulevard exudes a different aura thanks to extensive flood-lighting. The façades gain a certain plasticity and the architectural details become more obvious.

■ There are many shops on the Nevsky – and, in summer, cafés and restaurants increase their capacity with chairs and tables on the pavement. However, due to

Insider Tip the noise and the crowds it's not exactly relaxing. If you want a breath of fresh air turn down one of the side streets. Malaya Sadovaya Ulitsa (pedestrianised area) and Ulitsa Rubinsteyna are good choices.

■ The Nevsky is very long-drawn-out – and demands a lot from your feet. So don't forget that all bus lines (except for Line 22) and all trolley buses (except Line 17) run between the Admiralty and Moscow Station – and always in a straight line!

㉞ Russian Museum
(Russkiy Musey)

After the Hermitage the Russian Museum is the uncontested 'number two' among the city's art museums. Its collections are exclusively of Russian art that has, at times, defined art anew internationally. In this respect the works of Chagall, Malevich and Kandinsky spring to mind.

The Russian Museum was founded in 1895 at the behest of Tsar Nicholas II – just at the right time, in fact, as Russian art was entering its most creative phase with a shift towards the avant-garde and its transition to abstraction. In addition to artworks from past eras, the museum's mission is to collect works that reflect current artistic trends within the country. This also embraces the Soviet era when many artists and artistic styles were officially shunned.

The Russian Museum's main building is the impressive **St Michael's Castle** that was built in 1819–25 for Emperor Paul I of Russia. The grand building is a focal point within a greater Classicist ensemble. The whole of **Arts Square** was planned as one entity by Carlo Rossi although several of the buildings were actually only erected to his original plans decades later.

Apart from the many plaster ceilings, virtually all the historical interiors, however, were destroyed when the building was converted into a museum. Only the impressive **White Hall** (Room 11) and the entrance hall with its grand staircase give a hint of the former exuberant magnificence of the Romanov residence. By taking this staircase to the first floor you can embark on a chronological journey through 1000 years of Russian art history.

The Collections

The first works on display are exclusively **icons** and **frescos** as, up until the time of Peter the Great, painting in Russia was limited to religious motifs. The oldest icon, arguably the most beautiful, dates from the 12th century and shows the benevolent face of the archangel Gabriel. Its creator and place of origin are unknown. **Secular portraiture**, exhibited from Room 5 onwards, emerged at the turn of the 18th century. Apart from painting, another technique was popular in Russia at that time too, as a closer look will reveal. What sometimes first appears to be a delicately drawn portrait turns out to be a **mosaic**.

In the 19th century, Russian painting freed itself thematically from its tight corset and expanded, literally, to reach gigantic proportions. This can be seen in Rooms 14 and 15 where the dramatic, monumental works of Fyodor Bruni (*The Brazen Serpent*, 1840 – at 48m² (517ft²) the

Central District

largest painting in the museum) and Karl Bryullov (*The Last Day of Pompeii*, 1833) are hung. **Ivan Aivazovsky** (*The Ninth Wave*, 1850), the principal painter of the Russian Navy, achieved international fame through his Romantic colour compositions of harbour scenes, naval battles and of the sea in general.

In the second half of the 19th century, a group of socio-critical artists called *Peredvizhniki* ('The Wanderers') set the tone in Russian painting. **Ilya Repin** became one of its most famous representatives with his painting *Barge Haulers on the Volga* (1873) – a dramatic indictment of the exploitation and lack of rights of humble men. Repin, however, was also capable of pleasing the tastes of the ruling class, as you will see when you go downstairs again to the ground floor. His monumental *Ceremonial Sitting of the State Council in 1901* which measures 4m × 9m (13ft × 30ft), occupies a room of its own.

Pushkin memorial in front of the Russian Museum

The 20th Century

By going up and down stairs the upper storey of what is known as the **Benois Wing** is reached with its collection of 20th-century art. As otherwise in the history of Russia, things can be a little bewildering here too. Works by Vrubel, Serov, Bakst, Chagall and Petrov-Vodkin provide a link to the Russian avant-garde, Futurism and the beginnings of abstract art. The especially creative phase several years before and after the October Revolution is very well documented. The museum owns more than 20 paintings by **Wassily Kandinksy** and more than 100 by the great Minimalist **Kazimir Malevich**. Virtually the complete oeuvre of the once ostracised and later forgotten artist

The White Hall still largely looks the same as when it was first completed

Pavel Filonov can be found here, even if – unfortunately – only a very small part of this collection is on display. The propagandistic works of **Socialist Realism** and a few by contemporary Russian artists conclude this section.

TAKING A BREAK

Unlike the Hermitage, the Russian Museum has an attractive **museum café** in the atrium of the Benois Wing that is otherwise also freely accessible. Museum visitors can re-enter the exhibition area afterwards by presenting their entrance ticket.

➕ 206 A4 ✉ Inzhenernaya Ul. 4,
☎ 812-595-4248; www.rusmuseum.ru
🕐 Wed, Fri–Sun 10am–6pm, Mon 10am–8pm, Thu 1pm–9pm
🚇 Nevsky Pr. 🚌 P450

INSIDER INFO

■ Those only interested in the **masterpieces of the 20th century** are advised to use the side entrance on Griboyedov Canal. You are then already one level higher. The ground floor of the Benois Wing is reserved for **temporary exhibitions**.

■ The right-hand wing of St Michael's Castle – with a bombastic marble atrium – houses the **Museum of Ethnography**. Art and the traditions of all ethnographic groups which once lived within the borders of the Russian Empire are displayed here (www.ethnomuseum.ru, Tue 10am–9pm, Wed–Sun 10am–6pm, entrance fee: ₽250).

Insider Tip

㉟ Fabergé Museum
(Musey Faberzhe)

Just 150m (490ft) from Nevsky Prospekt is a gem of a museum, in the true sense of the word. The largest collection of works by the Russian court jeweller Peter Carl Fabergé is owned by a private foundation and is on display to the public. Among works exhibited here are some fifteen of the world-famous Fabergé eggs.

Fabergé eggs are the most expensive 'surprise eggs' in the world and the quintessence of the goldsmith's art. There were only seventy-one eggs in total. Fifty-four of these unique gems were made by the court jeweller **Peter Carl Fabergé** (1846–1920), who was of German descent, as commissions for the last two Russian tsars between 1885 and 1917. The remainder were for private customers. Every year on Good Friday Fabergé handed one or two of these filigree eggs from his workshop to the tsar who then gave them to his wife and mother for Easter. Ten eggs are now in the Kremlin in Moscow; the others were scattered around the world after the tsar was overthrown. Seven eggs have been lost.

The largest collection of Fabergé eggs, totalling fifteen in all (including eleven of the 'Imperial Eggs') can be marvelled at the Fabergé Museum that was first opened in 2014. It owes its existence to two multi-billionaires. In 2004 the heirs of the US publishing mogul Malcolm Forbes wanted to auction the Fabergé collection – including the 'Imperial Eggs' – that had been amassed over a period of several decades. The Russian oligarch Viktor Vekselberg succeeded in pulling off a coup by acquiring the complete collection at auction that is reputed to have set him back some 100 million dollars. In Russia this was celebrated as a patriotic move as Vekselberg promised to bring these items of jewellery back to Russia and make them accessible to the general public. In this way, a tiny piece of the enormous cultural damage caused

The grand staircase in Shuvalov Palace leads up to the Blue Room...

through the plundering and sale of cultural artefacts by Soviet authorities, hungry for foreign currency, could be put right. And Vekselberg seized the opportunity a second time when the city of

...and to the filigree Easter presents given by Tsar Alexander III and Tsar Nicholas II

St Petersburg offered him **Shuvalov Palace** on the bank of the Fontanka, the richly decorated, neo-Renaissance nobleman's palace from the mid 19th century. It cost his cultural foundation 27 million euros to have the palace renovated over a period of seven years. It now gleams like a polished diamond. The foundation also acquired a number of other works by Fabergé and other Russian jewellers, including a large collection of works in enamel by Fyodor Rückert.

The exhibition now comprises some 4,000 items including valuable icons and works in gold. They are displayed in twelve extremely impressive rooms on the first floor in the palace. Each of the 'Imperial Eggs' is presented in a glass showcase of its own in the **Blue Room** (Room 4).

TAKING A BREAK

Pelmeni that resemble ravioli to a certain extent are as popular among Russians as pizza is for Italians. And this can be turned into cult food simply by not offering anything else on the menu – as in the modern restaurant **Pelmenia** (nab. Reki Fontanki 25; tel: 812-415-4185; daily 11am–11pm). These are complemented by *pelmeni*-like creations from other countries: *manty* from Central Asia, *chinkali* from Georgia and *vareniki* from the Ukraine...

🚹 206 B3 ✉ Nab. Reki Fontanki 21
☎ 812-333-2655; www.fabergemuseum.ru
🕐 Sat–Thu 10am–8:30pm 🚇 Gostiny Dvor 🅿 P450

INSIDER INFO

A **guided tour** of the Fabergé Museum **in English** is usually offered once a day. It is recommended booking tickets in advance (P600 incl. entrance fee) using the museum's website, as the numbers of participants is limited.

Insider
Tip

㊱ Pushkinskaya 10 Art Center
(Art-Tsentre Pushkinskaya-10)

Ligovsky Prospekt is rather unattractive despite its central location. But it makes up for that by being a hotspot for the alternative crowd, especially in the self-managed 'Pushkinskaya 10 Art Center' where the non-conformist underground culture of the Soviet era still lives on in the studios, galleries and museums.

The name 'Pushkinskaya 10' may sound like an address but the art centre can only actually be accessed via Ligovsky Prospekt that runs parallel to Pushkinskaya Ulitsa. The shabby-looking entrance is at no. 53 – it stands out due to the mass of posters and advertisements randomly stuck on it. The alternative microcosmos begins in the second courtyard where there are two pubs, both confusingly called **Fish Fabrique**, and unfolds properly in the third courtyard where there is a big sign pointing to the individual galleries and museums.

This 'art biotope' came about as the result of a squatting campaign. In 1989 artists and musicians occupied the empty block of flats at Pushkinskaya Ulitsa no. 10. The liberal-minded, sub-culture commune became a trademark for a new post-Soviet era which is why the authorities were keen to find a compromise. While the flats in the front building were expensively renovated and sold, two side buildings lining the courtyard and two auxiliary buildings were turned into a foundation for some 40 artists – but the entrance to the complex was to be from the rear.

Insider Tip The studios and galleries can be accessed via two staircases which are worth seeing in their own right as they are filled with

The staircases in the art centre are also full of works of art

WHAT FLOOR?
Russian houses (and lifts) do not have 'ground floors' – instead they start counting floors at ground level which is therefore called the 1st floor (i.e. 'level 1').

A typically improvised stage for a concert in one of the inner courtyards in the art centre

installations, paintings and sculptures. The **Museum of Non-Conformist Art** with temporary exhibitions is reached up the stairs in Wing C (right). The entrance fee includes the interesting gallery opposite called **bridge over the styx** with *functio-collages* by Vadim Voynov (1940–2015), who transformed *objets trouvés* into testimonies to times past. Halfway up the next stairs is the mini-gallery **Dwer** that, as the name suggest, consists of just a door. There is no room behind it – just a wall with exhibits.

The **Samizdat Museum**, with underground publications from the Soviet era, acts as a link on the second floor to the staircas in Wing B where interesting exhibitions are staged by the galleries **2.04** (2nd floor), **Navicula Artis** (4th floor) and **Art Liga** (7th floor).

Art can be heard in the experimental **Museum of Sound** (Musey Svuka) under the roof in Wing D in the adjacent graffiti-filled courtyard. Unusual, specially-made instruments and early synthesizers are on display as well as an inter-active acoustic city map and graphic scores.

TAKING A BREAK

Tucked away under the roof in Wing D is the tiny but colourful **Art Buffet** (daily 3pm–11:15pm) – the perfect place to take in all the new impressions you have gained over a cup of coffee.

🚻 206 C3 ✉ Ligovsky Pr. 53 ☎ 812-764-5371; www.p-10.ru
🕐 Wed–Sun 4pm–8pm 🚇 Ploshchad Vosstaniya
💰 Free; individual museums each c. P100

Fish Fabrique
ℹ www.fishfabrique.ru 🕐 Both Mon–Fri from 6pm, Sat, Sun from 3pm, Thu–Sat live electronic music from 9pm

Central District

city, was reserved for the privileged classes and is now a magical labyrinth of more than 1,000 partly crumbling tombs. In Russia a grave remains untouched for eternity. The universal genius Michail Lomonossov, Pushkin's widow Natalia Lanskaya and the architect Carlo Rossi found their final resting places here.

To the right is **Tikhvin Cemetery** – the 'necropolis of masters of the arts'. Things are much tidier here as the cemetery was remodelled in the 1930s in line with Soviet ideology. Many tombs not considered worth preserving were destroyed. In their place other tombs deemed noteworthy were brought here from cemeteries that had been abandoned – although the mortal remains were not necessarily brought with them. The writer Fyodor Dostoyevsky's tomb is near that of the composers Rubinstein, Tchaikovsky, Rimski-Korsakov and Glinka.

The heart of the monastery, founded by Peter the Great in 1710 to honour the patron saint of the city, is **Trinity Cathedral** (1776–90), built by Ivan Starov in the Russian Neoclassical style. At the front on the right-hand side of the nave is the shrine with the relics of Alexander Nevsky – which is continuously visited by pilgrims and the devout. Between the cathedral and Metropolitan House, the archbishop's residence, another cemetery can be found within the monastery complex that seems rather out of place in its Orthodox surroundings. During the Soviet era 'worthy comrades' were buried here, some in quite avant-garde tombs.

On your way out of the monastery, have a look inside the **Church of the Annunciation** that looks more like a palace, located next to the gateway. It was consecrated in 1724 and, today, is the oldest church in the city.

🚇 207 E2 ✉ Pl. Aleksandra Nevskogo 1
🔗 www.lavra.spb.ru 🕙 Daily 6am–11pm.
Cathedral: 6am–7pm. Museum cemeteries:
10am–6pm 🚇 Pl. Aleksandra Nevskogo
✋ Donations welcome.
Museum cemeteries: P250

42 Smolny Cathedral (Smol'niy Sobor)

In the mid 18th century the 'star architect' **Bartolomeo Rastrelli** designed an extremely elegant convent for Empress Elizabeth of Russia. She was both building-mad and pious and intended the convent to be her home in old age. A two-storied Baroque range of cells surrounds a magnificent cathedral. Both of the buildings in Rastrelli's typical blue and white are in the shape of a Greek cross. However, the lack of funds during the Seven Years' War put a stop to the project. When the empress died in 1762 only the basic shell of the cathedral – a lively structure with five onion domes – had been finished. It was not completed and consecrated until 1835. The cathedral's valuable furnishings were plundered after the October Revolution and the building later used as an exhibition space and concert hall. It was restituted to the Orthodox Church in 2016 and

The monastery on Monastyrka Canal was named after the Russian national hero Alexander Nevsky

returned to its intended use. The plain walls are painted white; the floor covering and iconostasis are interim solutions.

Whether the viewing platform in one of the bell-towers of the 94m (308ft)-high cathedral will be accessible again after all the exterior façades have been restored is not known. The site of the convent that was abandoned in 1764 is, however, open to the public. It now houses a number of university institutes and local authority offices.

Just a little bit to the west of the cathedral is an old water tower and the **Water Museum** that shows the history of the water supply and waste water management over the course of time. It also includes a collection of related furnishings and fittings.

The **Tauride Palace** (1783–89) opposite was a present from Catherine II to her favourite, Prince Potemkin, who conquered the South Ukraine and the Crimea and annexed them to Russia. The honorary title 'of Tauride' (the Crimea) that he was given was transferred to his residence on the outskirts of the city. From 1906 until 1917, it became the seat of Russia's first parliament, the Imperial State Duma. The palace now houses the (politically irrelevant) Interparliamentary Assembly of Member Nations of the Commonwealth of Independent States and is, therefore, not open to the public.

The well-tended **Tauride Gardens** that lie beyond, however, are freely accessible. They form the largest public park in the city centre.

➕ 207 E/F5 ✉ Ploshchad Rastrelli 1
🕐 Service: daily 7am, 10am and 6pm
🚌 Trolley 5, 7, 11; bus 22 from Nevsky Pr.
💰 Free

Water Museum
➕ 207 D5 ✉ Shpalernaya Ul. 56
🏠 www.vodokanal-museum.ru
🕐 Wed–Sun 10am–7pm 💰 P150

THE 'SMOLNY'

The **Smolny Institut** that adjoins the convent was established in 1806 as a school for the daughters of the wealthy. In 1917, the year of the Revolution, the workers' and military councils set up their headquarters here. Until Moscow was made the capital city again in 1918 this representative building was the nerve centre of the young Soviet state. This accounts for the statue of Lenin outside the entrance and the busts of Marx and Engels in the park in the front. Today, the 'Smolny' is the official residence of the governor – the Lord Mayor – of St Petersburg.

Where to...
Eat and Drink

Prices
for a main course (without drinks):
£ under ₽450   ££ ₽450–₽900   £££ over ₽900

RESTAURANTS

Aragvi ££

Insider Tip

Georgian food – just the mention of the word 'Georgian' is enough to make any Russian's mouth water! Original recipes from the neighbours to the south – grilled fare using a wide variety of spices and accompanied by full-bodied wines – are celebrated is this tiny, rustically elegant restaurant.
🏠 206 B4 ✉ Nab. reki Fontanki 9
☎ 812-570-5643
🕐 Mon–Fri 11am–11pm, Sat, Sun from noon
🚇 Nevsky Prospekt/Gostiny Dvor

Biblioteka ££

Centrally located and chic. This eatery occupies three floors of a former bookshop on a corner of the Nevsky. There is a cake shop on the ground floor and a snack bar for those in a hurry; one floor up is a restaurant with an open kitchen for the hungry and, at the very top, there is a bar open in the evenings for the thirsty.
🏠 203 D1 ✉ Nevsky Pr. 20
☎ 812-244-1594; www.ilovenevsky.ru
🕐 Daily 8am–2am
🚇 Nevsky Prospekt/Gostiny Dvor

Bufet ££

Going by the sign it looks like a café; optically it looks like an antique shop. This mini restaurant has just five tables and you'll feel like a private guest in a St Petersburg intellectual's best parlour. The landlady Tatjana conjures up the very best food while mothering her guests attentively.

An oasis of individuality among the universally styled big restaurants on and around the Nevsky.
🏠 206 C3 ✉ Ul. Pushkinskaya 7
☎ 812-764-7888 🕐 Daily 11am–11pm
🚇 Mayakovskaya/Pl. Vosstaniya

Kaschmir £

Vegetarians still have a tough time in Russia's gastro scene. That makes this small Indian restaurant with its fiery and spicy meat-free dishes all the more appealing. Quiet and calming atmosphere and a wide variety of select teas.
🏠 206 B2 ✉ Bolshaya Moskovskaya Ul. 7
☎ 812-575-6369; www.cafe-kashmir.ru
🕐 Daily 11am until approx. midnight
🚇 Vladimirskaya

Kvartirka £

Nostalgic Soviet eateries are the in thing – but without red stars and CCCP logos. What the locals prefer are reconstructions of kitchen-cum-living rooms and that dacha feeling from the 1960s and 1970s. And Granny's delicious recipes are called for here too – with lots of bottled and pickled things and traditional puddings. Other branches can be found at Nevsky Pr. 20 (called 'Dachniki'), Nevsky Pr. 51 and on Vasilyevsky Island (Line 6, no. 25).
🏠 206 B3 ✉ Malaya Sadovaya Ul. 1
☎ 812-900-6550; www.reca.su
🕐 Daily noon–1am, Fri, Sat until 3am
🚇 Nevsky Prospekt/Gostiny Dvor

O! Cuba ££

This cellar restaurant and bar in the nightlife area along Ul. Rubinsteyna doesn't get its Cuban atmosphere just from the retro decoration with pictures of Fidel and Che. The entrance area resembles a beach bar in Varadero. The Buick convertible from 1956 is a real eye-opener. The largely barbecued food is a mixture of Cuban and Creole. To round off the day try one of the many cocktails – or how about testing the rums?

➕ 206 B3 ✉ Ul. Rubinsteyna 36
☎ 812-312-8892; www.o-cuba.ru
🕐 Daily 11am–11pm, Wed–Sat until 1am
Ⓜ Vladimirskaya/Dostoyevskaya

Shinok ££
Ukrainian food is very popular among Russians irrespective of any political tension. The cellar restaurant goes the whole hog with waiters in *sharovary* – wide trousers – and a folkloric duo performing every evening. Try the cabbage soup *kapustniak*, served in a bread bowl!

➕ 206 B3 ✉ Sagorodny Prospekt 13
☎ 812-571-8262; www.spbshinok.ru 🕐 Daily 11am–1am Ⓜ Vladimirskaya/Dostoyevskaya

Insider Tip

Terrassa £££
When the menu is as extensive and has the overall appearance of a lifestyle magazine then the restaurant itself has to match up to it! This is a place where people come to see and be seen – and because of the wonderful terrace. It is at the same height as the dome of Kazan Cathedral diagonally opposite. Inside, glass panels running the length of the restaurant (which has a Russian/Italian/Asian repertoire) separate guests from the kitchen. Another plus pont: 👪 there is a lovely play area for children.

➕ 205 E3 ✉ Kasanskaya Ul. 3 ☎ 812-640-1616; www.ginza.ru/spb 🕐 Mon–Fri from 11am, Sat, Sun from noon until the last guest leaves Ⓜ Gostiny Dvor

CAFÉS

Coffeeshop Company £
Three leading coffeeshop chains compete for dominance in the ob-viously notoriously caffeine-starved market in St Petersburg. In the case of 'Coffee House' and 'Idealnaja Tschaschka' a lack of coffee-know-how and service culture is evident. But in the case of the 'Coffeeshop Company' chain you can tell something is different: the founder comes from Vienna. The most exquisite of all the branches is reached up a grand flight of stairs and is housed in palatial rooms. In summer, there is a terrace overlooking the Nevsky, one floor up from the road itself. Pretty noisy but different.

➕ 206 B3 ✉ Nevsky Pr. 47
☎ 981-381-0809; www.coffeeshopcompany.ru
🕐 Daily 10am–11pm, Fri, Sat until midnight
Ⓜ Mayakovskaya

Du Nord £
A bar with baguettes and a display of delicious cakes is an open invitation to visit this bistro-café opposite Moscow Station. However, they don't give away this place's real secret – top-quality French food is served here in a down-to-earth style. Just perfect before catching the night-train to Moscow!

➕ 206 C3 ✉ Ligovsky Pr. 41 ☎ 812-578-1245; www.dunord.spb.ru 🕐 Daily around the clock Ⓜ Ploshchad Vosstaniya

Pyshki £
In this, the most down-to-earth café in the whole city, resolute ladies have been producing deep-fried *pyshki* – shamelessly delicious doughnuts – with their secret machine for a good 60 years. With a liberal sprinkling of sugar on top they are handed over the counter, generally half a dozen at a time! The queue of ad-dicted fans often stretches down the road. Locals like to wash things down with weak coffee sweetened with sticky condensed milk. The interior dates from the time when Gorbachev was still a young re-former. In short: this place is cultic!

➕ 205 F4 ✉ Bolshaya Konyushennaya Ul. 25
☎ 812-314-0868 🕐 Daily 9am–8pm
Ⓜ Gostiny Dvor/Nevsky Prospekt

Where to...
Shop

The central section of Nevsky Prospekt combines shopping with sightseeing – and several shops are themselves impressive sights.

Good shopping is also to be had in the side streets. There is a lot to be discovered if you turn off the main stretch between the Fontanka and Moscow Station.

CENTRAL NEVSKY PROSPEKT

Even if it does seem a little old fashioned the **Gostiny Dvor** department store block (Nevsky Pr. 35; www.bgd.ru, metro: Gostiny Dvor/ Nevsky Prospekt) is the epicentre of St Petersburg's shopping scene. What you can't find here you'll find just round the corner! Quality souvenirs that are not too kitschy are on the ground floor right in middle of the building facing the Nevsky. This is where **Caviar**, Russia's first specialist shop for black caviar, has set up shop too.

Insider Tip

On the west side of Gostiny Dvor is **Perinniye Rjadi** (Dumskaya Ul. 4) which stretches over three floors and comprises lots of little shops selling antiques, accessories and artworks.

Behind Gostiny Dvor and slightly to one side is the **Apraksin Dvor** market area (Sadovaya Ul. 28–30) – a place for the more adventurous – where forty old warehouses, some dilapidated, others renovated, form a city within the city. Everything that is not edible, primarily textiles and shoes, is traded in the buzzing, cobbled lanes of the *Apraksha*.

Insider Tip

As colourful and oriental this huge bazaar may be, it is better not to take any photographs. This way you will avoid any problems – just do as the locals do!

When on the north side of the Nevsky it is well worth making a short detour to see the **DLT** department store (Bolshaya Konyushennaya Ul. 9pm–11pm) where luxury labels present their wares in extremely elegant Art Nouveau surroundings.

Dom Knigi in the **Singer House** (Nevsky Pr. 28; www.spbdk.ru), where you can browse through the bookshelves until midnight, is equally stylish.

Another large bookshop is **Bukvoyed** (Nevsky Pr. 46). This shop, open round the clock, lies between two shopping centres: the **Grand Palace** (Nevsky Pr. 44) is ultra-modern and extremely pricey whereas the nostalgic **Passage** (Nevsky Pr. 48) is a good place to shop for jewellery and perfume.

One place to be visited at all costs is the food hall at **Eliseyev** (Magasin Kupzov Yeliseyevich, Nevsky Pr 56; www.kupetzeliseevs.ru).

If you can't find a suitable souvenir here among all the chocolates and drinks on sale, then head for the **Generator Nastroenia**, the 'Good Mood Generator' (Karavannaya Ul.9) where it would seem that no idea is too absurd not to be turned into something by designers and tinkerers as a gag.

Insider Tip

UPPER NEVSKY PROSPEKT

It is well worth turning off into the side streets between Fontanka and Moscow Station – to take a look inside **Art Lebedev** (Ul. Zhukovskogo 2; www.artlebedev.ru), for example. Tucked into the back room of a café the shop run by Russia's most successful designer is full of clever little things for nerds, hipsters and those who like to have a bit of fun.

Artistically elegant dresses as well as objects for the home by St Petersburg's top fashion designer, **Tatiana Parfionova,** can be found in her studio/boutique (Nevsky Pr. 51; www.parfionova.ru).

The best branch of the imperial china manufactory **Imperatorski Farfor** (www.ipm.ru) of St Petersburg is to be found at Vladimirsky Prospekt no. 7. The former purveyor to the tsarist court still produces tableware of the highest quality.

The product range at **Russki Lyon** (Pushkinskaya Ul. 3; www.linorusso.ru, metro: Mayakovskaya) is only traditional with regards to the material. This fashion store with a lot of Russian products is specialised in all things made of linen – for him, her and the bed.

A few doors further down the road is **Prialka** (Pushkinskaya Ul. 10; www.prialka.ru) that sells beautifully warm items that are as light as a feather made of *kosye puch* – otherwise known in the rest of the world as cashmere.

A shopping experience of quite a different kind awaits visitors to **Gallery** (Ligovsky Pr. 30; www.galeria.spb.ru) next to Moscow Station. This shopping mall, tarted up with lots of gold, comprises some 300 shops and 30 gastro areas, distributed across four levels. And, at the very top, is the 👪 children's fun area, **Happylon**.

Another shopping centre, the **Nevsky Zentr**, with 80 shops (Nevsky Pr. 116; www.nevskycentre.ru) is much more tasteful. Under the umbrella of the Finnish **Stockmann** company, it is the only true western European-style department store in the city.

Where to...
Go Out

CLASSIC

Arts Square (➤ 135) is next to Theatre Square (➤ 111), the city's second hotspot for classical music.

The **Shostakovich Philharmonia** (Ul. Mikhailovskaya 2; tel: 812-240 0100; www.philharmonia.spb.ru) is a concert hall of world renown in the magnificent festival hall of the former Nobles' Assembly and seats 1,450. The Music Director and Chief Conductor of the St Petersburg Philharmonic, Yuri Temirkanov, is responsible for a concert programme of the highest quality with performances by Russian and international musicians. There are, however, no performances from the beginning of July until the end of September.

Also concealed behind Rossi's uniform Neoclassical façade on the square, together with the **Mikhailovsky Theatre** (Pl. Isskusstw 1; tel: 812-595-4305; www.mikhailovsky.ru), is the Mariinsky Theatre (➤ 111), the second, large and famous home to opera and ballet in the city.

And just two doors down from the Philharmonia is the **St Petersburg Theatre of Music Comedy** (Italianskaya Ul. 13; tel: 812-570-5316; www.muzcomedy.ru) for less high-brow performances, including operettas and musicals.

JAZZ

There has been a State Jazz Philharmonic Hall in St Petersburg as well since 1989. The concerts are a wonderful trip down memory lane, especially when the founder David Goloshokin takes to the stage. The main jazz hall seats 180 around small tables, as food and drinks are served during concerts. Upstairs is the **Ellington Hall – the Jazz Philharmonia's piano bar** (Sagorodny Pr. 27; tel: 812-764-8565; www.jazz-hall.ru).

Central District

St Petersburg's best-known, do-what-you-like nightlife area can be found at the junction of **Dumskaya Ulitsa/Ulitsa Lomonossova**. Under the arcades of **Small Gostiny Dvor** – a listed building from 1790 that was last renovated 130 years ago – a good dozen bars, pubs and clubs have set themselves up. And there is nothing trendy or chichi about any of them. The motto here is the trashier, louder and darker the better. This fits with the old wooden doors in this run-down arcade and the uneven paving slabs that are witnesses to so many years of use where lots of guests sit or stand around having a drink. The idea for this conglomerate of bars that are open every day from 6pm until 6am, came from a young publican from Hamburg, Anne-Christin Albers, in 2006. Her legendary DJ bar Dacha was relaunched in 2016 under the name **Dachnlki** with the aim of turning it into an LGBT meeting place.

What Dacha was originally like can still be experienced in its neighbours and emulators **Belgrad, Duma Bar** and **Fidel**. Around the corner on the Lomonossovaya side is the small rock 'n' roll karaoke bar **Poison,** another 100 percent Russian, pop-free bar founded by Albers.

The disco bar **SSSR**, on the other hand, is pure Soviet punk.

The retro bar **Zhert poberi!** (Go to the Devil) is a rocker meeting place (to which some come on their custom-built bikes). There is generally no food served in these fringe bars.

But, in among them all, is **U Dshamala**, a ridiculously cheap oriental shawarma take-away (as kebabs are called in St Petersburg) with good portions – and tables outside in the Small Gostiny Dvor's otherwise inaccessible courtyard.

On the opposite side of the street (nab. kan. Griboedov 28/ Ul. Lomonossova 1), some ten bars, discos and clubs have established themselves in a row of old shops, including **Central Station**, the best-known gay bar in the city and **Rhino Bar**, one of the few red-light strip bars in St Petersburg.

Anyone wanting to extend their pub crawl should head for the other end of Ul. Lomonossova. After surviving the 1km (0.6mi) distance without a pint, the up-market gastro bar **Buddy** (no. 14) and the real dive **Na Broviach** (no 22) herald the start of the night-life district along **Ul. Rubinshteyna,** just to the left around the corner.

For the past few years night has been turned into day along this 750m (2,500ft) stretch as far as Nevsky Prospekt. There are some 50 places – most of them bars and cafés – and virtually all proprietors put tables and bar stools out on the pavement in the summer.

The Israeli venue **Bekizer** (no. 40) is popular especially among the hip crowd. The chic beleaguer **Vino Studia** (no. 38), the gastro bar next door.

Berlin-inspired **Café Mitte** (no. 27) (where you can even get a 'curry sausage') rubs shoulders with the cocktail bars **Zvetochki** (no. 11) and **Tesla Bar** (no. 30).

The craft beer oasis **Punk Brew** (no. 9) and **Café Rubinstein** (no. 20) immediately opposite, a favourite meeting place for well-known artists and actors – and all those who think they are or want get to know them – are the most packed of all.

What, you still haven't had enough? St Petersburg's third gastro district is along the short **Ulitsa Belinskogo** between the Fontanka and Liteyny Prospekt. Highlights here include the jazz bar **The Hat** (no. 9) and the long bar in the legendary **Terminal Bar** (no. 11).

Imperial Palaces Outside the City

 **Little Treats**

Skimming the Baltic

Taking a hydrofoil to **Peterhof Palace** (➤ 156) is rather like being on a plane – except that you can also stand outside at the back and let your hair blow in the wind at 60km/h (40mph)!

A shower with a difference

Several fountains in the **park at Peterhof Palace** (➤ 158) look unassuming but can easily catch you out: you walk up to them unsuspectingly and then suddenly get wet!

A park like in a painting

Pavlovsk Park (➤ 170) in the autumn is quite a sight – and the rustling of leaves is a treat for the senses.

Getting Your Bearings

The luxurious country seats of the Russian emperors – Peterhof Palace, Tsarskoye Selo and Pavlovsk – and their no less stunning parks, all fall within the administrative area of St Petersburg. However, to visit them you do have to leave the city quite some way behind you. The journey to the palaces takes at least an hour, passing huge, new housing estates on the way. The imperial palaces are not scattered around the countryside but form two distinct clusters – one to the southwest of the city, the other to the south.

A row of elegant Baroque palaces was built in Peter the Great's day along the southern shore of the Gulf of Finland. A natural terrace, some 10m–20m (33ft–66ft) above the waterline, runs parallel to the shore over a distance of several miles. It was on this elevated site that the residence in Strelna (Konstantin Palace), Peterhof Palace and Oranienbaum were built. Peterhof Palace became of central importance thanks to its famous fountains and cascades. It is not only the most magnificent of the palaces and parks in this direction but also where other buildings were erected for the tsarist family in the 19th century, including the grand 'Cottage' and 'Home Farm' in Alexandria Park, and the picturesque pavilions on Olgin Pond.

The Grand Cascade below Peterhof Palace is part of one of the most impressive fountain complexes in the world

The second palace complex is about ten kilometres (6.2mi) to the south of the present city boundary. In the town of Pushkin, formerly known as Tsarskoye Selo, is vast Catherine Palace. It is home to the world-famous Amber Room and is surrounded by a beautiful park. In the immediate vicinity is another imperial residence, the Alexander Palace, also with a large park, as well as several interesting museums and buildings from the early 20th century. This ensemble is complemented by the elegant palace of Pavlovsk, embedded in an unusually extensive landscaped park, located some five kilometres (3mi) further to the south.

46 The Court Entertainment Project
43 Alexandria Park
Tsaritsyn Pavilion and **48**
Olgin Pavilion
Saints Peter and Paul Cathedral **47**

2
Peterhof Palace

Strelna
45
Congress
Palace

0 — 10 km
0 — 5 mi

Memorial Lyceum
Museum
Catherine **49**
Palace **Pushkin**
51 **5** (Tsarskoye Selo)
Alexander Park **50** Court Carriages
  44
  Pavlovsk

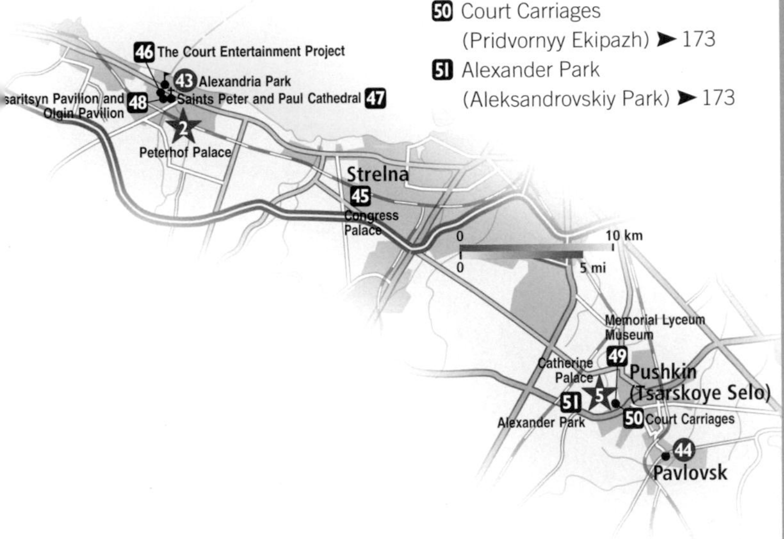

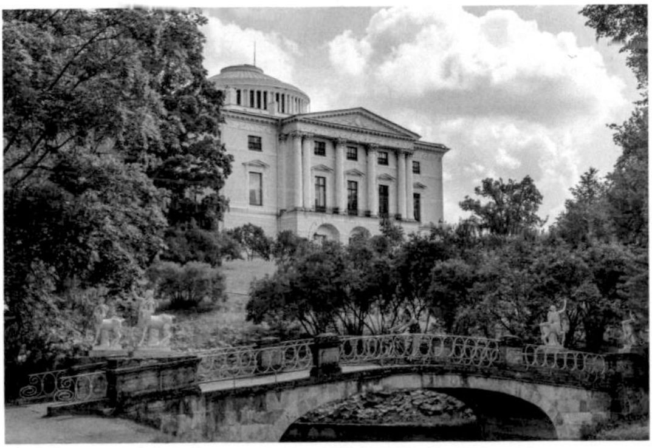

Pavlovsk –
the most
modern of
all the former
imperial
summer
residences

Two Perfect Days

The half-day excursions to Peterhof Palace or Tsarskoye Selo offered by many travel organisations only give you enough time to get a brief overall impression. If you would rather soak in the aura of these imperial sites you will need much more time. It is a shame to tour the palaces quickly and then not even be able to explore the parks at your own pace afterwards. If you follow our suggested route over two days you will see the most important palaces as well as several highlights in the area – such as elegant Alexandria Park at Peterhof Palace and the beautiful palace at Pavlovsk.

Day One

The Court Entertainment Project
46 Alexandria Park
Tsaritsyn Pavilion 48 43 47 Saints Peter and Paul Cathedral
and Olgin Pavilion
Peterhof Palace 45 Strelna
Congress Palace
0   10 km
0   5 mi
Memorial Lyceum Museum
Alexander Park 51 49 Tsarskoye Selo
5 50 Court Carriages
Catherine Palace 44 Pavlovsk

Morning
The first hydrofoils to
★2 **Peterhof Palace** (► 156) depart
at around 10am from Palace Bridge.
This means you will reach the park (fig. top right: The Hermitage), in good time before the **Great Cascade** is turned on to the sound of classical music. In the high season the queues outside the Great Palace can be very long indeed. If that is the case it is better to take a stroll around the extensive park with its various water features (fig. below) and take a look at **Monplaisir**, Peter the Great's original garden house.

Lunch
Instead of seeking out one of the overcrowded eateries in the park head for the village for lunch and the **Duck & Drake** (► 175), for instance. Afterwards

you can visit Olgin Pond and explore 47 **Peter and Paul Cathedral** (► 171) and the 48 **island pavilions** (► 172).

Afternoon
Some 1km (0.6mi) further to the east next to the **Telegraph Museum** (► 168) is 43 **Alexandria Park** (► 167). Don't miss a visit to the imperial residences, the **Cottage** and **Home Farm**.

Evening
You can eat in the tiny guesthouse **Old Kitchen** next to the park's eastern exit or, if it is already full, in much larger **Krasny Kabachok** a few yards further on. Even if it gets quite late buses to the various metro stations in the city still run frequently in the evening. On the way you will pass 45 **Konstantin Palace** (► 171) on the left.

Day Two

Morning

Take the metro and a bus right to ⑭ **Pavlovsk Palace** (➤ 169) itself. When the doors are opened at 10am it is still pleasantly quiet here. Afterwards, hire a bicycle for an hour to explore the Slavyanka valley and the pretty eastern part of the park (fig. left).

Lunch

After lunch in the restaurant **Podvorye** (➤ 175) take a bus (lines 370, 545, K-286 or K-545) from opposite Pavlovsk Station for the short trip of a few minutes to Pushkin (alight: Orangerienaya Ul. 7).

Afternoon

In Catharine Park head first of all for ⭐**Catherine Palace** (fig. below: Hall of Mirrors; ➤ 162) to be sure that you get on a tour to see the Amber Room. Afterwards take a walk around the park. From the palace head down towards the Hermitage and then around the large pond in a clockwise direction. Leave the park before getting as far as the palace so that you see it from behind. From here you can make a short detour to visit ⑤ **Alexander Park** (➤ 173).

Evening

After eating in the tiny Café **Bakenbardy** (➤ 175) or in the water tower restaurant **Sotschi** (➤ 176) walk past **Alexander Palace** (➤ 173) and take in the lovely view of the little town and **Feodor Church** (➤ 174) bathed in the evening light. Buses depart outside the Egyptian Gate to various metro stations in the south of the city.

⭐2 Peterhof Palace
(Petergof)

Water and gold have been blended into one coherent whole within this landscaped ensemble. The huge Baroque palace at Peterhof and its park with its numerous fountains and cascades were, in the 18th century, the epitome of the perfect country estate in the ostentatious taste of the tsar. Retrace the footsteps of the imperial family with an inevitable fresh breeze off the Baltic blowing in your face!

The founder of the city, Peter the Great, was impressed by the fashionable display of pomp at royal courts in Europe and also by seafaring. The choice of the site for his country residence and its design were to reflect these passions. The seaside location was obligatory just as the water features were too. Thanks to the terraced site that rises 16m (52ft) above the water just 400m (1,300ft) back from the shoreline and with water courses further inland that could be diverted, it was possible to create something at Peterhof Palace that the Russian emperor had so admired at Versailles and Marly-le-Roi in 1717, namely a series of fountains and cascades right in front of his palace. And better still: a side canal enabled the tsar to reach his palace from the capital exclusively on water.

The Grand Palace and the cascade at Peterhof – Russia's answer to Versailles

The Grand Palace

The first palace ensemble was completed in 1725. The present Grand Palace with its 286m (938ft)-long Baroque façade is, however, the result of extensions and revamping around 1750 by Bartolomeo Rastrelli, Empress Elizabeth's much sought-after 'star architect'. 27 rooms on the first floor of the palace are open to the public. The ballroom and the small audience chamber in the west wing, that seems to heave under the weight of its decorative gold ornamentation, are both especially magnificent. Most of the private imperial apartments are in the east wing. A small oak panelled study and a staircase from the time of Peter the Great have survived in the middle tract. The rooms in the centre, the portrait hall with paintings of 368 young ladies and two Chinese cabinets that flank it on either side date from the 1760s. They were designed by Jean-Baptiste Vallin de la Mothe, very much to the taste of Catherine the Great.

In Front of the Palace

Around the palace and in the park there are a number of pavilions and museums open to visitors. The golden Baroque **Palace Church** in the east wing, with its distinctive octagonal ground plan, and the exhibition **'The Special Treasury'** with exceptionally crafted jewellery in the west wing, can be recommended. You can also go under the palace to see the artificially created **grottoes** (entrance fee: ₽500) behind the **Grand Cascade**.

The Grand Cascade is Peterhof's chief attraction. Water sprays out of 138 jets down a regal composition of marble, gold and tuff stone. These jets, however, were merely intended to provide a backdrop for the **Samson Fountain**, installed in 1735 as the central element in the harbour basin at that time, depicting the biblical hero tearing open a lion's mouth.

This was intended as an allegory of the victory over the Swedes at the Battle of Poltava some 25 years earlier. The present version is a copy made in 1947, the original sculpture having been lost in World War II. At that time the palace and its park were both badly damaged as they lay on the front.

The Palace Park

To the left and right of the canal is the **Lower Park**, laid out in a linear form, running 1km (0.6mi) parallel to the coast. It offers plenty of room for a long walk. The tall trees in the eastern section provide a lot of shade; in the western part the setting next to the sea is more evident. Nowhere is it uninteristing as twenty-five historical fountains ensure variety. The most elegant is the **Lion Cascade** in the western section installed in 1855; the most original is the **Chessboard Hill Cascade** (of 1739) on a slope in the east, fed by three whimsical, water spouting dragons. Children love the 🏛️**trick fountains** in the park below which the tsars had built to amuse (and soak) their guests!

The smaller palace **Monplaisir** is an historical and architectural gem. It lies in the east section right on the shore.

INSIDER INFO

Insider Tip
- **Arriving** on the **hydrofoils** – called *meteors* – on the Baltic is not only fast (c. 30 mins.), they are also the most comfortable way to travel. From May to Sep there are three companies that shuttle back and forth. They depart from outside the Hermitage and the Admiralty. At Peterhof the pier leads immediately into the park without having to pay any additional entrance fee. Tickets cost around ₽750, one way. Booking in advance on the companies' websites (citycruises.ru, neva-shipping.ru, peterhof-express.ru) guarantees you a seat at the time you want and is often a bit cheaper. If you want to return by the same route, do not leave the Lower Park or else you have to pay to re-enter. Anyone wanting to explore the little town around Peterhof or visit sites outside the park is best advised to return by bus. Virtually every line operating along the main road at Peterhof will take you back to the city to one of the metro stations.

Insider Tip
- With some 5 million visitors a year Peterhof Palace is the most popular tourist site in St Petersburg – and almost all of them visit in summer. During the high season plan your visit on a week day when it is not quite as busy as at weekends. If you would like to tour the Grand Palace, it is better to take a slot in the afternoon when the queues are a little bit shorter.

Monplaisir: Peter the Great's delightful 'garden house'

Built in 1714–23 it was Peter the Great's favourite dacha and is the oldest building at Peterhof. The furnishing is puritanically plain but nevertheless elegant with blue-and-white Dutch tiles being an inherent design element. The tsar had his collection of West European paintings hung in two naturally lit galleries; his collection of chinoiserie is displayed in a lacquer cabinet.

TAKING A BREAK

There are a number of expensive snack bars and one large restaurant in the park, none of which are particularly good. A more fitting place to seek out is perhaps the old **Orangery** (in the east section of the park, immediately below the main entrance, May–Sep daily 11am–7pm). From the wonderfully positioned small tables outside the restaurant you have a view of the Triton Fountain.

Insider Tip

THE NEPTUNE FOUNTAIN
The large Neptune Fountain is in the Upper Park on the side of the palace facing inland. It was made in Nuremberg in 1668 but never installed and sold to Russia in 1797. A replica was erected in Nuremberg in 1902. In 1942 the original turned up there having been looted during the war but was returned to the Soviet Union by the Allies in 1945.

🚩 208 B2 ✉ Petergof, St Petersburgsky Pr. 45–47
☎ 812-450-5287; www.peterhofmuseum.ru
🕐 Lower Park: mid-April until 20 Oct daily 9am–8pm, Sat until 9pm, in winter 9am–5:45pm; Palace: Tue–Sun 10:30am–6pm, in summer for individual visitors: Tue–Fri, Sun noon–2pm, 4:15pm–5:45pm, Sat until 7:45pm (closed last Tue in the month); Grand Cascade: operates mid-April–end Oct daily 11am–6pm, Sat until 8:50pm; Monplaisir: daily except last Mon in the month 10:30am–6pm (closed when raining).
🚇 Pravlenskaya Ul. (from Avtovo metro station, lines 200, 210, K-224, K-300, K-404, K-424) 🎫 Lower Park: P700 (free in winter), Palace: P600, Monplaisir: P500

Russia's Versailles

Peterhof, the imperial summer residence on the sea, consisting of the Grand Palace, the magnificent park and its wonderful water features is considered Russia's answer to Versailles. Anyone arriving by boat is treated to an overwhelming panorama of the palace from the landing stage with the Samson Fountain in the foreground.

❶ Grand Palace The Grand Palace, erected in 1714–25, is a relatively plain, three-storey building. Inside, its is exquisitely furnished with priceless works of art.

❷ Upper Park The central feature of the Upper Park, laid out in the French style, is the Neptune Fountain.

❸ Lower Park In this carefully laid out Baroque garden, considerable variety can be found not only in the form of the Grand Cascade, the Lion Cascade and the Chessboard Hill Cascade with its water-spurting dragons, but also in a further twenty fountains.

❹ Grand Cascade The Grand Cascade, created in 1714–24, is one of the most impressive fountains and cascades anywhere in the world.

❺ Samson Fountain The fountain in front of the Grand Cascade commemorates the victory of Russia over Sweden at the Battle of Poltava in 1709. A spout of water shoots 22m (72ft) up into the air out of the lion's mouth, forced open by Samson.

❻ Sea Canal Peter the Great normally travelled to Peterhof by boat and sailed right up to the palace along the sea canal.

Sturdy but elegant: the Lion Cascade with its 8m (26ft)-tall columns made of granite and marble

Peterhof Palace

Historical parade outside the palace with a view of the Great Cascade and the canal leading to the sea

★⑤Catherine Palace
(Yekaterininskiy Dvorets)

While Peterhof Palace is seen as Russia's 'Versailles', the 'tsar's village' of Pushkin is straight out of a fairy tale. The imperial seat of Tsarskoye Selo with Catherine Palace lies to the south of St Petersburg. The original Amber Room came from Berlin and, in its time, was considered an 'Eighth Wonder of the World'. Its reconstruction draws visitors from all over the world. To be able to enjoy a stroll around the interestingly varied palace park you should plan plenty of time.

The palace's name did not come from Catherine II (the Great) but from Catherine I, Peter the Great's wife who was the first woman to ascend the Russian throne following the death of her husband. It was for her that a small country residence was erected from 1718 onwards, a day's journey south of the capital. The slope was terraced and a geometrically laid out park with two ponds created. This garden still exists, by and large, other than the palace and its successor on the site which were both demolished in the middle of the 18th century by Empress Elizabeth in her craving for building ever bigger and more pompous palaces.

The palace with its blue, white and golden Baroque façade, 308m (1,010ft) long, pierced by the many windows, still largely bears the traits of the building completed in 1756 by the court architect Bartolomeo Rastrelli.

While tour groups enter the palace across the vast cour d'honneur on the northwest front, visitors travelling under their own steam have to queue on the side facing the park. In the high season it may well take a good two hours to reach the ticket desk.

The palace
A tour of the palace begins up the marble staircase that, however, did not gain its elaborate Rococo ornamentation until 1860. Passing through two ante-chambers the **Great Hall** is reached. Covering an area of 860m² (9,260ft²), it actually seems much bigger thanks to the many windows and mirrors on the long side walls and the mass of gilded, carved ornamental work. The huge ceiling painting with allegorical depictions of Peace, Victory and Russia (in the middle) make the room seem optically one storey taller.

THE TSAR'S VILLAGE
The whole museum complex with its palaces, parks and museums is known today simply as **Tsarskoye Selo** ('the tsar's village'). This was the name originally given to the settlement that had grown up around the imperial seat. In 1918 it was renamed Detskoye Selo ('the children's village') and, in 1937, it was christened **Pushkin**, commemorating the 100th anniversary of the poet's death who went to school here. Today, Pushkin has a population of around 100,000.

Catherine Palace

Catherine Palace is the home of the legendary Amber Room

From the Great Hall visitors enter three magnificent smaller rooms, formerly used by guests to access the ballroom. Beyond these is the **Arabesque Hall** that was only restored a few years ago. This is the furthest point of the tour. You now return in the other direction that takes you 300m (985ft) in a straight line through the **Golden Enfilade** – a grand suite of twenty-two richly decorated state rooms.

The sixth beyond the Great Hall is the **Amber Room** (▶ 165) that covers 96m² (1,033ft²). Visitors find themselves in a room with walls covered with some 500,000 pieces of amber that have been fitted together with great precision. The variety and skill of the craftsmen who created the ornamental works and filigree engravings is overwhelming. Like almost all the rooms in the palace, the Amber Room is also a reconstruction of the original that is presumed to have been looted during World War II. This replica was completed in 2003. Only one chest of drawers and a Florentine mosaic are original. Both appeared on the art market at the end of the 1990s in Germany.

The next room, the large **Portrait Hall** with paintings hung very close to one another across all the walls, represents the last Baroque room of the tour, the following ones being in the Neoclassical style.

The **Palace Church** at the end of the enfilade has not yet been renovated and is, therefore, not open to the public. A hint of its rich ornamental interior is suggested by the five golden onion domes.

Catherine the Great valued the palace greatly. Her favourite architect Charles Cameron not only re-designed

Imperial Palaces Outside the City

a number of rooms but also introduced the Neoclassical style that was fashionable at the time. The **Cameron Gallery** complex forms an extremely elegant building that divides the older Baroque garden from the more contemporary English landscaped park. On the upper storey of the so-called 'Cold Baths' that were built after 1780 and which had their own entrance, Cameron designed a day-time apartment with a roof garden for the empress – the **Agate Rooms** – employing twenty-five tons of precious stones. Although only two of the seven rooms were panelled with dark-red agate, they gave their name to this additional palace highlight.

The whereabouts of the original Amber Room remains a mystery to this day; a replica has been open to visitors since 2003

THE AMBER ROOM

The disappearance of the Amber Room has not only turned into a myth but is also a symbol of the ups-and-downs of the German-Russian relationship. In 1716 Frederick William I of Prussia gave Peter the Great an exquisite amber room that had been built in his palace in Berlin. In return he received 55 Russian soldiers – 'Lange Kerls' (lit.: 'tall guys'). The room was initially installed in the Winter Palace but then transferred to Tsarskoye Selo in 1755. As the wall surface there was considerably larger, the amber panels were supplemented with dados, mirrors and decorative woodwork. Four Florentine stone mosaics with allegorical depictions of the senses were also integrated. The Amber Room was completed in 1770. In 1941 the German occupying forces looted the *gesamtkunstwerk*, that by this time was badly in need of renovation, as spoils of war and displayed it temporarily in a palace in Königsberg (Kaliningrad). From there all traces of it were lost at the end of the war. First begun in 1979, the reconstruction was completed in 2003, having been made possible by a donation of 3.5 million dollars by Ruhrgas AG to the Amber Workshop that suffered from a notorious lack of funds.

The Park

The park is best explored clockwise around the **Large Pond** Insider Tip as this follows the chronology of the park's creation. N.B.: When it is raining the pavilions in the park are closed.

In the 1750s Rastrelli built the pavilions, the **Grotto** (on the water) and the **Hermitage** (in the woods), at the same time with façades designed in a similar manner to the palace. The latter is a playful *maison de plaisance* in which courtly society could withdraw to the upper floor without being seen by the servants. That explains why the table is fitted with a food lift – its operation is demonstrated during tours.

Two bathhouses, built in the 1770s, are close to the palace. A detailed reconstruction of the art of bathing is shown in the **Lower Bath**. The **Admiralty**, once a boathouse built in the 1770s in the Gothic style, is located on the Large Pond and is flanked by two aviaries. A ballroom can be found on an island in the lake near the **Chesme Column** which rises out of the water, erected to commemorate the Russian victory over the Turkish fleet in 1770. This explains why a (Russian) eagle is picking a (Turkish) crescent to pieces.

The last building erected in the park, in 1850, is also a reminder of another military triumph, this time in 1829. The **Turkish Bath** pavilion resembles a mosque with an interior entirely in the oriental style. The idyllic marble bridge of 1774 marks the western-most end of the lake. The colonnade superstructure in the Italian Renaissance style was made in Yekaterinburg and transported from the Ural Mountains in sections.

The sad **Milkmaid** (1816) on the north bank became a symbol for Tsarskoye Selo. It is a touchingly romantic fountain with water pouring out of a broken jug.

A granite terrace (1810) with a number of statues leads to the upper park. A puristic Neoclassical **concert hall** was built on an island in the park in 1784 and a 1800-year old Roman mosaic incorporated in the floor. Fragments of

INSIDER INFO

Getting there Tsarskoye Selo is not as easy to reach as one would expect. For those travelling under their own steam and bearing the very long queues in the high season in mind, it makes good sense to visit Catherine Palace on an organised trip. If, however, you do decide to go there on your own, you have a number of different alternatives: Insider Tip

■ From Vitebsky Station (➤ 116) or Kupchino metro station all **district line trains** go to Tsarskoye Selo station (30 or 15 mins. respectively). From there you have to walk 2.5km (1.5mi) through the town of Pushkin; or take a bus (lines 371, 382, 385, K-377 as far as the stop Parki).

■ From Kupchino metro station (leave the platform in the opposite direction and go through the pedestrian tunnel to the left under the road) and take one of the following **buses**: 186, K-342, K-286, K-287, K-342, K-347. Most of these lines go to Tsarskoye Selo station first and then to the park.

Imperial Palaces Outside the City

sculptures from Antiquity are also to be found in the adjacent ruins of the kitchen.

After a short detour to the colourful **Creaky Pavilion** (c. 1780; the name refers to the noisy weather vane) in the Chinese style, leave the park at the nearby exit. This gives you the opportunity of seeing Catherine Palace through the **Parade Gates** at the back.

TAKING A BREAK

A very good cake shop, a branch of the **Wolkonski chain** (daily 11am–11pm), in the left-hand section of the Admiralty, is the perfect place for a cup of tea.

The Cameron Gallery in Catharine Park

✛ 208 C3 ✉ Pushkin, Sadovaya Ul. 7
☎ 812-415 7667; www.tzar.ru.
Park: ◑ Daily from 7am, Sep–April until 9pm, May–July until 11pm, Aug until 10pm 🖐 May–Oct 9am–7pm: ₽120 (otherwise free)
Palace: ◑ Closed Tue; June–Aug noon–8pm, May and Sep noon–7pm, Oct–April 10am–6pm (except 1st Mon in the month) 🖐₽1,000
Agate Rooms: ◑ Fri–Wed 11am–7pm 🖐 ₽300
Hermitage: ◑ June–Sep Tue–Sun 11am–7pm; guided tours: noon, 12:30pm, 3pm, 3:30pm 🖐 ₽300
Lower Bathhouse: ◑ Thu–Tue 11am–7pm 🖐₽150
Turkish Bath: ◑ June–Sep Thu–Tue 11am–7pm 🖐 ₽200
Concert Hall: ◑ June–Sep Wed–Sun 11am–6pm 🖐 Free

Getting there: Insider Info ➤ 165

INSIDER INFO

Insider Tip

- If you plan long in advance the eternal queues outside Catherine Palace can be avoided. **Entrance tickets** for a specific date can be bought online under www.tkt.tzar.ru. This contingent of tickets, however, is often sold out many days beforehand. In summer, an entrance ticket for the park must be shown before you can visit Catherine Palace itself. Anyone who has thrown their ticket away or entered the park before the ticket booths open, has to pay (again).
- **Tours of the park** on an electric buggy that last one hour depart from outside the Admiralty (₽250 per person). You see considerably more of the park this way than on horse-and-carriage rides that start at the lake outside the palace (25 mins., ₽400).

㊸ Alexandria Park
(Park Aleksandriya)

The absolutist display of pomp at Peterhof Palace is not everyone's cup of tea. This was even the case in the 19th century within the Russian imperial family itself. Tsar Nicholas I yearned for a much less ostentatious summer residence for himself and his wife, Alexandra Feodorovna, a Prussian princess by birth.

The Gothic
Chapel in
Alexandria
Park at
Peterhof
Palace was
designed by
the famous
Berlin
architect
Karl Friedrich
Schinkel

The idea of an intimate dacha for the tsar actually became reality on a 110ha (272-acre) site to the east of Peterhof. The **Cottage**, a romantic summer residence in the Gothic Revival style that was becoming increasingly popular in England at that time, was built in 1826–29 on a terrace above the Baltic. The architect was the Scot, Adam Menelaws. In the 1840s Andrei Stackenschneider added a dining room with a marble terrace to this, by far the most intimate imperial palace in the St Petersburg area. The villa is bewitching with its pointed gables, intricately cut woodwork and numerous balconies. Today, it has a nostalgic feel; in its day it very much reflected the spirit of the era and was 'very British'. Nicholas I even jokingly called himself 'Lord Cottage'!

As there were six children in the imperial family a 👫 **play area** (now restored) was created near the house in addition to a rose garden. A farmhouse in the park, 700m (2,300ft) further to the west, provided the large family with fresh milk and eggs. The next in

line to the throne, later Emperor Alexander II, loved it there so much when he was a child that he had it gradually turned into a country seat over the years up until 1860. The result is the generously proportioned **Farmers' Palace** (or Home Farm) in the Victorian style that was popular at the time in the British Isles. With a lift, running water, bathrooms and lavatories, the elegant farm was also technically up-to-date. In 1860 Alexander II signed the decree abolishing serfdom in the elegant study, the Blue Cabinet. Hordes of children – including six boys –

belonging to the imperial household ran around the corridors of this house too and enjoyed playing in the mock fortress in the garden where they also had a mini fire station.

Some 200m (650ft) to the west is the small but highly unusual **Gothic Chapel**, built to a design by the famous Berlin architect Friedrich Schinkel and consecrated in 1834 as a private place of worship for the Romanovs. The steep path down to the shore with its mass of reeds cannot really be recommended unless you have lots of time on your hands or have bicycles – that are permitted everywhere in Alexandria Park. The only building there is the **Lower Dacha** of the last tsar, Nicholas II. It was shelled in World War II and the ruin blown up in 1961. Only a pile of rubble amidst the undergrowth marks the site today.

Inland, heading towards the road, is the **Telegraph Museum** that is well worth a visit. A telegraph outpost was built here in 1858 to serve both the royal residences and the local community. On the ground floor of the little building the technology of the times has been lovingly recreated as well as everyday life in such an office, right down to its store of supplies. An exhibition under the roof explains how the optical telegraph between St Petersburg and Kronstadt worked.

Nicholas I felt very much at home in the more modestly proportioned 'Cottage'

TAKING A BREAK

There is a delightful guards' house on the other side of the road outside the east entrance to the park. It is now home to the **Old Kitchen** (Sankt Peterburgski Pr. 2; daily noon–11pm, in summer only) which serves Italian fare and is a cosy place to sit either under a roof or at tables outside.

➕ 208 B2 ✉ Peterhof, Sankt Peterburgski Pr. 1–7
☎ 812-450-5287; www.peterhofmuseum.ru
🕐 Park: daily 9am–10pm. All buildings/museums in summer: Tue–Sun 10:30am–6pm (Cottage and Gothic Chapel only open in dry weather); opening times in winter: see website 🚌 Alexandria (same lines as to Peterhof Palace) 💵 P300, free after 5pm. Cottage: P500; Farmers' Palace: P400; Gothic Chapel: P250; Telegraph Museum: P250

44 Pavlovsk

Is this just another imperial palace outside the city boundary? No, not really – this comparatively intimate royal residence in the town of Pavlovsk is especially noteworthy due to its exquisite artistic furnishing. Sophistication rather than ostentation was also the motto when landscaping the surrounding park that is impressive if only thanks to its sheer size.

Pavlovsk Palace is located in the town of the same name with a population of around 16,000 some 5km (3mi) to the southeast of Catherine Palace. All those interested in seeing the sights while yearning for a bit of peace and quiet will find it refreshingly different to Tsarskoye Selo as many fewer tourists make their way here. On top of that the palace park covers a huge 5.5km² (2mi²) and merges with the surrounding countryside where it is easy to get lost.

The estate was created by the later tsar, **Paul I** who commissioned Charles Cameron with the task of erecting a palace high above the right-hand bank of the little river Slavyanka. The English architect specialised in Italianate architecture which explains why the three-storey main building resembles a Renaissance Palladio-style villa. To each side, low, semi-circular galleries frame the building and enclose an oval courtyard. The palace has a grand east façade whereas, from the west, it appears more like a gracious country villa.

The Great Palace of Pavlovsk was planned in a uniform neo-Classical style

While the palace was being built between 1782–84, Paul and his wife, Maria Feodorovna, a German princess by birth, travelled extensively around Europe buying furniture, porcelain and exquisite materials in a big way. Together with no less noble presents given to the successors to the Russian throne by their various hosts, these acquisitions served as a source of inspiration and a stylistic guideline while planning the interiors. Pavlovsk is a uniquely composed synthesis of decorative work and furnishing. After Paul's assassination in 1801 the palace became the principal home of his widow who devoted herself to elaborating on the building.

Imperial Palaces Outside the City

Cameron and his colleagues set about landscaping the **park** with the same perfectionism. With pavilions, temples and little bridges they conjured up idyllic areas in the Slavyanka valley.

Ultimately, the Italian theatre scenery painter Paolo Gonzaga proved that he also knew how to create a variety of different backdrops and whole new landscapes through the felling and planting of trees in the far eastern corner of the park.

The Temple of Friendship – also designed by Charles Cameron

TAKING A BREAK

The food in the **Grand Column Hall Restaurant** inside the palace (daily 10am–6pm) is very average but you can enjoy the privilege of eating in an imperial palace!

➕ 208 C3 ✉ Pavlovsk, Ul. Sadovaya 20 ☎ 812-452-1536; www.pavlovsk museum.ru 🕐 Park: daily 6am–midnight; Palace: daily 10am–6pm (closed first Mon in the month and, in winter, on Fri too; on Tue and Fri only the state rooms on the 1st floor are accessible) 🚌 Pavlovsk, Dvorez (K-299 from Moskovskaya metro station; K-286, K-521 from Kupchino metro station 🚇 Pavlovsk (district line trains from Vitebsky Station or Kupchino metro line) 💵 Park: 10am–6pm ₽100 (free at other times); Palace: ₽500 (Tue, Fri ₽400); temporary exhibitions: each ₽150

INSIDER INFO

Insider Tip

- **Pavlovsk Palace Park** is so extensive that it is best explored by **bicycle**. These can be hired at three of the park entrances (from the station, at the entrance leading from the town centre and in the car park to the east of the palace) as well as at Café Slavyanka. Price per hour: ₽300, tandems ₽500. Large groups should reserve bicycles in advance (www.velopark.spb.ru; daily 10am–8pm). There are two places where boats can be hired on the largest lakes in the park. In winter, cross-country skis and Finnish sledges (one persons pushes or stands on the skids, the other person sits) are available.
- A **Costume Museum**, in which the elegant original garments worn by various Russian empresses are on display, lies hidden in the northern arc of the courtyard wing. The museum is only open at weekends from 11am–6pm and on days when the palace itself is closed. Entrance fee: ₽150

Insider Tip

- On the top floor of the palace there is a **'walk-through manual of style'** for antique lovers: 16 rooms reflect the quickly changing fashions in furniture in the 19th century.

At Your Leisure

45 Congress Palace (Dvorez Kongressov)

The official name of this massive building conceals its real name – **Konstantin Palace**. Located in the Strelna district of St Petersburg it is halfway between the city centre and Peterhof Palace (➤ 156). Peter the Great first started building this palace on the shore before shifting his ambitions to create 'Russia's Versailles' 9km (5.5mi) further east. The lay of the land here made it impossible to generate enough pressure for the fountains he so much wanted to have.

In the 19th century the palace in **Strelna** served as an out-of-town residence for three Romanov grand dukes – and as all three were called Konstantin the name stuck. The palace was badly damaged during the Siege and used as a school after World War II. In 1990 the building was empty and falling into disrepair. It was Vladimir Putin who awakened the palace from its Sleeping Beauty-like slumber. Within just eighteen months the ruin was turned into a stately, representational building of the first degree. On the occasion of the city's 300th anniversary the palace was inaugurated as a luxury conference centre with a 5-star hotel and a showy colony of villas for state visitors.

When not in use for a political event the state rooms can be visited on a guided tour (in Russian only). There are four other tours available too to suit a variety of interests, one of which is through the park. As the number of participants is strictly limited it is advisable to book in advance via the Internet, especially in the high season.

🚩 208 B2 ✉ Strelna, Beriosovaya Alleya 3 ☎ 812-438-5360; www.konstantinpalace.ru 🕙 Thu–Tue 10am–6pm 🚌 Konstaninovski Dvorez (lines as for Peterhof Palace) 🚊 Strelna (Line 36) 💵 P250–P400

46 The Court Entertainment Project (Gosudarevy Potekhi)

In this exhibition in **Peterhof Palace** (➤ 156), first opened in 2014, life in a country residence is realistically displayed with original exhibits and multimedia presentations. The journey back in time shows the court theatre and the garden parties and fireworks displays enjoyed in the country in the 19th century, and finishes with a picture of the mass of bicycles kept at the ready for members the imperial Romanov family. This display can be found in the single-storey building immediately opposite the main entrance to the Lower Park.

🚩 208 B2 ✉ Ul. Pravlenskaya 1 ☎ 812-450-5287; www.peterhofmuseum.ru 🕙 Tue–Sun 10:30am–6pm 🚌 Pravlenskaya Ul. (from Avtovo metro station: lines 200, 210, K-224, K-300, K-404, K-424) 💵 P500

47 Saint Peter and Saint Paul Cathedral (Petropavlovski Sobor)

Anyone travelling to **Peterhof Palace** (➤ 156) by hydrofoil will see its pointed silhouette from quite a distance as, reaching a height of 70m at the top of the dome, this colourful place of worship on the bank of Olgin Pond is the tallest historical building in the residential borough. The cathedral was built in 1895–1905 in the neo-Russian style popular at the time. It includes elements of ecclesiastic

Imperial Palaces Outside the City

architecture from the 16th and 17th centuries that turn it into a little piece of picture-postcard Russia seldom found in the St Petersburg area. The traditional painting of the interior that reaches right up into the dome has been executed with unusual delicacy. For a small fee visitors can climb to a gallery half-way up from where a window provides a distant view over the Gulf of Finland – and the skyline of St Petersburg on the horizon.

✚ 208 B2 ✉ Petergof, St Petersburgsky Pr. 32
☎ 812-450-6268; www.spp-petergof.ru
◷ Service: daily 9:30am and 5pm
🚇 Torgovaya pl. (from Avtovo metro station: lines 200, 210, K-224, K-300, K-404, K-424)
✋ Free

48 Tsaritsyn Pavilion and Olgin Pavilion (Zarizyn i Olgin Paviliony)

At the behest of Emperor Nicholas I a swampy area in the middle of the town of Peterhof was turned into a lake, **Olgin Pond**, with two islands created from the earth removed in the process. In the 1840s the German-born court architect Andrei Stackenschneider was commissioned to build two highly individual buildings. The first was created for the tsar's wife, **Alexandra Feodorovna**, as a place to withdraw from the limelight. Designed in the style of a Roman villa, the atrium with its basin and fountain in col-oured marble, in particular, exude something of the luxury of Ancient Rome. The furnishings were also made in the Roman style.

The island is accessed over a dyke. The second island is reached via a long footbridge. **Olga Pavilion** was a wedding present for the emperor's daughter, Olga, who later married King Charles I of Württemberg. From the outside, the three-storey, tower-like building in the austere Sicilian style seems devoid of any ornamentation. It was intended to be reminiscent of Palermo where the couple were

first introduced to one another. There is only one room on each floor: a dining room and two cabinet rooms – one for the tsar's daughter, the other for the ruler himself.

✚ 208 B2 ✉ Peterhof, Olgin prud
☎ 812-450-5287; www.peterhofmuseum.ru
◷ Daily 10:30am–6pm 🚇 Torgovaaa pl.
(from Avtovo metro station: lines 200, 210, K-224, K-300, K-404, K-424) 💳 ₽600

49 Memorial Lyceum Museum (Memorial'niy Musey-Litsey)

The imperial Tsarkoye Selo Lyceum was the first school in Russia open exclusively to the children of the aristocracy and was housed in the north wing of **Catherine Palace** (▶ 162). Pushkin was among the first pupils to start at the school in 1811 as a 12-year old. He wrote his first works here and his talent became evident during the six years he spent at this school. The building now forms a branch of the **Pushkin Museum** (nab. reki Moyki 12; www.museumpushkin.ru, Wed–Mon 10:30am–6pm, ₽120). Classrooms, the library, a teacher's flat and the pupils' tiny rooms, equipped merely

Peter and Paul Cathedral was built c. 1900 in the Old Russian style

with the bare necessities, have been faithfully reconstructed. The history of the school and the biographies of other prominent alumni are documented in a separate exhibition on the 2nd floor (entrance fee P100).

🏛 208 C3 ✉ Pushkin, Sadovaya Ul. 2
☎ 812-476-6411; www.museumpushkin.ru
🕐 Wed–Mon 10:30am–6pm
🚌 Srednaya Ul. (lines 382, 385, K-377 from Tsarskoye Selo station) 💰 P120

50 🎎 Court Carriages (Pridvornyy Ekipazh)

The former palace mews lie opposite the main entrance to **Catharine Park** (➤ 165) and now house a collection of carriages and sledges in which Russia's rulers once rode. Breathtakingly ornate, huge horse-drawn coaches from the time of Catherine the Great are on show in all their splendour as well as elegant carriages made for the coronation of Alexander II. Of all the some two dozen exhibits, children are

Thought was given to everything: A coach with a latrine

particularly fascinated by the imperial coach with a latrine hidden under the cushion.

🏛 208 C3 ✉ Pushkin, Sadovaya Ul. 8
☎ 812-415-7667; www.tzar.ru 🕐 Thu–Tue 10am–6pm (closed last Thu in the month)
🚌 Srednaya Ul. (lines 382, 385, K-377 from Tsarskoye Selo Station) 💰 P200

51 🎎 Alexander Park (Aleksandrovskiy Park)

A wooded park covering a good 2km² (495 acres) spreads out behind **Catherine Palace**. The side of the palace facing the park is actually the main façade and includes the extremely impressive main gateway. Even in the high season the park is little used. And like any huge landscaped area there are many surprises to be discovered. These include the exotic **Chinese Bridge** that leads from the palace into the park and, some 300m (985ft) further on, the **Chinese Theatre** (or rather the ruins thereof) as, since the end of World War II, it has been left to crumble. If you explore this former imperial hunting ground more closely, you will come across curiosities such as the tower of a ruined Gothic cathedral or that of a play castle erected for the tsar's children, an old stable for lamas and a horses graveyard for the Russian ruler's favourite steads.

Insider Tip

Grand **Alexander Palace** (Dvortsovaya Ul. 2a) is located in the northeastern corner of the park. Russia's last tsar **Nicholas II** chose this neo-Classical palace, built by the architect Giacomo Quarenghi in 1796, as his principle residence in 1904. It was from here that the tsar, deprived of his power, left in August 1917 with the other members of the imperial family, having been banished into exile. One year later it would culminate in their murder.

The palace is being restored at the moment and is expected to be re-opened in mid 2018.

A complex covering 400m (1,300ft) to the north of the imperial

Imperial Palaces Outside the City

Alexander Park: In the 19th century buildings in the Chinese style were very much in fashion

residence and created just before and during World War I is unusual. The **Feodor ensemble** (Feodorovski Gorodok, Akademicheski Pr. 14–18) has a mystical air about it. It owes its appearance as a miniature citadel to buildings in Novgorod and Pskov from the 16th century. The now half-ruined complex was built to accommodate palace staff and as a brracks for the imperial bodyguard.

Feodor Church (Akademicheski Pr. 34) with its golden-topped tower looks as neat as a pin. Consecrated in 1912, this place of worship was also designed in the style of Ivan the Terrible. Originally intended to be used by the household guard, it was officially given the name 'Rulers' Church' in 1914. It was here that the imperial family attended services.

Some 250m (820ft) to the west of the church, **Ratnaya Palata** is both the last building and a highlight. With the construction of this picturesque ensemble in the Old Novgorod style in 1913, the collection of military artefacts was given its

first home. The building was completed towards the end of World War I and included a museum on the war in progress from the very beginning. After the October Revolution the collection was split up and the building bombed in World War II. After its rebuilding it was decided to establish a museum highlighting Russia's role in World War I – which explains why a hundred-year-old type Nieuport 17 biplane is hanging in the medieval-like vaulted main room.

🚇 208 C3 ✉ Pushkin, entrances to the west and north of Catherine Palace 🛈 www.tzar.ru ⏰ open daily, 24-hours 💵 Free

Ratnaya Palata
✉ Fermskaya Doroga 5 ☎ tel: 812-415-7692; www.tzar.ru ⏰ Thu–Tue 10am–6pm (except for the last Thu in the month) 💵 P300

INSIDER INFO

Due to the large distances to be covered, cycling is allowed in Alexander Park. Alternatively, **tour the park on an electric vehicle** that departs from the Rastrelli memorial on the north side of Catherine Palace (daily 11am–6pm; P150)

Insider Tip

Where to...
Eat and Drink

Prices
for a main course (without drinks):
£ under P450   ££ P450–P900   £££ over P900

PETERHOF

Brynsa £
It's well-worth remembering the word *chebureki*. This is the name of a dough speciality with a variety of different fillings. In this restaurant on the west side of the palace (there are another eight branches within the city) *chebureki* are the main feature on the menu.
🕂 208 B2
✉ Peterhof, Ul. Morskogo desanta 3
☎ 812-944-4490; www.cafebrynza.ru
🕐 Daily 10am–11pm, Sat until 1am
🚇 Rasvodnaya Ul. (from Avtovo metro station: lines 200, 210, K-224, K-300, K-404, K-424)

Coffee Love £
This little café is not only refreshingly different – with its mixture of pop-art and bric-a-brac – but has friendly staff and quick service. It serves good food with a Mexican and Asian lean.
🕂 208 B2
✉ Peterhof, St Petersburgsky Pr. 41
☎ 812-925-0043   🕐 Daily 10am–11pm
🚇 Torgovaya pl. (from Avtovo metro station: lines 200, 210, K-224, K-300, K-404, K-424)

Duck & Drake ££
Sound gastro pub in the newly-built, swish hotel Novy Petergof (New Peterhof) (➤ 42), well located between the palace park and Olgin Pond. Despite its touristy location a low-priced business lunch is available during the week. Although the dishes tend to be pretty 'hearty' the menu also takes vegetarians, allergy sufferers and teetotallers into account.

🕂 208 B2
✉ Peterhof, St Petersburgsky Pr. 34
☎ 812-319-2699; www.new-peterhof.com
🕐 Daily 11am–11pm
🚇 Torgovaya pl. (from Avtovo metro station: lines 200, 210, K-224, K-300, K-404, K-424)

PAVLOVSK

Podvorye £££
Whoever unabashedly calls themselves 'Russia's most Russian restaurant' certainly has a reputation to live up to! The restaurant on the edge of Pavlovsk Park is in a huge log cabin. Inside, it also looks like something out of a folksy picture-book – complete with a stuffed bear. Vodka from their own distillery helps wash down the filling Russian classics.
🕂 208 C3
✉ Pavlovsk, Filtrovskoye Chaussee 16
☎ 812-454-5464; www.podvorye.ru
🕐 Daily noon–11pm   🚇 Pavlovsk station

PUSHKIN / TSARSKOYE SELO

Bakenbardy £
For an eatery right next to a kitschy souvenir market outside Catherine Palace this is a pleasant surprise. Pushkin's whiskers (*bakenbardy*) appear time and again like a running gag through this revamped old building. The restaurant is small, the menu too – and the atmosphere is totally cosy. There is a cafeteria on the ground floor which sells blinis.
🕂 208 C3   ✉ Pushkin, Lizeyski per. 1
☎ 921-996-0235; www.bakenbards.ru
🕐 Mon–Thu 11am–8pm, Fri–Sun 11am–10pm
🚇 Insider info ➤ 165

Imperial Palaces Outside the City

Sotschi £ / Odessa ££

A renovated water tower right next to Catherine Palace is home to two restaurants. Sotschi on the ground floor is in a spacious and bright room. At lunchtime guests can put together their own personal meal at the cafeteria with its wide range of choices. In the evenings, from Wednesday to Sunday, there is live music. The Odessa, one floor up, is a chic restaurant serving fish specialities from the Black Sea. Further up again, there is a vodka bar and a roof terrace.

�︎ 208 C3
✉ Pushkin, Lizeyski per. 7 (in courtyard)
☎ 812-901-0808; www.bashnya-pushkin.ru
🕐 Daily noon–11pm
💻 Insider info ➤ 165

Mox £

A complete and utter contrast to the many eateries for tourist groups and wedding parties close to the palace. This little, freaky vegetarian café lies hidden in an inner court-yard in the middle of Pushkin near Gostiny Dvor. Apart from the much-praised falafels, good coffee, smoothies, wine and craft beer are served too. And sometimes there is live music – if and when someone fancies performing.

🚫 208 C3 ✉ Pushkin, Oranzhereynaya Ul. 15a (in courtyard)
☎ 981-958-3990; www.vk.com/pushkinmox
🕐 Wed–Mon 2pm–10pm
💻 Insider Info ➤ 165

Where to...
Shop

Both Pushkin and Peterhof are comparatively provincial places. There are several souvenir shops near the imperial residences and a little further away shops for the locals' everyday needs.

If you fancy some fresh fruit Pushkin market is held in the courtyard of lovely old Tsarskoselskiy **Gostiny Dvor** (Ul. Moskovskaya 25, Mon–Sat 8am–7pm, Sun until 5pm), some 800m (2,500ft) from Catherine Palace. At Peterhof Palace the **market** is right on Olgin Pond (Zaryzinskaya Ul.; daily 8am–8pm).

Amber Room

The highly professional **Amber Workshop at Catherine Palace** was not dissolved once the reconstruction of the Amber Room was completed but, in-stead, now produces exquisite amber objects, some based on historical pieces. The shop has the feel of a museum with a collection of old amber pipes on display. Prices are high but then both the source of the material and the standard of the work is of the highest quality too.

🚫 208 C3
✉ Pushkin, Sadovaya Ul. 7 (in Catherine Palace below the palace church; shop in the ticket desk area)
☎ 812-476-9918; www.amberroom.ru
🕐 Wed–Mon 10am–5pm
(closed last Mon in the month)
💻 Insider Info ➤ 165

Where to...
Go Out

There is no nightlife to speak of in this area. Pubs and restaurants shut quite early in the evening rather than late. And locals either go to bed or head for the centre of St Petersburg. Anyone who wants to have a good time out after visiting the palace and park should do the same.

Excursions

Excursions

A city with a population of five million can be tiring at times – so there's no better antidote than a trip to the country. Although every visitor to St Petersburg who takes a trip to one of the imperial residences, Peterhof Palace or Tsarskoye Selo, leaves the city, very little of the countryside or the flatlands are actually ever seen. The following two excursions take you that little bit further and give you the chance to breathe in the country air! St Petersburg is, after all, a port 'between two seas' – Europe's largest land-locked area of water, Lake Ladoga, is only 30km from the city boundary but seems all that much further away than the Baltic that narrrows to form the shallow Neva Bay near St Petersburg.

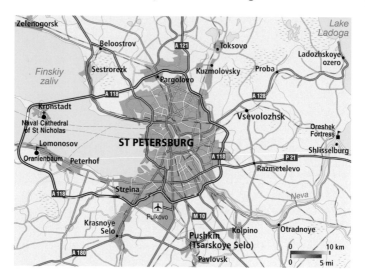

Oranienbaum & Kronstadt

Oranienbaum is – in addition to Strelna and Peterhof Palace – the third imperial palace on the south shore of the Gulf of Finland. The Chinese Palace, Catherine the Great's luxury dacha in the landscaped park is the main attraction. Afterwards, take the bus across the flood protection dyke completed in 2011 to Kronstadt on Kotlin Island where a huge cathedral dominates the eastern-most corner of the Baltic.

Originally, Oanienbaum was not an imperial seat but the country palace of Prince **Alexander Menshikov**, the first Governor General of St Petersburg. Completed in 1720, his palace was initially more magnificent than that of Peter I's Peterhof Palace (➤ 156) ten kilometres (6.2mi) away. Menshikov, however, had to do without the water features.

Oranienbaum & Kronstadt

From 1745 until 1762 **Grand Menshikov Palace** was occupied by the unhappily married, German-born heir to the throne, later (briefly) Peter III, and his conspiring wife, later Catherine II. Hardly on the throne, she declared the far end of the 1.5km² (370 acre)-park as the site of 'her own country house' and had a *maison de plaisance* designed by Antonio Rinaldi to suit her taste. The **Chinese Palace** looks unassuming from the outside but its beguiling interior boasts incomparably magnificent rooms in the Rococo style, such

The Grand Palace in Oranienbaum was once the home of Prince Menshikov

as the Glass Beaded Salon that is unique anywhere in the world. Its silvery shimmering wall-hangings incorporate strings of glass beads and silk embroidery with intricate depictions of plants and birds. Several rooms are decorated in the Chinoiserie style popular at that time – hence the name of this hideaway that was only built to be used in mild weather. The Chinese Palace is, in fact, much more interesting than the main palace building.

A stroll around the landscaped park brings you to the tall **Sliding Hill Pavilion** in the northwest corner, also built by Rinaldi. This served as the starting point for a wooden rollercoaster-type slide that members of the royal party once rode on. In the southeast is what is left of **Peterstadt**, the mock-fortress in which Peter III played war games with his household guards from the Holstein region of Germany.

Across the dam to Kronstadt

Technically-speaking Kronstadt is no longer on an island. The St Petersburg Ring Road crosses the 22km (13.5mi)-long **flood protection dam** built between 1979 and 2011 which now means that the town can be easily reached by bus. Coming from the south, from Oranienbaum, you pass through a 2km (1.2mi)-long tunnel under the main shipping channel. At this point the road is 28m (92ft) below sea level.

The fortified town is the same age as St Petersburg. The Russians started building bastions on Kotlin Island and in the shallow waters of Neva Bay in 1704 so as to gain control of the Neva estuary. In the mid 19th century Kronstadt was the main civilian and military port of St Petersburg – and had twice the number of residents as today (43,000). Although officially a borough of the city of St Petersburg, it is a peaceful spot that still boasts a number of old fortifications,

Excursions

barracks, docks and harbour buildings. The Russian navy only has a small base here today.

The focal point of the town centre is the 70m (230ft)-high **St Nicholas Naval Cathedral** that can be seen from afar. It was re-opened to visitors and worshippers in 2013 following extensive renovation work. The neo-Byzantine domed building, stylistically akin to the Hagia Sophia, was only consecrated in 1913. Only the wide-eyed angels at the main entrance show it is from the Art Nouveau era. The intricate marble mosaic floors, the stained glass windows and the soaring dome painted with much gold give this church its exceptionally festive atmosphere.

St Nicholas Naval Cathedral is Kronstadt's focal point

Some 800m (2,500ft) to the south of the cathedral is the harbour from where **⛴ boat trips** depart that take you past several of the island's forts at close quarters. Longer trips include an excursion on land to explore Alexander I's rather gruesome, kidney-shaped 'Pest Fortress'.

Insider Tip

One of the excursion boats itself is an attraction. The *Reeperbahn*, built in 1954, was once a legendary music steamer that chugged around the harbour in Hamburg. Its ferried the Beatles, the Rolling Stones and Queen down the Elbe River – as photos on board prove!

✚ 208 A1/2

Oranienbaum

✉ Lomonossov, Dvorzovy Pr. 44 ☎ 812-450-5287; www.peterhofmuseum.ru
Palace Park 🕐 Daily 9am–8pm 💷 P140 (free after 5pm)
Grand Menshikov Palace 🕐 Wed–Mon noon–2pm and 4pm–4:45pm
(closed last Wed in the month) 💷 P400
Chinese Palace 🕐 June–Sep Tue–Sun noon–2pm and 4pm–4:45pm
(closed last Tue in the month) 💷 P500
🚌 Lomonossov, Voksal (bus 200, K-300, K-424a from Avtovo metro station)
🚆 Oranienbaum-1 (district line trains from Baltic Station)

St Nicholas Naval Cathedral

✉ Yakornaya pl. 1 ⓘ www.kronshtadtsobor.ru 🕐 Daily from 9am until just after evening service (that begins at 6pm) 💷 Free

Fort cruise with the *Reeperbahn*

✉ Arsenalny per. ☎ 921-309-4850; www.forthotel.ru
🕐 In summer: daily 1pm, 3:30pm, 5:30pm 💷 P550–P1,100
How to get to Kronstadt 🚌 Kronstadt (bus K-405 from Chyornaya Rechka metro station, 101 from Staraya Derevnya metro station, 175 from Oranienbaum station)

Shlisselburg Fortress

Orekhovets (Nut) Island sits like a plug in the water where it drains out of Lake Ladoga – a huge expanse of water that is just slightly smaller than Wales! It is hardly surprising that this strategic position at the southern end of the lake was settled and fortified at the beginning of the 14th century, long before St Petersburg was founded. The original wooden fortress was replaced by a stone structure that was heavily fought over and later served as a high-security prison.

The island and its fortress are reached after a short ferry ride. There are connections from both banks of the Neva but the best starting point is the little town of Shlisselburg itself on the south shore of the lake where there are also a couple of cafés. Next to the jetty is a canal lock from the mid 19th century. Lake Ladoga, that stretches from here to the horizon, was a body of water much feared by sailors due to its violent storms. This prompted Peter the Great to dig a canal along the southern shore so that boats could circumnavigate the lake.

Both the Swedes and the Russians claim to have founded the fortress. This took place in 1299 according to the Swedish version – in 1323 according to the Russians – when an agreement was signed establishing the border between Sweden and the former Russian republic of Novgorod. Both the Swedes and the Russian named the fortress **Nut Castle** – Nöteborg or Oreschek

The walls of Shlisselburg Fortress are between 4.5 and 6m (15ft–20ft) thick

Excursions

respectively – and, in its history, it has indeed turned out to be hard to crack!

In 1352 the people of Novgorod began building a small, stone fortress. During excavations the remains of a gateway from that period came to light. The roofed-over site is open to visitors. There is also a **viewing walkway** around the partially rebuilt walls and towers from the 16th century that are between 4.5m and 6m (15ft–20ft) thick.

After several aborted attempts the Swedes finally took the fortress in 1612. In 1702 Peter the Great recaptured it and, as this site was vital to ensure access to the Baltic, he rechristened it 'Shlisselburg' – 'Key Fortress'.

The fortress gained its present appearance in the 16th century

After the founding of St Petersburg the fortress immediately lost its strategic importance. The island, however, proved to be the perfect place to incarcerate perpetrators of court intrigues and political prisoners. Supporters of the Decembrist Revolt, freedom fighters and revolutionaries were imprisoned in Shlisselburg Fortress, including Michail Bakunin and Lenin's brother, Alexander Ulyanov, who was hanged here in 1887. Two tracts of the prison building that have been reinstated as a museum are a reminder of that time.

The imposing ruins in the courtyard include a prison structure from 1911 and the old fortress church that is now a commemorative site. Both buildings were destroyed in World War II when the fortress once again proved to be a hard nut to crack. For 500 days a small Soviet garrison held out against the German army that had occupied the town of Shlisselburg.

✚ 208 E2 ✉ Shlisselburg, Orekhovets Island

☎ 812-230-6431; www.spbmuseum.ru

🕐 June–Sep Mon–Fri 10am–6pm, Sat, Sun until 7pm, May and Oct Mon–Fri 10am–5pm, Sat, Sun until 6pm 🎫 P200

🚌 Slisselburg (bus 575 from Ulitsa Dybenko metro station)

🚆 Petrokrepost (district line train from Finland Station)

🚢 from Shlisselburg or Morosov (north bank) 🎫 P250 (return)

Walks

1 ART NOUVEAU IN ST PETERSBURG
Walk

DISTANCE: 4km (2.5mi)
DURATION: 2 hours (without museum visits)
START/FINISH: Gorkovskaya metro station ✚ 203 D3

Apart from Baroque and neo-Classical architecture St Petersburg's historical cityscape is characterised by Art Nouveau as well. Nowhere else in the city are there so many Art Nouveau buildings as in the district of Petrograd Side – testimony to a building boom at the beginning of the 20th century. This walk not only takes you along elegant boulevards but also down narrow lanes to hidden courtyards and flaking façades.

❶–❷

Just a stone's throw from Gorkovskaya metro station is one of the first buildings in the 'Northern Art Nouveau' style which generally has less exuberant floral ornamentation than 'classical' Art Nouveau

and clearly defined quoins, so typical of St Petersburg. By contrast, the façade of **Barsowa House** (1911; Kronverkski Pr. 11) has cladding in natural stone that reaches high up the building, together with extremely playful decorative elements around the windows. The cavernous door-ways are watched over by owls and amusing looking sphinxes. **Maxim Gorki** lived here from 1914–21.

About 100m (300ft) from the metro station on Kamenoostrovski Pr. you will reach an unusual **monument** commemorating the sinking of the **torpedo boat Steregushchiy** in the Russo-Japanese war in 1904. The Art Nouveau memorial is a lively interpretation of the legend according to which two sailors

The villa where the ballerina Matilda Kschessinskaya once lived now houses the Museum of the Political History of Russia

scuttled their own boat after it had become disabled so that it could not fall into enemy's hands.

❷–❸

The architect of the monument, Alexander von Hohen, also built two other buildings of exceptional quality in the immediate vicinity. No. 1 Kronverkski Pr. is the luxurious **villa once owned by Matilda Kschessinskaya,** a prima ballerina at the

Mariinsky Theatre. She was tsar Nicholas II's mistress before he became engaged. The brick villa (1904–10) now houses the **Museum of the Political History of Russia**. In 1917, the year of the Revolution, the

Bolsheviks used the building as their headquarters.

❸–❹

Two buildings further down is the massive **mosque** (1910–14, open outside prayer times). Its close proximity to the tombs of the Orthodox Russian rulers testifies quite clearly to the high degree of religious tolerance in the multi-ethnic empire. The towering blue dome with intricate majolica ornamentation and the main entrance were modelled on the Gur-e Amir mausoleum in Samarkand.

❹–❺

Now turn onto Kamenoostrovski Pr. where Nos. 1 and 3 (1902–04) are in the 'Modern Style', as Art Nouveau was called in Russia. The architect and owner of this **residential complex** was **Fyodor Lidval** who cleverly combined a variety of different window shapes, diverse surface areas and animal and plant motifs. Can you see the balcony railings in the shape of a spider's web?

❺–❻

The next highlight is **Austrian Square** – the only complete Art Nouveau ensemble in the city. The St Petersburg architect Va... Schaub was fortunate to have been able to build a total of... private apartment blocks... 1901–06 that are chara... by their asymmetry, tu... animated façades.

Map labels

- ❽ Benois Apartment House
- ❼ Cavos House
- ❾ Kolobovych House
- ❿ Frenkel House
- ❻ Austrian Square
- ⓫ Sytnyy rynok
- ❶ Barsova Apartments
- ❺ Lidval House
- Aleksandrovskiy
- Ⓜ Gorkovskaya
- ❷ Monument to the Torpedo-Boat Steregushchiy
- ❹ Mosque
- ❸ Matilda Kschessinska Mansion
- Park
- Baltiyskiy Dom Theatre
- Music Hall
- Planetarium
- Kronverk

Streets: Kamennoostrovskiy prospekt, Bolshoy prospekt, ul. Rentgena, Monetnaya ul., Bol. Kronverkskaya ul., ul. Mira, Puskarskiy per., ul. Krapotkina, ul. Voskova, Sytninskaya ul., Kronverkskiy prospekt, ul. Markina, Kamennoostrovskiy, Kronverkskaya nab.

0 200 m
0 200 yd

MUSEUMS
Museum of the Political History of Russia
⏱ Fri–Tue 10am–6pm, Wed until 8pm
ℹ www.polithistory.ru 💲 P200

Kirov Museum
⏱ Thu–Tue 11am–6pm
ℹ www.kirovmuseum.ru 💲 P150

Walks

Examples of the 'Modern Style', as the Russians call Art Nouveau, can be seen on Austrian Square

6–8

At the next crossroads is **Kavoss House** (Bolshaya Monetnaya 10), built in 1896–1912, with decorative red brickwork, green tiles and lions' heads.

On reaching the elegant, neo-Classical **Benois building complex** (nos. 26–28, 1911–14) turn into the first open courtyard that leads through to a labyrinth of nine rather run-down courtyards in total. The complex, originally built by an insurance company, is not in the Art Nouveau style but boasts instead the most advanced luxurious attributes of the day such as dozens of garages for cars, a waste incineration and power plant and an integrated vacuum cleaning system. One of the 250 flats houses the **Kirov Museum** and is open to visitors. This was the home of the popular Bolshevik leader Sergei Kirov in the 1930s.

9

... the complex at the back onto ...rkskaya Ulitsa. After cross-...ark opposite you will reach ... **House** (Ulitsa Lenina 8, ... This exclusive residence ... is neo-Baroque ...ever layout for its

day – to the south, facing Pushkarski per., the building opens up into a 'W' shape which allows as much sunlight to reach as many flats as possible.

9–10

Follow Pushkarski per. and turn left into Sablinskaya Ul.: no. 8, **Frenkel House** (1911/12), is also by Vassili Schaub. He did without ornamentation here, creating instead a seven-storey block of flats of interconnecting geometrical shapes. This building can be seen as a precursor of the architectural style that was then to sweep across Russia – Constructivism.

10–11

Cross nearby **Sytny Rynok**, the oldest market in the city with a lovely market hall from 1913, to return to Gorkovskaya metro station.

TAKING A BREAK

The corner coffee shop, **Coffee Room** (Kameno Ostrovski Pr. 22, Mon–Fri 9am–11pm, Sat, Sun from 10am), halfway through the tour, offers all sorts of food and snacks in a trendy designer-style environment.

Insider Tip

2 YELAGIN ISLAND
Walk

DISTANCE: 5.5km (3.5mi) **DURATION:** 2.5 hours
START: Krestovsky Ostrov metro station 🚌 202 west A1
FINISH: Sausadebnaya Ul. 37, Staraya Derevnya metro station
🚌 202 northwest A1

Three small islands in the north-west of the Neva Delta provide city dwellers and tourists alike with a place for relaxation and recreation. Yelagin Island in particular, with its network of nine ponds, is a favourite place to escape to. The imperial dacha and its park have been turned into an idyllic landscaped area open to the public.

1–2

Krestovsky Ostrov metro station is right next to extensive **Victory Park** and opposite 🎡 **Divo Ostrov amusement park** (www.divo-ostrov.ru) which has some pretty hair-raising fun rides. For children and the young at heart this is without doubt a real attraction. Pass by these parks unless you are there on a weekday and you would rather hire a bike for the day. The Velogorod blue hire bikes available online, however, are cheaper. One 'dock station' is located at the metro station.

Insider Tip

All the thrills and fun of the fair are to be found at Divo Ostrov amusement park

2–3

Some 300m (985ft) to the north is a bridge leading to Yelagin Island. Officially, the island is known as the **Central Kirov Recreation and Leisure Time Park** (ZPKiO im. Kirova; www.elaginpark.org). Its founder, however, was not the Party Secretary Sergei Kirov, who was murdered in 1934, but **Ivan Yelagin**. Under Catherine II he was the director of the Imperial Theatre and owned this island from 1777 onwards, on which he built a country seat and laid out an English landscaped park.

WHEN?
Insider Tip

On weekdays, especially in the morning, Yelagin Island is a haven of peace (opening times: April–Oct daily 6am–midnight, Nov–March until 11pm). At weekends, on the other hand, it is well visited even though there is an entrance fee of ₽100 on Sat and Sun from 10am–10pm. Please note: cycling is not permitted during these hours.

187

3–5

After the bridge follow the right-hand bank to **Yelagin Palace** (closed for renovation). Although it is still named after its first owner, the building was largely remodelled by Carlo Rossi after the island was acquired by the imperial family in 1817. As an ensemble specialist, he conjured up this idyllic summer residence and included elegant pavilions for the **kitchens, stables** and an **orangery** located towards the edge of the central lawns.

bridge to the island. In winter there is a small ice rink.

6–8

Pass the **mini zoo** (freely accessible at all times) – with its reindeer from the Russian Tundra, among other animals – and you will reach the **western-most point on the island**.

Staraya Derevnya Ⓜ
Shopping Center Gulliver 12
Torfyanaya doroga
Zausadebnaya ul.
Hermitage Restoration Department and Depot
Shkolnaya ul.
Dibunovskaya ul.
ul. Savushkina
ul. Savushkina
Buddhist Temple 11
Lipovaya alleya
Primorskiy prospekt
Bolshaya Nevka
5-y Severnyy prud
4-y Severnyy prud
3-y Severnyy prud
2-y Severnyy prud
1-y Severnyy prud
8
Mini Zoo 7
Café Nota 6
Chalet of Creation
Orangery 5
Sredniaya Nevka
Yelagin Island
4-y Yuzhnyy prud
4
Yelagin Palace
Green Beach 9
2-y Yuzhnyy prud
Srednyaya Nevka
Pier 10
0   200 m
0   200 yd
3
nab. Martynova
Kemskaya ul.
Divo Ostrov 2
ul. Krupina
Victory Park 1
Krestovskiy Ostrov Ⓜ
Morskoy prospekt

5–6

Take a short stroll down the main winding path in the shade of the trees, heading west. This can be quite memorable if you take some nuts with you as the local squirrels will eat out of your hand! If there are too many inline skaters on the tarmac road that goes right round the island, take the unmade track. Or simply hire a pair of roller or inland skates yourself from the boat and skate hire company behind **Café Nota** next to the northern-most

Insider Tip

The romantic statues of lions on either side frame what used to be an unrestricted view of the Baltic. In the meantime, how-ever, new monumental buildings block the panorama. Slightly to the left is the bombastic bowl of the football stadium which seats 68,000 spectators and, after all sorts of scandals and delays, cost some 600 million euros. It was opened in 2017 – Russia is hosting the World Cup in 2018.

TAKING A BREAK
There are four cafés on the island as well as a number of tents during the summer months where beer and grilled food is sold.

Gliding past gleaming Yelagin Palace on inline skates

Slightly to the right is the Lakhta Center (www.lakhta.center). The needle-like Gazprom skyscraper will be 462m (1,515ft) high when completed and will be the tallest building in Europe. Its opening is planned for 2018. On the 86th floor, at a height of 378m (1,240ft), there will be a viewing platform. A restaurant is planned at 330m (1,082ft).

Right in front of you is one of the bridges on the motorway that runs north/south across the Neva Estuary. It was inaugurated in 2016.

🔟–🔟

The way back along the southern side of the island takes you past a **large grass area** for sunbathing and beach volleyball courts with a view to the opposite bank where the impressive yachts of the super-rich lie at anchor.

🔟–🔟

If that makes you want to take to the water yourself you can take a **boat trip** from the landing stage at the point where the path joins the tarmac road.

🔟–🔟

Head northwards for **Café Nota** where you can cross to the mainland. The pedestrian subway under the heavily used Primorskiy Pr. brings you directly to the most northerly **Buddhist temple** in the world – further proof of Russia's strong multi-religious tradition. The **Datsan Gunzechoinei** was consecrated in 1913.

🔟–🔟

Staraya Derevnya metro station is some 500m (1,500ft) further north down Lipovaya Alleya.

A highlight for the culturally interested is near here. After the railway crossing turn right, pass the Gulliver shopping centre and you will reach the **Hermitage Museum's state-of-the-art restoration and depot complex** (Sausadebnaya Ul. 37, Wed–Sun 11am–3:30pm, guided tours, in Russian only, ₽550). Apart from the many paintings, other treasures kept here include the tsars' luxurious golden carriages, an Ottoman sultan's magnificent tent and a huge collection of furniture.

Insider Tip

Children love feeding the squirrels on a walk around the island

3 ON DOSTOYEVSKY'S TRACKS
Walk

DISTANCE: 3km (1.9mi) **DURATION:** 1.5 hours
START/FINISH: Hay Square (Sennaya, Spasskaya, Sadovaya metro stations) ✠ 205 F3

The most romantic district in St Petersburg can be found along Griboyedov Canal just where it bends. It was here that the brilliant author Fyodor Dostoyevsky lived for some time and it was here that he based the action in his novel *Crime and Punishment*. The beginning and end of this tour through quieter corners of the city is the all-the-more turbulent Hay Square; but then it can also be easily reached on three metro lines.

buildings are of a more recent date and there is no more bartering to be heard. Since the city council ordered the demolition of all the kiosks and stands on the square in 2016 the search for a new identity for the city's former central market has begun.

The western corner of the square opens up just where Griboyedov Canal bends. Cross the footbridge, turn right and go as far as the first side road. The red building

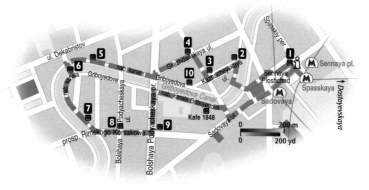

1–2

Opposite the entrance to the metro station in the northeast corner of Hay Square is the old **Guard House** (1820) where Dostoyevsky had to spend two days in a cell in 1874 for an infringement of the censorship law. It is now the municipal **tourist information** office that makes visiting very practical! The square has, however, changed a lot since Dostoyevsky's day. Virtually all the

(no. 1/61) was the **first place Dostoyevsky lived** in this district from 1861–63. It was here that he wrote *The House of the Dead*. Like all of the houses he lived in, this is on a corner too. However, he would not have been able to see a church from the windows here – something he generally placed great value on whenever he moved, which was frequently.

Dostoyevsky was once held prisoner for two days in the former guard house

2–3

Follow Kaznacheyskaya Ul. and, at the next crossroads, you will find yourself in front of **Kaznacheyskaya Ul. 7/Stolyarny per. 14**, where Dostoyevsky wrote *Crime and Punishment* and *The Gambler* in 1864–67 – the latter in just twenty-six days as the writer was badly in debt at the time. The young stenographer Anna Snitkina assisted him. When the work was completed Dostoyevsky proposed to her – with success.

3–4

One block further on, the **corner of Stolyarny per./Graschdanskaya Ul.** is the address Dostoyevsky used for the garret room lived in by the tragic hero in *Crime and Punishment*. There is a plaque to the figure of

Rodion Raskolnikov. Right next to this, stones engraved in Russian and German are a reminder of the high water mark reached during the catastrophic flood on 7 November 1824. During the worst flood in the city's history the level of the Neva rose within just a few hours by four metres (13ft). The raging mass of water that thundered down the streets damaged thousands of buildings and caused the death of hundreds of people. It was from here, so the story goes, that Raskolnikov set out to walk the 730 paces with an axe concealed under his coat to murder the shameless pawnbroker. You follow the same route across Graschdanskaya Ul. as far as the canal. It is best to keep to the right bank – it is, after all another 750m (2,500ft) to the ostensible

DOSTOYEVSKY MUSEUM *Insider Tip*

If you want to immerse yourself completely in Dostoyevsky's world, pay a visit to the Dostoyevsky Museum (▶ 142) before starting out on your tour. It is located next to Dostoyevskaya metro station and from here it is just one stop to where the walk begins.

Walks

DOSTOYEVSKY DAY
A celebration is held every year on the first Saturday in July to honour St Petersburg's most famous writer. It is organised by the Dostoyevsky Museum that mobilises all sorts of troupes of artists, theatre ensembles and bands for an unconventional street festival (noon–3pm) in the nearby streets and lanes. Other museums and libraries also have their own Dostoyevsky-inspired programmes of events on this day.

scene of the crime. The details given in the novel, however, do not match the actual lay of the land.

4–5

House no. 91 on the canal, on the other hand, was the scene of a real-life murder that shocked modern Russia. The popular Russian politician **Galina Starovoytova** who promoted democratic reform lived here. She was murdered on the staircase in 1998. A commemorative plaque has since been unveiled.

5–6

The picturesque **Bridge of Four Lions**, a footbridge on the next bend of the canal, was designed by Wilhelm von Traitteur in 1826 and built with the same supporting structure as Bank Bridge (► 142). White lions hold the cables here rather than griffins and even if these big cats do look like marble sculptures from a distance they are actually made of cast iron.

TAKING A BREAK
At the end of the tour, just before reaching Hay Square where things start to get hectic again, is the retro **Kafe 1848** (nab. kan. Griboedov 68; daily 11am–11pm). Russian fare is served in surroundings rather like an antique shop.

6–7

Follow the canal now walking down the left-hand side. No. 104 fits the description as the place **where the nasty old pawnbroker lived**. The courtyards and stairways of this once infamous block of flats are not open to the public.

7–8

When you reach Pr. Rimskogo-Korsakova turn left. Many St Petersburg artists love the view from the next crossroads but one: at **Bolshaya Podyacheskaya Ul.** where the dome of St Isaac's Cathedral (► 106) rises right above the middle of this alignment of streets.

8–9

Insider Tip

When turning into Voznesensky Prospekt keep an eye out for the little **Memorial to the Nose** on number 11. It commemorates **Nikolai Gogol's** satirical short story, *The Nose*, first published in 1836 in which the collegiate assessor Kovalyov's olfactory organ develops a life of its own.

9–10

Until you cross the next bridge you will have the golden needle of the Admiralty (► 118) right in front of you. Turn right here to return to Hay Square. On the opposite bank is the house where the character Sofya (Sonya) Marmeladova lived who provided Raskolnikov with support in the novel (no. 73).

Practicalities

Practicalities

WHAT YOU NEED

- ● Required
- ○ Suggested
- ▲ Not required

	UK	USA	Canada	Australia	Ireland	Netherlands
Passport	●	●	●	●	●	●
Visa	●	●	●	●	●	●
Onward or Return Ticket	▲	▲	▲	▲	▲	▲
Health Inoculations	▲	▲	▲	▲	▲	▲
Health Insurance (➤ 198, Health)	○	○	○	○	○	○
Travel Insurance	○	○	○	○	○	○
Driver's Licence (national)	●	●	●	●	●	●
Car Insurance Certificate (if using own car)	○	n/a	n/a	n/a	○	○
Car Registration Document (if using own car)	●	n/a	n/a	n/a	●	●

WHEN TO GO

High season   Low season

JAN	FEB	MAR	APRIL	MAY	JUNE	JULY	AUG	SEP	OCT	NOV	DEC
−5°C	−4°C	1°C	8°C	16°C	20°C	21°C	20°C	15°C	8°C	2°C	-2°C
23°F	25°F	34°F	46°F	61°F	68°F	70°F	68°F	59°F	46°F	36°F	28°F

☀ Sun   ⛅ Sunshine and showers   🌧 Wet   ☁ Cloudy

The temperatures given are the **highest average daytime temperatures**. The most popular time to visit St Petersburg is during the White Nights from the beginning of June until mid July. There are lots of events and festivals in the city from May until July. In August there is virtually nothing going on; there are hardly any performances in the theatres and opera houses until well into September. Many tourists visit St Petersburg over Christmas and New Year. However, Russian winters can be unpredictable, with the first snow often falling in October. Regardless of what time of year you visit you should be prepared for changeable, wet weather. Sturdy shoes are advisable bearing in mind the considerable distances to be covered in the city.

GETTING ADVANCE INFORMATION

Websites
- www.visit-petersburg.ru/en
- http://eng.ispb.info/news
- https://eng.russia.travel/peterburg

Travel agencies (with visa service)
- https://realrussia.co.uk
- http://www.visitrussia.org.uk
- https://www.justgorussia.co.uk/en

Practicalities

GETTING THERE

By Air British Airways (www.britishairways.com) operates regular, direct flights from London to St Petersburg Pulkovo Airport (www.pulkovoairport.ru), with 7 flights a week. Several other airlines fly via Moscow. For the best choice consult your travel agent or check routes and alternatives online, e.g. flying via a Scandinavian country (SAS, Air Baltic, etc.). The flight time from London is around 3hrs 45 mins.

By Train Modern Allegro express trains operate four times a day between Helsinki and St Petersburg (travelling time: 3.5 hrs). There are no longer any direct trains from mainland Europe. If you travel via Minsk or Brest a transit visa for Belarus is required.

By Coach Eurolines (www.europebus.co.uk/russia/) offer cheap fares to Russia (journey time from London to Russia: approx. 60 hrs.). Lux Express (https://lux express.eu) operates via Vilnius and/or Riga. There are more and better connections from Finland.

By Car Possible but exhausting and not a choice for most people. From Helsinki it is about 400km (250mi) along good roads. From Central Europe, e.g. Berlin, the journey via Poland, Lithuania and Letland is approx. 1,800km (1,120mi), with few stretches on motorways.

TIME

St Petersburg is permanently in the **Moscow Time Zone** (MSK); there is no change to daylight saving time. The time difference to Grenwich Mean Time (UTC) is +2 hours in summer and +3 hours in winter.

CURRENCY & FOREIGN EXCHANGE

Currency: The currency in Russia is the rouble (R. or RUB; Cyrillic: ₽). Banknote values are ₽5,000, ₽1,000, ₽500, ₽100 and ₽50, coins ₽10, ₽5, ₽2 and ₽1, 50 and 10 kopeks. £1 = approx. ₽78; ₽100 = £1.28; US$1 = approx. ₽60; ₽100 = approx. US$1.67

Exchange: Bureaux de change (recognisable by their illuminated displays of euro and dollar exchange rates) can be found on most squares in the city centre. Other currencies are generally not accepted. Banks which do not display exchange rates either do not offer this service or only at low exchange rates (as is the case with the omnipresent Sberbank). A passport must be shown when exchanging money to a value of ₽40,000 or more.

Cash dispensers (ATMs) (*bankomat*) are all over the place and in at least two languages (Russian/English). Depending on the bank, the maximum amount that can be paid out is between ₽5,000–₽20,000, in the VTB Bank up to ₽100,000. Most shops, hotels and restaurants accept standard **credit cards**.

Cancelling credit cards: Note the number of your credit card institution that has to be rung to cancel your credit card and freeze your account in the case of theft or loss, before leaving home.

VISA CENTRES

UK: http://ru.vfsglobal.co.uk/tourist.html;
Tel. 0905 889 0149; Mon–Fri 8.30am–5.30pm

15–27 Gee Street,	Peter House,	64 Albion Road
Barbican	Oxford Street,	(back entrance),
London, EC1V 3RD	Manchester, M1 5AN	Edinburgh, EH7 5QZ

USA: www.russianembassy.org/
page/russian-visa-centers
1680 Wisconsin Ave NW,
Suite 100
Washington D.C., 20007

Practicalities

WHEN YOU ARE THERE

NATIONAL HOLIDAYS

1–8 January	New Year's Day	1 May	Spring and
7 January	Christmas Day		Labour Day
23 February	Defender of the	9 May	Victory Day
	Fatherland Day	12 June	Russia Day
	(Men's Day)	4 November	Unity Day
8 March	International		
	Women's Day		

If a public holiday falls on a Saturday or Sunday, the following Monday is generally declared a holiday, as in the UK.

OPENING HOURS

○ Shops   ● Post Offices
● Offices   ● Museums/Monuments
● Banks   ● Pharmacies

8am 10am noon 1pm 2pm 4pm 6pm 8pm 10pm

☐ Day   ▨ Midday   ☐ Evening

There are no fixed closing times for shops. Alcohol can only be sold from 11am–10pm. **Banks** and **post offices** are also open on Saturdays; virtually all **shops** and **markets** are also open on Sundays and public holidays (with shorter opening hours). In **museums**, ticket desks generally shut one hour before closing time.

ETIQUETTE

Old-fashioned gallantry is still valued in Russia: men open doors for women and help with heavy luggage, etc. Shaking hands is only common among men (but never across a threshold due to superstition). Blowing your nose when other people are around is considered uncouth. In Orthodox churches men should remove any head covering, whereas women should cover their heads with a scarf. There are often headscarfs available at the entrance.

ELECTRICITY

The standard power supply is 220 Volt. Most power points are of the thin-pinned Continental European type. The thicker variety will not fit many power points from the Soviet era. Taking an adapter is advisable.

TIME DIFFERENCES (in summer)

St Petersburg (MSK)
12 noon

London (GMT)
← **10am**

New York (EST)
→ **5am**

Los Angeles (PST)
→ **2am**

Sydney (AEST)
→ **8pm**

Practicalities

STAYING IN TOUCH

Post The slow, unreliable and much frowned upon *Potschta Rossii* hardly plays a role in modern-day Russia any more. As a result letter boxes are few and far between and stamps can only be bought at post offices – where you have to queue for ages, too. The main post office is at Pochtamtskaya Ul. 9 and is open daily around the clock. To buy stamps go to the kiosk in the middle of the hall.

Public Telephones: The area code for St Petersburg is 812, from the UK 007–812; from the USA/Canada: 011 7 812 and then the phone number. Three digit dialing codes that start with 9 are mobile phone numbers. When making a national or an international call from a landline, dial 8 and wait for the dial tone. In the case of calls abroad this is then followed by the prefix 10, then 44 for the UK or 1 for the US followed by the area code without the 0. Calling the UK, e.g., from a mobile phone simply dial the prefix +44; calling a number in Russia +7 then the code and the number. Telephone boxes have now disappeared.

International dialling codes (landline/mobile):

UK	8 (wait for dial tone)	1044 / +44
USA/Canada	8 (wait for dial tone)	101 / +1

Cell Phone Providers and Services Your mobile phone will connect up with the Russian network via roaming without any problem. The mobile phone network coverage is very good. For travelling to more distant locations it may be worthwhile buying a local prepaid SIM card (from around ₽200) for one of the major mobile phone networks such as Megafon, MTS or Beeline; all of them have offices opposite Moscow Station: Ligovsky Pr. 43. You must show your passport as identification. You can top up your card at terminals in many shops.

WiFi & Internet Free access to the Internet is standard in hotels; many pubs and restaurants as well as shopping malls have free hotspots too (either ask the staff for the password or get authorisation as a text message via the website). Free access to the net is available under 'SPB Free WiFi' in Nevsky Prospekt, in metro stations, Peter and Paul Fortress and in the large parks.

PERSONAL SAFETY

St Petersburg is a very safe city. Muggings, harassment and attacks of any kind in public places are virtually non-exisitent, even at night, as long as you keep to well-lit streets where there are other people and you are not drunk. Modern housing estates are less safe.

- Pickpocketing has become a big problem, esp. in the metro and in buses where gangs use a whole range of tricks especially aimed at tourists. Longfingers also like busy museums and cafés.
- A stolen or lost passport can ruin your holiday. Leave it in your room safe and only take a copy of the main page and your visa with you.
- LGBTs are much less well tolerated than in western Europe – not helped by the laws of the land. Same-sex couples are well advised not to flaunt their sexual orientation publically so as not to provoke a violent homophobic reaction.

Emergency	0112
Police	002
Fire Brigade	001
Ambulance	003
Tourist Hotline	800-303-0555

Practicalities

HEALTH

 Insurance: An international health insurance policy is a prerequisite for a visa. Check the scope of services provided carefully beforehand. The state-run medical care does not always inspire confidence and reacts slowly even in emergencies.

The **private clinic Skandinavia** (tel: 812-600-7777, Liteyny Pr. 55a) employs a number of specialists, has a 24-hour emergency service and an out-patients facility. All the consultants and other doctors at the **American Medical Clinic AMC** (tel: 812-740-2090, emergency: 812-336-0033, nab. reki Moyki 78) speak English. The **eye-clinic** at Liteyny Pr. 25 runs a 24-hour emergency service.

 Dental Services In addition to the private clinics AMC and Skandinavia there are many private dental practices. Ask the locals if they can recommend a *stomatolog*.

 Pharmacies There are lots of *apteky* and they are well stocked. Medicines are often much cheaper and sold under different names. If you want a specific medicine, a member of staff can check for you.

 Drinking water In principal tap water is clean but there is always a slight inherent risk due to the ancient pipes. It is recommended buying mineral water to drink. Tap water is fine for showering or cleaning your teeth.

CONCESSIONS

Palaces, parks and museums have a complex system of concessions for different social groups but these are only valid for Russian citizens (who often enjoy reduced rates as a matter of course). Foreign children up to 16 years of age, however, also have free admission to Peterhof Palace (▶ 156), Tsarskoye Selo (▶ 162), the Hermitage (▶ 54) and all branch museums. Students are admitted free of charge to the Hermitage.

TRAVELLING WITH A DISABILITY

St Petersburg has a long way to go to catch up here. Curbs are often very high and there are either no ramps or lifts or they are in a poor state of repair. Stairs have to be negotiated as a matter of course in all metro stations at the entrances and when changing trains (generally they have rails or ramps at the side). More and more buses and trams adapted to the needs of the disabled are now coming into service.

CHILDREN

Special attractions for children are marked in this guidebook with the logo shown above.

TOILETS

Public lavatories are often like little kiosks with two cubicles and a cashdesk in between. Special toilet buses are parked at tourist hotspots. If a toilet roll is hanging at the cash desk then there will not be any paper in the cubicle. The lavatories in bars and museums are generally of a high standard. The 'Gents' is marked with an 'M', the 'Ladies' with 'Ж'.

EMBASSIES & CONSULATES

UK	USA	Ireland	Australia	Canada
☎ 812-320-3200	☎ 812-331-2600	☎ 812-326-2598	☎ 812-325-7334	☎ 812-325-8393

Useful Words and Phrases

You can usually get by, more or less, with English in hotels and restaurants. Street names, signs in the metro and virtually all menus are in English too. Nevertheless, you should familiarise yourself with the Cyrillic alphabet in order to be able to decipher signs and labels – and a lot of things then become self-explanatory. A lot of Russians have at least a basic knowledge of English but many of them have little occasion to use it.

Cyrillic letters	Transcription	Transliteration	Cyrillic letters	Transcription	Transliteration
Аа	a		Чч	ch	č
Бб	b		Шш	sh	š
Вв	v	v	Щщ	shch	šč
Гг	g		Ъъ	hard pronunciation	
Дд	d		Ыы	y	
Ее	ye		Кк	k	
Ёё	yo		Лл	l	
Жж	zhe		Мм	m	
Зз	ze		Нн	n	
Ии	i		Оо	o	
Йй	y		Пп	p	
Сс	s		Рр	r	
Тт	t		Ьь	soft pronunciation	
Уу	u		Ээ	e	
Фф	f		Юю	yu	
Хх	kh	h	Яя	ya	
Цц	ts	c			

AT A GLANCE

Yes	Da	Да
No	Net	Нет
Please	Pozháluysta	Пожáлуйста
Thank-you	Spasibo	Спасибо
Not at all	Ne za chto.	Не за что.
Sorry!	Prostite!	Простите!
I don't understand	Ya Vas ne ponimáyu.	Я Вас не понимáю.
I would like ...	Ya khochý...	Я хочý...
Good/bad	khoroshó/plókho	хорошó/плóхо
Have you got ...?	U Vas yest'...?	У Вас есть...?
How much does that cost?	Skól'ko eto stóit?	Скóлько это стóит?
Where's the toilet?	Gde zdes' tualét?	Где здесь туалéт?

GREETINGS

Good morning!	Dóbroe ýtro!	Дóброе ýтро!
Good afternoon!	Dóbryy den'!	Дóбрый день!
Good evening!	Dóbryy vécher!	Дóбрый вéчер!
Welcome!	Zdrávstvuyte!	Здрáвствуйте!
How are you?	Kak u Vas delá?	Как у Вас делá?
Good-bye!	Do cvidániya!	До свидáния!

EN ROUTE

left/right	nalévo/naprávo	налéво/напрáво
straight on	pryamo	прямо
near/far	blizko/dalckó	близко/далекó
Excuse me, where is...?	Skazhite, pozháluysta, gde...?	Скажите, пожáлуйста, где...?
Help!	Pomogite!	Помогите!
Beware!	Vnimánie!	Внимáние!
Please ring for .... quickly	Vyzovite bystro ...	Вызовите быстро...
... an ambulance ...	...skóruyu pómoshch'.	...скóрую пóмощь.
...the police ...	...politsiyu.	...полицию.
...the fire brigade.	...pozhárnuyu komándu.	...пожáрную комáнду.

Useful Words and Phrases

FOOD AND DRINK

Where can I find a good restaurant here?	Gde zdes' khoróshiy restorán?	Где здесь хоро́ший рестора́н?
Is there a nice pub here?	Yest' zdes' uyutnoe kafé ?	Есть здесь уютное кафе́?
I would like to reserve a table for four this evening, please.	Zarezerviruyte nam na segódnyashniy vécher stol na chetyryokh chelovék, pozháluysta.	Зарезервируйте нам на сего́дняшний ве́чер стол на четырёх челове́к, пожа́луйста.
Cheers!	Za Váshe zdoróv'e!	За Ва́ше здоро́вье!
The bill, please	Schet, pozháluysta.	Счет, пожа́луйста.
Did you enjor your meal?	Vam ponrávilos'?	Вам понра́вилось?
It was very good.	Bylo prevoskhódno.	Бы́ло превосхо́дно.

CHANGING MONEY

Where can I find a bank/ bureau de change?	Gde zdez' bank/ punkt obména valyuty?	Где здезь банк/ пункт обме́на валюты?
would like to change... (sum)	Ya khochu obmenyat'...	Я хочу обменять...
...pounds Sterling	...funt	...фунт
...dollars	...dóllarov	...до́лларов
...euros	...évro	...е́вро
...into roubles.	...na rubli.	...на рубли.

NUMBERS

0	nol	ноль
1	odin (m), odná (f), odnó (n)	один/одна́/одно́
2	dva (m/n), dve (f)	два/две
3	tri	три
4	chetyre	четыре
5	pyat'	пять
6	shest'	шесть
7	sem'	семь
8	vósem'	во́семь
9	dévyat'	де́вять
10	désyat'	де́сять
11	odinnadtsat'	одиннадцать
12	dvenádtsat'	двена́дцать
20	dvátsat'	два́цать
30	tritsat'	трицать
40	cópok	со́рок
50	pyat'desyat	пятьдесят
60	shest'desyat	шестьдесят
70	sem'desyat	семьдесят
80	vósemdesyat	во́семдесят
90	devyanósto	девяно́сто
100	sto	сто
200	dvésti	две́сти
300	trista	триста
400	chetyresta	четыреста
500	pyat'sot	пятьсот
1000	tysyacha	ты́сяча
2000	dve tysyachi	две ты́сячи
10 000	désyat' tysyach	де́сять ты́сяч
½	polovina	половина
¼	chétvert' (f)	че́тверть

Street Atlas

For chapters: See inside front cover

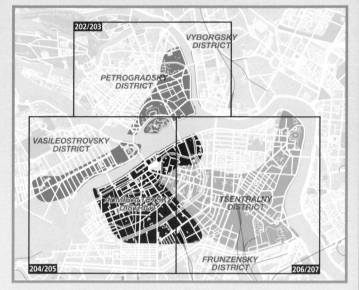

202/203

VYBORGSKY
DISTRICT

PETROGRADSKY
DISTRICT

VASILEOSTROVSKY
DISTRICT

ADMIRALTEYSKY
DISTRICT

TSENTRALNY
DISTRICT

FRUNZENSKY
DISTRICT

204/205

206/207

Key to Street Atlas

Ṁ	Museum	⎯⎯⎯	Railway
🎭	Theatre, opera house	Ⓜ	Metro line/station
⌂	Indoor swimming pool	▨	Public building, building of interest
📖 ✉	Library / Post office		Built up area
👤	Monument		Park area
✚	Hospital		Undeveloped area
✪	Police station		Pedestrian precinct
✚ ⚲	Church		
⚲	Mosque	★	TOP 10
♟ ♟	Palace / castle	26	Don't Miss
🐘 ⓘ	Zoo / Information	22	At Your Leisure

1 : 25 000

0	500	1000 m
0	500	1000 yd

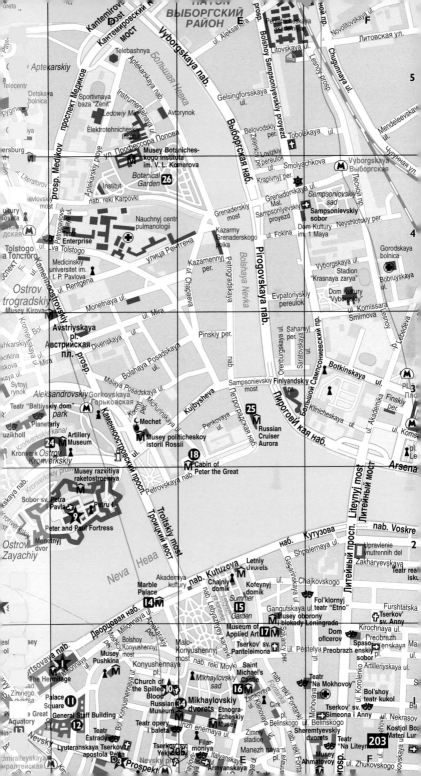

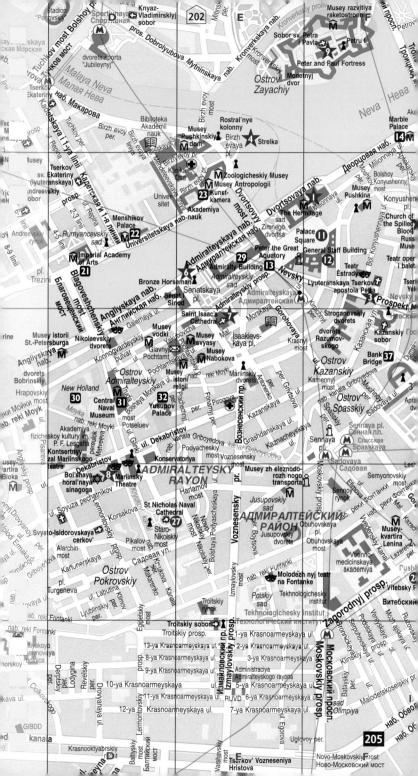

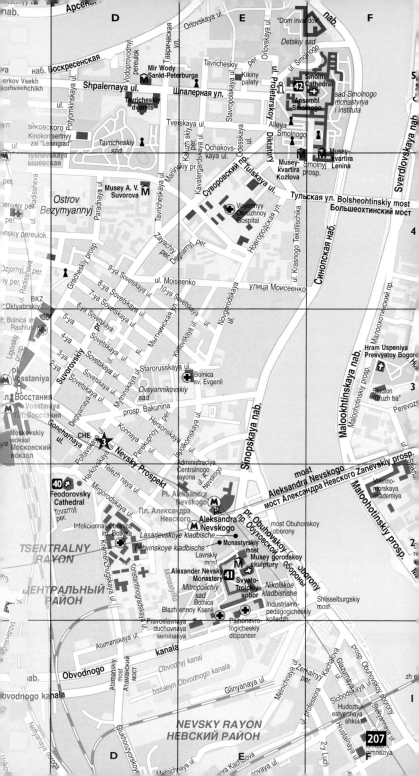

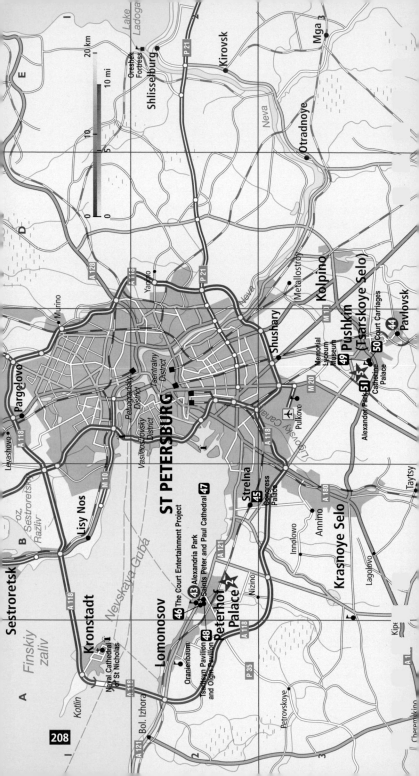

Lake Ladoga

Oreshek
Fortress

Shlisselburg

P 21

Kirovsk

Mga

Neva

Otradnoye

E

D

20 km

10 mi

10

5

0   0

Murino

A 128

A 118

Yanino

P 21

Neva

Metallostroy

Kolpino

Pushkin
(Tsarskoye Selo)

Pavlovsk

Memorial
Lyceum
Museum

Court Carriages

Catherine
Palace

49
50
51

Alexander Park

Parnas

C

Vasileostrovsky
District

Petrogradsky
District

Tsentralny
District

ST PETERSBURG

Shushary

M 11

M 20

Pulkovo

A 118

Neva

Levashovo

Sestroretsk

A 118

Finskiy
zaliv

oz.
Sestroretsky
Razliv

M 10

Lisy Nos

B

The Court Entertainment Project

Alexandria Park

Saints Peter and Paul Cathedral 47

43

46

48

Oranienbaum

Tsarevna Pavilion
and Olgin Pavilion

Strelna

Congress
Palace

45

A 121

Nizino

Peterhof
Palace

A 118

P 35

Innolovo

Annino

A 180

Krasnoye Selo

Lagolovo

Taytsy

Kipe

A 1

Kronstadt

Naval Cathedral
of St Nicholas

Kotlin

Lomonosov

Nevskaya Guba

Petrovskoye

Bol. Izhora

A 121

Cherepa

Parnas

Pargolovo

A 118

Street Index

nab. = naberezhnaya (embankment)
pl. = ploshchad (square)
per. = pereulok (alley)
prosp. = prospekt (avenue)
ul. = ulitsa (street)

Street Index

Street Index

Index

Index

Index

Picture Credits

Credits

1st Edition 2018

Worldwide Distribution: Marco Polo Travel Publishing Ltd
Pinewood, Chineham Business Park
Crockford Lane, Chineham
Basingstoke, Hampshire RG24 8AL, United Kingdom.
© MAIRDUMONT GmbH & Co. KG, Ostfildern

Author: Lothar Deeg
Translation: Christopher Wynne, Bad Tölz
Program supervisor: Birgit Borowski
Chief editor: Rainer Eisenschmid

Cartography: © MAIRDUMONT GmbH & Co. KG, Ostfildern
3D-illustrations: jangled nerves, Stuttgart

Printed in China

Despite all of our authors' thorough research, errors can creep in.
The publishers do not accept any liability for this. Whether you
want to praise us, alert us to errors or give us a personal tip –
please don't hesitate to email or post to:

MARCO POLO Travel Publishing Ltd
Pinewood, Chineham Business Park
Crockford Lane, Chineham
Basingstoke, Hampshire RG24 8AL
United Kingdom
Email: sales@marcopolouk.com

FSC
www.fsc.org
MIX
Paper from
responsible sources
FSC® C124385

10 REASONS
TO COME BACK AGAIN

1. The **Hermitage and its branch museums** are so vast that you will have to come again.

2. A holiday in Russia is **not expensive** as long as the rouble is weak due to the price of oil.

3. The **bar scene** is evolving so fast and taking over new districts in the city centre.

4. You can never have seen enough of the **avant-garde art of the 1920s.**

5. There are **dozens of interesting museums** that you will not have been able to visit.

6. You can **really unwind** in the parks surrounding the imperial residences if you have time.

7. The **historical city centre** extends over such a huge area.

8. Few other metropolises with populations of so many million are as **clean and safe**.

9. The **restaurant scene** has a great variety to offer – with lots of dishes you don't know to try.

10. The **party mood during the White Nights** in June and July is simply out of this world.